SEXTUS POMPEY

SEXTUS POMPEY

BY

MOSES HADAS

AMS Press, Inc.

New York

1966

TO

PROFESSOR CHARLES KNAPP

PREFACE

The years during which Rome underwent the transition from Republic to Monarchy constitute one of the most dramatic periods in the history of the western world. In such a period even the deuteragonists and the tritagonists deserve study, particularly since their rôles have been minimized and disparaged because universal attention was focussed on the protagonist. A fairer estimate of the career of Sextus Pompey should give a truer appreciation of the work of Octavian.

Works cited more than two or three times in this monograph are referred to by abbreviations in the footnotes. The full titles are given in the List of Abbreviations (pages 167–170). For ancient authors I used the latest texts available to me. The extensive quotations of Greek authors in English translation may appear somewhat unusual in a work of this character. But (as I suggest on page 145), when Appian or Dio Cassius is our only authority for an event, it serves the interest of economy as well as of accuracy to reproduce the source rather than to attempt a paraphrase. I quote a translation rather than the original because a translation will, I think, serve the convenience of the greater number of possible readers; I quote a printed translation rather than my own in the interest of objectivity.

I am obliged for information on specific points to my friends Professor Jacob Hammer, of Hunter College, Professor Clinton W. Keyes, of Columbia University, and Professor Allen B. West, of the University of Cincinnati. Professor W. L. Westermann, of Columbia University, read my manuscript and made several important suggestions. I feel bound to say that in one or two significant points his suggestions were not followed; he is therefore not to be held accountable for any faults in method or in fact.

An indebtedness far greater than may be acknowledged here is that to Professor Charles Knapp, under whose direction this study was undertaken.   He has several times scrutinized my work, in manuscript and in proof, and his long editorial experience has been of the greatest help in seeing the book through the press.   But beyond such assistance, his constant encouragement and accessibility even at a period of great stress in his own life deserve my deepest gratitude.   To him I owe a new conception of the methods, aims, and ideals of scholarship, and of the obligation of teacher to pupil.

MOSES HADAS

Cincinnati,
    March 31, 1930.

CONTENTS

		PAGE
	Preface	v
I.	Introduction	1
II.	The Date of Sextus's Birth	3
III.	Youth and Education	10
IV.	From Rome to Pharsalus	21
V.	Pharsalus to the Ides of March	36
VI.	The Ides of March until the Peace of Misenum	56
VII.	The Peace of Misenum to 36 B. C.	100
VIII.	Naulochus	123
IX.	The End of the House of Pompey	148
X.	Appraisal of Sextus: Sources	161
	List of Abbreviations	167
	Index	171

I. INTRODUCTION

The central theme of Roman history during the first century before Christ is the struggle between the incipient monarchy and the expiring but obstinate Republic, or, more precisely, oligarchy. The political abuses at Rome and the grossly inefficient administration of the provinces seemed to cry aloud for the rule of a single man. The republican traditions of Rome, on the other hand, tended to obstruct the consummation of monarchy. But even under the forms of democracy there had already grown up a precedent for what amounted to autocratic power in the extraordinary military commands which were granted to outstanding generals. Roman armies, unlike those of the earlier Republic, were now composed not of citizens who were disbanded after a short campaign, but of professional soldiers under professional generals.[1] Under such generals, it is true, the armies became more efficient, but they ceased to be national; they lost their devotion to the government and bestowed their loyalty upon their leaders, to whom they swore allegiance and of whom they expected booty and bounties. So radical was the change in the constitution and the motives of the Roman armies that they were ready to defy the authority of the State at the bidding of their leaders.[2] Furthermore, the personal power enjoyed by the great military leaders tended to become hereditary. A great general's adherents, military or civilian, at home or in the provinces, would be likely to transfer their loyalty to his successor.[3]

In the great struggle in which Julius Caesar and Pompey the Great were the opposing leaders Caesar was successful and

---

[1] The first professional army was created by Scipio Africanus. His command in Spain was the forerunner of the great commands such as those of Sulla, Marius, Caesar, and Pompey. See Kromayer-Veith, 294–295, and W. Schur, Scipio Africanus, 104 (Leipzig, 1927); compare also Parker, 9–46.

[2] Domaszewski, 1.12; Holmes, 1.37–38, 115, 134, 162–163; Heitland, 2. 262, 368, 3.22, 120; L. Hahn, Das Kaisertum, 3–5 (Leipzig, 1913). Compare also Frank, 269–271, 357.

[3] See especially Kromayer-Veith, 464–465, and compare pages 152–154 below.

Pompey lost his life. Octavian arose as the successor of Julius, and won the loyalty of his adoptive father's following. The most obstinate defender of the traditions of Pompey was Pompey's younger son Sextus, and he, similarly, won over a large part of his father's following. It shall be the purpose of this monograph to trace the career of Sextus, and to make it clear that he was not merely the corsair chief that history has painted him, but the legitimate successor to the claims of his father, and the active representative of a considerable section of Roman sentiment.

II. THE DATE OF SEXTUS'S BIRTH

The marital life of the ill-starred Pompey the Great shows the same diversity as does his political career. He was married five times.[1] Of his wives only the third, Mucia,[2] bore him offspring that survived for any considerable period. Mucia had three children,[3] two sons, Gnaeus and Sextus,[4] and a daughter, Pompeia.[5]

Of the ancient historians only Appian gives information concerning the birth and the death of Sextus Pompey, and even Appian's information on the subject is incomplete, since only the date of Sextus's death is given specifically. Relating the events of 35 B. C., Appian says:[6] καὶ Πομπήιος . . . ἑαλώκει, Τίτιος δὲ . . . αὐτὸν δὲ Πομπήιον, τεσσαρακοστὸν ἔτος βιοῦντα, ἐν Μιλήτῳ κατέκανεν. . . . According to Appian, therefore, Sextus Pompey was in his fortieth year when he was killed in 35 B. C.; this would fix the year of his birth as 74 or 75. The year 75 is in fact accepted by many scholars as the correct date.[7] However, Appian's statement requires close scrutiny.

If Sextus were born in 75, we should naturally expect to find that his father was in Rome at least as late as 76. But, as we shall see, this was not the case. The year 78 witnessed the counter-revolution of Marcus Aemilius Lepidus, who attempted

---

[1]For a list of his wives see Drumann, 4. 560–561.

[2]Appian 5.69 (references to Appian are to the *Civil Wars* unless it is otherwise noted); Dio 48.16.3; Plutarch, Pompey 42.7. Mucia was the daughter of Q. Mucius Scaevola, consul in 95.

[3]Suetonius, Iulius 50.1; compare Dio 37.49.3.

[4]Compare Appian 2.105, 2.122, 4.83, 5.143; Plutarch, Cato Minor 55.3, 56.1; Dio 42.2.3; Aurelius Victor 78.8, 79.2; Orosius 6.18.2; Velleius 2.72.4; Eutropius 6.24, 7.4.

[5]Suetonius, Tiberius 6.3. It may be mentioned that Pompey's fourth wife, Julia, daughter of Julius Caesar, bore him a son who died shortly after his mother in 54. See Velleius 2.47.2; Suetonius, Iulius 26.1. Dio, however, mentions (39.64) a daughter. Shipley (154) says: "Son is supported by Livy, *Epit.* 106." This note is not correct, for in that Periocha we read: Iulia, Caesaris filia, Pompei uxor, decessit; honosque ei a populo habitus est, ut in campo Martio sepeliretur. There is no mention of a son. Compare also Valerius Maximus 4.6.4.   [6]5.144.

[7]Compare Lübker, 836.

3

to undo the reforms of Sulla.[8] The Senate displayed its cus-. tomary irresolution and hesitated to employ stringent measures. But, when Lepidus raised an army and marched on the capital, the issue of public safety became paramount. Since no other competent general was at hand, Pompey was entrusted with an extraordinary command, and together with the ex-consul Q. Lutatius Catulus succeeded in crushing the rebellion, in 77.[9]

After the defeat of Lepidus, Pompey returned to Rome, but did not disband his army.[10] Sertorius had reached the height of his power in 77[11] and constituted a great menace in Spain. Pompey received the command in Spain for the purpose of bringing the Sertorian War to an end. After forty days of preparation[12] he set out; he crossed the Alps during the early autumn of 77 and entered Spain in the early spring of 76.[13] Perperna, a lieutenant of Sertorius, murdered his chief and assumed command in his place, in 72. Pompey crushed him immediately, and, after devoting some time to reorganizing affairs in Spain, set out for Italy, in 71.[14]

From the above outline it may be seen that Pompey spent part of 77 fighting against Lepidus. He had to blockade Marcus Brutus,[15] the lieutenant of Lepidus who held Cisalpine Gaul, at Mutina, and then disperse the remnants of Lepidus's army in Etruria;[16] it is clear, therefore, that he was away from Rome. Again, he cannot have been in Rome after the early autumn of 77, since he crossed the Alps at that time. Therefore the only remaining portion of 77 during which it was possible for Pompey to be at Rome is the period during which he was

---

[8]Livy, Periocha 90: M. Lepidus cum acta Syllae temptaret rescindere, bellum excitavit. See Appian 1.107; Florus 2.11; Plutarch, Pompey 16. Compare Suetonius, Iulius 3; Orosius 5.22.1–2, 16–18.

[9]For a discussion of the rebellion of Lepidus see Holmes, 1.134–138, 365–369; Drumann, 4.346–357; Heitland, 3.1–7. Compare also Meyer, 7, and Schulten, 96.

[10]Plutarch, Pompey 17.3.   [11]Schulten, 85.

[12]Sallust, Historiae 2.98.4.

[13]Holmes, 1.145, 370–372; compare Schulten, 97–99.

[14]Livy, Periochae 91–97; Orosius 5.23.14; Appian 1.113–115; Plutarch, Pompey 20.2–21.1, Sertorius 36–37; Florus 2.10.8–9. See also Drumann, 4.391–392; Holmes, 1.152; Heitland, 3.14, 26.

[15]The father of the assassin of Caesar. Compare Livy, Periocha 90; Appian 2.111; Plutarch, Pompey 16.5.

[16]Livy, Periocha 90; Florus 2.11.4–8; Plutarch, Pompey 16.2–5.

trying to secure from the Senate the command against Sertorius, and the forty days he devoted to the preparations for this expedition. If we assume that September is the 'early autumn' during which he crossed the Alps (and time should really be allowed for his reaching the Alps), the logical conclusion would be that Sextus must have been born before 75. If Pompey, then, was present at Rome as late as September 77, Sextus may have been born in June or July of 76, but not in 75.[17]

Groebe, in his revision of Drumann, introduces a correction of Drumann by pointing out that Pompey on his return to Italy in 71 had been absent not 'almost six years' but more than six years.[18] It is, therefore, the more surprising that he leaves unchallenged the statement that "wurde der jüngere Sohn Sextus schon im J. 75 v. Chr. geboren."[19]

There is yet another point of view from which our problem must be approached. That 75, the date generally accepted, is the correct date for the birth of Sextus has been denied by Emil Hitze,[20] who maintains[21] that Sextus was born in 67. Hitze bases his argument chiefly on the expressions denoting youth, ambiguous at best, applied by ancient authorities to both Gnaeus and Sextus.[22] The passages in question are the following:

(1) Plutarch, Caesar 56.2: . . . εἰ μηδὲν αἰδοῦνται λαβόντες αὐτὸν ⟨Caesar⟩ ἐγχειρίσαι τοῖς παιδαρίοις ⟨in the Battle of Munda⟩.

(2) Appian 4.83: νεώτερος ὢν ὅδε τῶν Μάγνου Πομπηίου παίδων ὑπερώφθη μὲν τὰ πρῶτα ὑπὸ Γαίου Καίσαρος περὶ Ἰβηρίαν, ὡς οὐδὲν μέγα διὰ νεότητα καὶ ἀπειρίαν ἐργασόμενος....

(3) Appian 5.143: Οὕτω μὲν ἑάλω Πομπήιος Σέξστος, ὁ λοιπὸς ἔτι παῖς Πομπηίου Μάγνου, νεώτερος μὲν ὑπὸ τοῦ πατρὸς ἀπολειφθεὶς καὶ ὑπὸ τοῦ ἀδελφοῦ μειράκιον ἤδη. . . .

(4) Plutarch, Caesar 56.1: Συντελεσθέντων δὲ τούτων ὕπατος ἀποδειχθεὶς τὸ τέταρτον εἰς Ἰβηρίαν ἐστράτευσεν ἐπὶ τοὺς Πομπηίου παῖδας, νέους μὲν ὄντας ἔτι. . . .

(5) Appian 5.133: ⟨Sextus⟩ ἐς δὲ Μιτυλήνην καταχθεὶς διέτριβεν, ἔνθα αὐτὸν ἔτι παῖδα μετὰ τῆς μητρὸς ὑπεξέθετο ὁ πατήρ, Γαίῳ Καίσαρι πολεμῶν, καὶ ἡττηθεὶς ἀνέλαβεν.

---

[17]Though Mucia subsequently proved faithless, there are no aspersions on her character at this time. See below, page 11.

[18]4.392, note 11. [19]4.561; the statement is repeated at 4.564.
[20]De Sexto Pompeio (Dissertatio Inauguralis, Breslau, 1883).
[21]9–10.   [22]7.

(6) Bellum Africanum 23: . . . ⟨Gnaeus⟩ adulescentulus profectus ab Utica est in Mauretaniam.

(7) Bellum Hispaniense 1.1:[23] Pharnace superato, Africa recepta, qui ex his proeliis cum adulescente Gn. Pompeio profugissent. . . .

(8) Ibidem 3.1: Ipse autem Gn. Pompeius adulescens. . . .

(9) Ibidem 40.1: Interfecto Gn. Pompeio adulescente. . . .

(10) Ibidem 42.6: Privatus ex fuga Gn. Pompeius adulescens. . . .

(11) Velleius 2.55.2: Gn. Pompeius Magni filius adulescens impetus ad bella maximi. . . .

(12) Ibidem 2.73.1: Hic ⟨Sextus⟩ adulescens erat studiis rudis. . . .

(13) Eutropius 6.24: Caesar . . . se voluerit occidere ⟨Mundae⟩ ne . . . in potestatem adulescentium . . . veniret.

(14) Valerius Maximus 9.15.2: . . . C. Caesar, Cn. Pompeio adulescente in Hispania oppresso. . . .

(15) Iulius Obsequens, Prodigiorum Liber 126: . . . ipse adulescens Pompeius victus et fugiens occisus.

(16) Cicero, Phil. 13.8: . . . Magnum Pompeium, clarissimum adulescentem. . . .

(17) Ibidem 13.12: . . . quod adulescenti ⟨Sexto⟩, patres conscripti, spopondistis. . . .

An examination of these passages yields interesting results. The Latin passages establish the consistency of Roman terminology in the use of *adulescens*. Added significance may be found in the fact that it is used by two nearly contemporary writers who were both military men, Velleius and the author of the Bellum Hispaniense.[24]

Considering the Greek passages we see that Plutarch's use of παιδαρίοις (Caesar 56.2) is derisive, and can therefore have no bearing on the respective ages of Pompey's sons. Neither can Appian 4.83 help us to determine Sextus's age. It is true that Sextus was young (νεότητα), as it is true that he was inexperienced (ἀπειρίαν). Caesar's disregard for him is explained, but his age is not defined.

Much more important is Appian's statement in 5.143: 'He had been deprived of his father when he was rather young ⟨νεώτερος⟩ and of his brother while he was himself still a stripling ⟨μειράκιον⟩.'

---

[23]This and the following passages are referred to by Hitze only.
[24]Hitze does not mention *Pompei iuvenes*, to be found in Florus **1.41.10**, and in Pseudo-Victor 78.8: Pompeios iuvenes in Hispania apud Mundam . . . vicit.

Before we proceed to a discussion of this passage it may be in place to point out that Appian is not always a dependable source. His interest in Roman history was that of a dilettante; when he deviates from his sources and attempts originality, he frequently displays an amazing ignorance.[25] His striving for rhetorical effect is another source of inaccuracy that is too well known to require discussion here.[26] Passages in his writings must be carefully weighed, therefore, before they can be accepted as proof.

In the passage under consideration Appian employs the word μειράκιον, a word flexible in meaning. A careful investigation of this term[27] has demonstrated that in classical authors it denotes an age of from fourteen to twenty years; it is also occasionally applied to bad generals as a term of derision.[28] With writers of the κοινή however, among whom is Appian, its meaning is twofold:

Bei den Schriftstellern der κοινή hat das Wort μειράκιον eine doppelte Bedeutung; an denjenigen Stellen nämlich, an denen wir das Alter des μειράκιον aus dem Autor selbst oder aus einem andern ersehen, ergibt sich, dass sich dasselbe von 14-22 Jahren erstreckt; aus den andern Stellen dagegen, wo wir auf die Berechnung dieses Alters angewiesen sind, geht hervor, dass dasselbe vom 2.-36. Jahre reicht.[29]

Our passage in Appian belongs to the second category ("aus den andern Stellen . . . wo wir auf die Berechnung dieses Alters angewiesen sind. . ."). On the basis of Appian 5.143 and 5.144 Amend fixes the date of Sextus's birth as 75, the date heretofore accepted by all scholars with the exception of Hitze. His conclusion follows:

S. Pompeius war also im Jahre 75 geboren; er war demnach im Jahre 48, als sein Vater starb, ca. 27 Jahre alt; sein Bruder Gn. Pompeius starb im Jahre 45; S. Pompeius war also damals als μειράκιον ca. 30 Jahre alt.[30]

We must also consider Appian's leaning toward rhetorical turns of speech. In the sentence under consideration there is manifest straining for effect in the chiasmus νεώτερος μὲν ὑπὸ

---

[25]Rosenberg, 204–205. See also White, 1.xi. Compare pages 164–165, below.

[26]Compare White, 1.x; H. Peter, Die Geschichtliche Literatur über die Römische Kaiserzeit bis Theodosius und ihre Quellen, 1.429, 2.279, 281 (Leipzig, 1897).   [27]Amend.

[28]Amend, 13, 70; compare 57.   [29]Amend, 57.   [30]Amend, 36.

τοῦ πατρὸς . . . ὑπὸ τοῦ ἀδελφοῦ μειράκιον ἤδη, as well as in the antithesis νεώτερος . . . μειράκιον. It is, therefore, difficult to discover in this passage with Hitze[31] that "Appianum ipsum Sexti miseret, quod et pater et frater maturius ei decesserint; a patre enim puerulum, a fratre adolescentulum illum esse relictum."

Similarly, the expression νέους . . . ἔτι in Plutarch, Caesar 56.1, is of little help in fixing a later date for Sextus's birth. The passage refers to 45; if my suggestion that Sextus was born in 76 is correct, he was 31 in 45, and a man of that age may certainly be called νέος.

The last Greek passage cited (Appian 5.133) refers to 48, the year in which Pompey sent his (fifth) wife, Cornelia, and his son Sextus to Mitylene for safety.[32] In this passage Appian calls Sextus παῖς, but the word cannot be taken literally, for in 5.144 Appian states that Sextus was 40 years old in 35, which would make him 27 years old at the time when Appian himself calls him παῖς.

The loose use of μειράκιον referred to above illustrates Appian's carelessness in terminology. Another example may be found in 5.136, in which Sextus's legates excuse his conduct (in B. C. 36) as being that of a νέος ἀνήρ. Appian's inconsistency is all the more striking in view of the fact that the various terms are used in almost consecutive chapters: 5.133, παῖς; 5.136, νέος ἀνήρ; 5.143, μειράκιον. Apparently Appian is consciously trying to give variety to his expressions.

Against the variety of terms employed about Sextus by Greek writers, the united front, as it were, of the Roman writers offers a bold relief, and their testimony is made the more acceptable by the fact that some of them were more nearly contemporary with the events they are describing.

Hitze's reasoning suffers from another contradiction. He maintains (8) that Gnaeus, the older brother of Sextus, was born in 70 or in the beginning of 69; there would then be a difference of two or three years in the ages of the brothers (9). He applies the term *adulescens* to Gnaeus (8), but denies it to Sextus, who was only two or three years younger, although *adulescentia* includes the period from fifteen to thirty years.[33]

---

[31]7. [32]Plutarch, Pompey 66; Dio 42.2.3 (compare 42.5.7).

[33]F. G. Moore, Cicero De Senectute, Edited, page 64, note (New York, 1903).

Faulty too is the *argumentum ex silentio* in the following statement (9):

Cum Gnaeus ab Africa proficiscens in Hispaniam in insula Ebuso (Ivica) morbo aliquamdiu retineretur, peropportuna ex improviso facultas Sexto data est, ut fratris aegrotantis vice fungeretur experireturque, quid suis viribus polleret. Qua occasione nemo scriptorum memorat aut usum Sextum esse aut uti voluisse.

It is dangerous to draw conclusions from the silence of historians.

Though the passages in the ancient authorities will not, in my opinion, support the late date advocated by Hitze, they do seem to emphasize the youth of Sextus. For this emphasis a conjectural explanation may be offered. We shall consider below[34] the possibility that most of our ancient literary evidence for the career of Sextus is derived from a single source, no longer extant, which was hostile in tone to Sextus. It may be that this source used some expression denoting youth in order to disparage the ability of Sextus. I have in mind some such word as μειράκιον, which, as we have seen,[35] need not, in such disparaging use, imply actual youth. In English, for example, it is almost natural for us to prefix 'young' to 'upstart,' without meaning to emphasize the youth of the upstart. This disparaging expression in the original source may well have colored all our extant accounts of Sextus, so that they all, unnecessarily as it seems to us, speak of Sextus as being very young.

To make his date for the birth of Sextus more plausible Hitze (11–14) rejects 81, the date generally accepted,[36] for Pompey's marriage to Mucia. His arguments here are as strained as in his 'proof' of the year of Sextus's birth.

We may safely assume that Sextus's birthplace was Rome, for he was born *in absentia parentis*.[37]

-----

[34]Pages 164–165. [35]Page 7.

[36]See Drumann, 4.560. [37]Dorn Seiffen, 34.

III. YOUTH AND EDUCATION

For the education of Sextus Pompey the evidence is scanty, and frequently so contradictory in nature that its proper evaluation seems almost hopeless. This evidence derives from two periods: imperial, as represented by Velleius (and Strabo), and republican, as represented by Cicero.[1] The passages in question follow:

(1) Velleius 2.73.1: ⟨Sextus Pompeius⟩ . . . adulescens erat studiis rudis, sermone barbarus. . . .

(2) Cicero, Att. 16.4.1: . . . Libo intervenit. Is Philonem, Pompei libertum, et Hilarum, suum libertum, venisse a Sexto cum litteris ad consules, sive quo alio nomine sunt. Earum exemplum nobis legit, si quid videretur. Pauca παρὰ λέξιν, ceteroqui satis graviter et non contumaciter.

Normally Cicero's testimony is sufficient to refute Velleius, but, since Cicero's statement on this point has been called into question,[2] it may be well to adduce arguments to show that Velleius's statement is an exaggeration.

We have seen that Sextus was born probably in the metropolis. There is the strongest likelihood that he enjoyed the educational and other opportunities that the son of a noble family would enjoy. The statement of Velleius, that a son of Pompey the Great was devoid of education and barbarous in speech, is therefore remarkable, and requires verification.

In his dissertation on Sextus, C. Risse[3] limits himself to the casual remark: "De Sexti educatione nihil constat; eadem usus esse videtur quam Tacitus in dialogo suo ⟨c. 29⟩ acerrimis verbis vituperat." Such a dismissal of the problem of Sextus's education is facile, and gives its author the sound of a modern Velleius. He ignores the information gathered by Dorn Seiffen[4] on the subject, which, while not exhaustive, is, nevertheless, illuminating.

Let us turn to the passage in the Dialogus of Tacitus to which Risse refers. The chapter (29) denounces contemporary evils

[1]Noted by Dorn Seiffen, 4, 6, 34, 136–137.
[2]By Drumann, 4.591, and by Blok, 64–65.
[3]Page 1. The view of Blok is similar to that of Risse, except that Blok mentions the passage in Strabo cited below.
[4]136–137.

in Roman education, particularly the negligence of parents who make no effort to train their children in virtue and self-control. The preceding chapter offers a contrast between this deplorable state of things and education in earlier times:

nam pridem suus cuique filius, ex casta parente natus, non in cella emptae nutricis, sed gremio ac sinu matris educabatur, cuius praecipua laus erat tueri domum et inservire liberis.

Much of the criticism voiced here by Tacitus might be applied to the case of Sextus. For one thing, he seems to have lacked a real childhood, which moderns have learned to appreciate, but which the Romans neglected.[5] During Pompey's absence (67–61 B. C.) Mucia may have taken care of her children in the traditional way, at least up to 62, when she began to play the wanton[6] and became Caesar's mistress;[7] but it is at least as likely that she did not, for the heavier burdens which fell upon women by reason of their husbands' long absences and the ease of procuring divorces in the first century B. C. tended to diminish their interest in children.[8] In any case, Mucia's influence ceased in 62, the year in which Pompey sent her a bill of divorce, even before he entered Italy (61 B. C.).[9]

It was customary for fathers to take part in the training of their children when the children grew older, and especially to associate with their sons and to instruct them in their future duties; but it is clear that Pompey could not have followed this custom. As we have seen, Sextus was born in 76 B. C., in his father's absence from Rome, and did not see his father until the latter's return from Spain in 71, that is, until he was five years old. Pompey remained at Rome until 67; he was then dispatched (by the Gabinian Law) to crush the pirates, and later (by the Manilian Law) to the East. In the four years of his stay at Rome he was kept too busy by affairs of state to have time to supervise personally the education of his children.[10]

---

[5]Fowler, 171.

[6]Plutarch, Pompey 42.7, limits himself to this general remark.

[7]Suetonius, Iulius 50.1. Jerome, Adversus Iovinianum 1.48, calls her *impudica uxor*.   [8]Fowler, 181.

[9]Plutarch, Pompey 42.7. Cicero, Att. 1.12.3, expresses the satisfaction of Cicero and others at Pompey's action. The divorce cost Pompey the support of the Metelli; see Dio 37.49.3, and Cicero, Fam. 5.2.6.

[10]Cicero says (Ad Quintum Fratrem 3.17) that he could accomplish wonders with Quintus's son, if the latter were with him in Arpinum; but at Rome he <Cicero> hardly has time to breathe. Pompey was as busy a man as Cicero.

When he returned from the East in 61, Mucia was already
divorced and Sextus was fifteen years old. Sextus's education
could not, therefore, have run along the traditional lines
eulogized by Tacitus, nor could Sextus have made any such
statement as Cicero[11] puts into the mouth of Scipio, that he was

. . . unum e togatis patris diligentia non inliberaliter institutum
studioque discendi a pueritia incensum, usu tamen et domesticis
praeceptis multo magis eruditum quam litteris.

But, granted that ". . . a real interest in education as distinct
from the acquisition of knowledge was . . . much wanting in
Cicero's day . . .,[12]" and that not many persons expressed the
desire, as did Cicero,[13] to teach their own sons if they only had
the time, nevertheless means of a kind for teaching children
were available. Roman education had long passed the stage
of being exclusively Roman. In its altered character it was
based on Greek models and entrusted to Greek hands,[14] especially when neither parent had the leisure or the inclination
to educate the children or to supervise their education. Wealthy
parents possessed the means of giving their children an education without themselves participating in it; this fact in itself
should serve to refute Velleius's charge that Sextus was *studiis
rudis, sermone barbarus*. The new education may have neglected
the moral and ethical side of his development—as indeed his
later life would serve to prove—, but he cannot have been
'almost illiterate.'

Let us consider the steps in the education of any Roman boy,
and presumably, therefore, of Sextus also. The rudiments of
his education the boy received at home[15] under the direction of
a freedman in the household, a *litterator* or *ludi magister*, who
taught him the so-called *elementa*, while the *paedagogus* looked
after his manners and took care of his Greek. The next stage
was the school of the *grammaticus*,[16] whose training was
equivalent to that of our secondary education. We may safely

---

[11]De Re Publica 1.36.   [12]Fowler, 176; compare 170.
[13]See note 10.

[14]For a recent discussion of the Graeco-Roman ideal of education see
Gwynn, 22–33, 46–58.

[15]Compare Tacitus, Dialogus 34.

[16]Suetonius, De Grammaticis 4, remarks that the term *grammaticus*
became current under Greek influence. For a definition of the term see
Sandys, 1. 6–9.

assume that Sextus received the elementary education, as outlined above; but do we have proof that he attended the school of a *grammaticus?* The answer is positive. Strabo, enumerating some of the illustrious natives of Nysa,[17] where he himself studied, mentions among them a certain Aristodemus, a distinguished *grammaticus*, who taught even at Rhodes. At Nysa he taught both rhetoric and grammar, but at Rome, in the capacity of superintendent of the education of Pompey's children, ἐν δὲ τῇ ῾Ρωμῇ τῶν Μάγνου παίδων ἐπιστατῶν . . ., he was satisfied with a school of grammar: ἠρκεῖτο τῇ γραμματικῇ σχολῇ. In Rome, then, as Strabo informs us, Aristodemus was a teacher of secondary subjects,[18] and Sextus was his pupil.

In the school of a *grammaticus* a boy remained until he assumed the *toga virilis*. Cicero and Quintilian inform us concerning the course of study pursued in such a school. Cicero (De Oratore 1.187; compare also 3.127) says: in grammaticis poetarum pertractatio, historiarum cognitio, verborum interpretatio, pronuntiandi quidem sonus. Quintilian (1.4.5) believed the study of literature a necessity for boys, and does not fall short of the ideal of Cicero. The profession of *grammaticus* Quintilian considers under two headings: he is a teacher of the art of correct speaking and an interpreter of the poets (1.4.2). Quintilian describes the art of writing as going hand in hand with speaking (1.4.3), and adds music, astronomy, and philosophy.[19] Considered as a whole, the education in the school of the *grammaticus*, unlike the old-fashioned utilitarian education, was not calculated to prepare for the service of the State; but it did build up a fair degree of culture, derived from

---

[17]14.1.48. For Nysa, near Tralles in Caria, see Strabo 14.1.43–48.

[18]Compare Quintilian 1.4.1: Primus in eo, qui scribendi legendique adeptus erit facultatem, grammaticis est locus. Quintilian goes on to say that his words apply equally to Roman and to Greek *grammatici*, since they used the same method. A distinction was made between a *grammaticus Graecus* and a *grammaticus Latinus* (compare Blümner, 324). We may thus suppose that Sextus had a *grammaticus Latinus* also.

[19]For the future orator Quintilian suggests other subjects also as preliminary to the study of rhetoric. Their completion is equivalent to the ἐγκύκλιος παιδεία (1.10.1), for a discussion of which see Gwynn, 85–91. See also the note in F. H. Colson, M. Fabii Quintiliani Institutionis Oratoriae Liber I, 121–122 (Cambridge, 1924). Compare also Apuleius's outline of education, Florida 21 (Halm).

careful reading of the poets, both Greek and Latin, and a knowledge of pronunciation, diction, and even composition, in the two languages.[20]

Strabo is considered a good authority, and his testimony scores an important point against Velleius (and Risse). Sextus's education was no doubt *praeter morem maiorum*, but otherwise normal and in accordance with the accepted standards of his age. We have no evidence that he studied rhetoric. This was the highest step in Roman education, and upon it Sextus should have entered, (if he entered upon it at all), after he assumed the *toga virilis*, that is, somewhere between his fourteenth and his seventeenth year[21] (62–59 B. C.). This was the period during which his father divorced his mother Mucia and contracted the marriage with Julia,[22] the daughter of Caesar, which was to cement the bond between Caesar and Pompey.[23]

There is no further evidence for the activity of Sextus up to the year 49 B. C. which marks the outbreak of the Civil War, but some suggestions may be advanced which would indicate that his education did not suffer. For this purpose it is necessary to review some events of his father's life. The political events from 61 to 49 B. C. were of a character to keep Pompey extremely busy. We know also that during this time (after 59) he travelled among the pleasure resorts of Italy with his newly wedded wife Julia,[24] and that he left Rome in 56 to go to Africa and Sardinia in the capacity of *curator annonae;* on this journey he also, at Luca,[25] settled his differences with Caesar and Crassus. In 54 Julia died. In 52 Pompey married again, this time Cornelia, the daughter of Metellus Scipio.[26] In 50 he was again absent from the metropolis and was ill at Naples.[27] All this excludes the probability of personal care (though

---

[20]Cicero would even include rhetoric as part of the *puerilis institutio;* compare Gwynn, 96.   [21]Blümner, 332, 335–336.

[22]Compare *inter alios* Cicero, Att. 8.3.3; Appian 2.14; Dio 38.9.1; Plutarch, Caesar 5.3, 14.4.

[23]This marriage was criticized because Pompey married the daughter of the man who seduced the mother of his children; see Suetonius, Iulius 50.1.

[24]Plutarch, Pompey 53.1.   [25]Cicero, Fam. 1.9.9; compare Appian 2.18.

[26]Appian 2. 24; Dio 40.51.3; Plutarch, Pompey 55.1.4; compare also Drumann, 3.685 and notes, 2.40.

[27]Plutarch, Pompey 57.1; compare Velleius 2.48.2.

not of affection) for his children in accordance with the old standards, but the following considerations may be offered in support of the view that Sextus was reasonably well educated.

(1)   Though he did not himself supervise the upbringing of his children, Pompey was certainly in contact with them, and we know that he had a genuine respect for scholarship. While he was at Rhodes, he listened to the sophists there; while he was at Athens, he heard the philosophers. While he was on his expedition against the pirates, he attended the lectures of the philosopher Posidonius of Rhodes, the teacher of Cicero, and he revisited Posidonius on his return from Syria. At Mitylene he listened to poetic contests.[28] He was fond of the Iliad,[29] and could compose and recite speeches in Greek. Cicero calls him *scriptor luculentus*.[30] Since he had these qualities, Pompey's influence upon the culture of his children could only be beneficial.

(2)   Pompey's children had two step-mothers after their mother Mucia was divorced. But there can be no question of step-mother treatment in the proverbial sense, for Caesar's daughter Julia was extremely fond of Pompey, though he was much older than she,[31] and Pompey reciprocated her affection.[32] We may assume without evidence that Julia was well educated, and we have proof that Cornelia, Pompey's last wife, was a beautiful and charming woman.[33] Her *sophrosyne* is eulogized in a Greek inscription found at Pergamum.[34] She was well versed in music, literature, and geometry, and also interested in philosophy.[35] We know further that Pompey sent Sextus to Lesbos with her when the Civil War was in progress, and that they spent some time together there.[36] The influence of both step-mothers, and especially the latter,[37] could only be favorable.

---

[28]Plutarch, Pompey 42.5; Strabo 11.1.6 (according to Strabo, Posidonius wrote a history of Pompey); Cicero, Tusc. Disp. 2.61; Pliny, N. H. 7.112 (Pliny pays a fine compliment to Pompey: fasces litterarum ianuae summisit is cui se oriens occidensque summiserat).

[29]Photius, quoted by Drumann, 4.554.   [30]Cicero, Att. 7.17.2.

[31]Plutarch, Pompey 53.1–2; the reasons for her devotion are there mentioned.   [32]Ibidem 53.4.   [33]Appian 2.83; Plutarch, Pompey 55.1.

[34]Dittenberger, 2.758.   [35]Plutarch, Pompey 55.1.

[36]See below, page 124.

[37]Pompey's fondness for Cornelia and consideration for her may be inferred from his sailing to Egypt for her sake after the debacle at Pharsa-

(3) We read in Suetonius that many noble families kept freedman 'professors' in their households. So Marcus Antonius Gnipho gave instruction in the house of Caesar when Caesar was a boy; and Cicero, when he was praetor, attended the school which Gnipho had by that time opened.[38] The freedman Epicadus was a member of Sulla's household and finished Sulla's incomplete autobiography.[39] The freedman Caecilius Epirota was the teacher of the daughter of Atticus, and later gained the friendship of the poet Cornelius Gallus.[40] Luckily for our purpose Suetonius also mentions two teachers in the household of Pompey: Nicias, who was dismissed, and the famous Lenaeus, who accompanied Pompey on his campaigns, and, because of his ability and learning, was set free.[41] Lenaeus was a good scientist, and well versed in the Latin language.[42] The presence of so learned a man in Pompey's household was certainly to the advantage of Pompey's children. If a conjecture is in place, inasmuch as a distinction was made between the *grammaticus Latinus* and the *grammaticus Graecus*,[43] it is possible that Lenaeus was the Latin *grammaticus*, while the Aristodemus whom Strabo mentions was the Greek *grammaticus*.

(4) In this connection another member of Pompey's household should be mentioned, a Greek, Theophanes of Mitylene, a poet and historian. He exercised so great an influence upon Pompey as to embitter the nobles, since they had to placate Theophanes in order to get Pompey's favor.[44]

These various circumstances combine to demonstrate that

---

lus; he might have gone to Africa or Corcyra where he had both military and naval forces. See Plutarch, Pompey 76.6; Appian 2.83.

[38]Suetonius, De Grammaticis 7.   [39]Ibidem 12.

[40]Ibidem 16.   [41]Ibidem 14–15; compare also 2.

[42]Pliny, N. H. 25.5; Gellius 17.16.2. Lenaeus translated into Latin Mithridates's treatise on poisons, and bitterly satirized the historian Sallust, who tried to detract from his patron's memory. Compare Suetonius, De Grammaticis 15; Schanz-Hosius, 315, 377, 582, 634.

[43]See note 18, above.

[44]For Theophanes see Drumann, 4.554–557; W. Christ, Geschichte der Griechischen Literatur, 2⁶.399–400. The influence exercised by Theophanes and by Greek freedmen upon Pompey is an anticipation of conditions under the Emperor Claudius. The descendants of Theophanes became members of the *ordo equester*, and later even entered the Senate. See Stein, 176–178, 301, 397. A stemma showing the descendants of Theophanes is given in the Prosopographia, 3.67.

Sextus enjoyed abundant cultural opportunities. His education went far beyond the mere knowledge of Greek and Latin. Even the possession of such linguistic knowledge would make it unfair to call Sextus *studiis rudis, sermone barbarus*. It is true that Sextus was for a time in concealment among semicivilized people in Spain and in contact with pirates, but in Sicily, until his defeat in 36, he associated with the many noble Romans whom he saved from the proscriptions in 43. It must be clear, therefore, that Velleius's statement is unjustified. It remains to find the motives for his malicious *testimonium*.[45]

Born not later than 18 B. C.,[46] Velleius may be included among those whom Tacitus (Annales 1.3.6) calls iuniores post Actiacam victoriam . . . nati: quotus quisque reliquus, qui rem publicam vidisset! His history is full of ". . . enthusiasm which amounts to a bias for Tiberius in particular and the Caesars in general."[47] Velleius owed everything to the Empire and especially to Tiberius. His spirit of adulation of the Empire and Tiberius did not permit him to give due credit to the man who, after Antony, was the most formidable enemy of Augustus; this same spirit, to cite an instance, prompted him to extol Messala Corvinus, who preferred to change his allegiance and to be indebted for his safety to Augustus, to the latter's satisfaction,[48] and, to cite another instance, to invent the story that Asinius Pollio distinguished himself against Pompey in Spain,[49] the truth being the reverse.

[45]Risse admits (54) that Velleius wrote *infestissimo animo*, but says that his charges against Sextus are not without grounds: "Verisimile est enim, liberalis et ingenuae doctrinae ac eruditionis expertum Sextum fuisse." He may have lacked *eruditio*, but I have made it clear, I believe, that he was not without *doctrina*. Velleius's charge is due to his *infestus animus*. Niebuhr (Lectures, 3.110) makes a generalization on the authority of this passage of Velleius: "It is remarkable to see how, at this time, men who did not receive a thorough education neglected their language, and spoke a corrupt form of it." This generalization is remarkable, in view of the fact that Velleius was a courtier of the Caesars, and was strongly prejudiced against the enemies of the family.

[46]Duff, 83.

[47]Duff, 85. For Velleius as a historian see Rosenberg, 221; Schanz, Geschichte der Römischen Literatur, 2².258.

[48]Velleius 2.71.1. For the career of Messala see J. Hammer, Prolegomena to an Edition of the Panegyricus Messalae (New York, 1925).

[49]Velleius 2.73.1.

Opposed to Velleius's biased evidence we have the testimony of Cicero (quoted above, 10). On July 10, 44 B. C., Cicero wrote that Scribonius Libo, the father-in-law of Sextus, came to see him, bringing a copy of a letter written by Sextus to the consuls. This copy Libo read to Cicero, and asked him what he thought of it. Cicero's comment is confined to the notice of a few odd expressions[50] (*pauca παρὰ λέξιν*); in other respects he found the letter sufficiently dignified (*satis graviter*), and not aggressive in tone (*non contumaciter*). We must remember that Cicero's letters were not written with a view to publication, and that this criticism is therefore a candid expression of his opinion. That opinion is rather complimentary, and implies that on the whole the letter was, in his judgment, well written; the mention of the oddities of expression probably signifies that Sextus did not maintain Cicero's own standard of formal language which would be proper for a communication to a consul. That this is the spirit of Cicero's criticism is evident from his suggestion (in the next line) that the simple address 'To the Consuls' should be expanded into 'To the Consuls, Tribunes of the People, and Senate.' This suggestion is made 'for fear,' as he says, 'that they ⟨the consuls⟩ may publish the letter sent to them.' One who could earn even the moderate praise of Cicero, as expressed in the confidence of his personal correspondence, must have been able to write reasonably well. The criticism implies that Sextus did not attain the felicity of a practised orator; we have seen that he probably did not study oratory.[51]

Except for this very meager evidence from Velleius, Cicero, and Strabo, we have nothing to help us reconstruct the life of Sextus up to 49–48 B. C., in which years the historical evidence concerning Sextus begins. The only bit of information, or rather misinformation, we find about the earlier years is in Florus (1.41.9). In his account of the war waged by Pompey

---

[50]Or, 'a few solecisms in language'; compare Tyrrell and Purser, 5.380, note.

[51]Drumann concedes that Velleius's statement is exaggerated, but only if Sextus was himself the author of the letter, which Drumann appears to doubt: see note 2 above. Drumann says (4.591): "Das <the judgment of Velleius> ist übertrieben, wenn sein Brief an die Konsuln des Jahres 44 von ihm selbst <Sextus> verfasst wurde." It is clear from the foregoing, even without Cicero's testimony, that Sextus had an education. In general, Drumann's attitude toward Cicero is too notorious to merit discussion.

the Great against the pirates (67 B. C.) Florus speaks of
Pompei iuvenes, i. e. Gnaeus and Sextus, as holding the office
of *legati*. At the time Sextus was only nine years old;[52] he
was, therefore, not a *legatus*: in fact he could hardly have been
with Pompey at all.[53]

A passage in Caesar (B. C. 3.5) has been wrongly applied to
Sextus by some scholars. In enumerating the naval preparations of Pompey the Great in 48 Caesar says, Praeerat Aegyptiis
navibus Pompeius filius. Commenting on this passage Charles
E. Moberly[54] says: "Sextus Pompeius." Even the very competent J. Kromayer, in a learned article[55] assumes that the

---

[52]According to Hitze (see above, page 5) he was born in this year.

[53]Drumann suggests (4.562) that Sextus's older brother Gnaeus could
participate "nur zu seiner Belehrung," but not in the capacity of a *legatus*.
Dorn Seiffen says (34) that no one will believe Florus (see also Drumann, 4.
562, note 5, and 564, note 6), and then adds (35): "quamquam discendi
gratia patrem comitari potuerunt <Gnaeus and Sextus>"; his contradiction
is obvious. Drumann's statement that Gnaeus could not be a *legatus* is
correct, but it is difficult to agree with his conclusion that Gnaeus went
with his father to learn naval warfare. Drumann's date for Gnaeus's birth
is 80–75 B. C. (4.562), which would make him at most only thirteen years
old at the time of the war with the pirates. For a *tirocinium militiae*, such
as Drumann's statement implies, but for which there is no proof, this age is
too low. Blümner says (337–338): "die Zeit, die zwischen jenem Akte
<the assumption of the *toga virilis*> und dem Eintritt in den Kriegsdienst
oder in die öffentliche Tätigkeit lag, hiess jenachdem *tirocinium militiae*
oder *tirocinium fori* und war in den letzten republikanischen Jahrhunderten
in der Regel auf ein Jahr, also das 17. Lebensjahr, ausgedehnt." There
are instances in which this happened earlier, e.g. Cicero, at 16, Octavian, at
15, and Antony's son, at 14. See Fowler, 191–192; compare Drumann, 5.
238–239. These examples can hardly be adduced as parallels, however, in
view of the uncertainty of the date of Gnaeus's birth. Florus must not
be taken very seriously, for he is panegyrist rather than historian, and his
account is without value for the historian (Rosenberg, 152; Duff, 647), as
Drumann and Dorn Seiffen both agree. One may conjecture that Florus
here confused events, as he often does. In 49 Pompey sent Gnaeus to the
East to raise a fleet (Plutarch, Pompey 62.2; Drumann 4.562), with which
he was on the sea until 47. After the death of Pompey the Great in Egypt,
Cornelia and Sextus fled, met Gnaeus on the sea, and proceeded with him
to Africa. It is quite possible that Florus was thinking of this occasion
when both brothers were on the sea together, and inserted it by mistake
into his account of the Pirate War.

[54]The Commentaries of Julius Caesar on The Civil War, 195 (Oxford,
1925).

[55]Entwicklung, 434.

Pompeius filius was Sextus. A. G. Peskett[56] and Maurice W. Mather[57] say correctly that the *Pompeius filius* here is Gnaeus.

It is impossible, therefore, to reconstruct the story of the years of Sextus's adolescence and early manhood.[58] We may assume, however, though we cannot prove it, that he participated fully in the life of the metropolis and its brilliant society. How close was his contact with the distinguished personages and the men of letters of his day we cannot say; certainly the enormous reputation of his father and the charm and wit of his step-mother would make his home much sought after by the great and the near-great, and there was no society into which he might not have entrée, if he wished it. It cannot be established that he held any public office, though it is quite likely that he held the offices that a young man of his class would normally hold. By 49 he was twenty-seven years old, and he would by that time have been *tribunus militum* and have held one or more of the minor civil offices included in what was later called the vigintivirate.[59] It is quite in the character of the scanty information we have regarding the early years of Sextus that there is no mention of his having held these offices. On the other hand, we know of no reason for an exception to be made in his case, and the fact that Cicero speaks of him as an exemplary young man[60] would indicate that he went through the usual forms.

Sextus surely witnessed the glory of his father's Triumph, as he was destined to witness his father's fall. He could remember such historic events as the consulship of Cicero and the conspiracy of Catiline; and, if he remained in the city and not on one or the other of his father's estates,[61] he witnessed the anarchy of 53 B. C.

---

[56]Bellum Civile III, 72 (Cambridge, 1900).

[57]Caesar, Episodes from the Gallic and Civil Wars, 404 (New York, 1905).

[58]It may be worth mentioning that even a nephew of Pompey the Great, also named Sextus Pompey, was considered of sufficiently distinguished lineage to be appointed leader in the game called Troy. See Plutarch, Cato Minor 3. This other Sextus Pompey is Number 6 in Lübker, 835.

[59]For the vigintivirate see Lübker, 1110.   [60]See below, page 82.

[61]Besides his splendid mansion in the residential quarter called *Carinae*, between the Caelian Hill and the Esquiline Hill (Velleius 2.78.1; Suetonius, Tiberius 15.1), Pompey also owned beautiful gardens outside the city, as well as many estates and villas throughout Italy. See Drumann, 4.541–543. Two villas of Pompey are mentioned in T. Ashby, The Roman Campagna in Classical Times, 194, 229 (London, 1927).

IV. FROM ROME TO PHARSALUS (49–48 B. C.)

After the formation of The First Triumvirate the political situation at Rome grew darker, and matters were not improved even by the second convention of Caesar, Pompey, and Crassus, which was arranged at Luca in 56 B. C. On the contrary, the situation grew steadily worse, especially after the death of Julia (54 B. C.) and the disastrous defeat of Crassus and his death at Carrhae (53 B. C.), by which the triumvirate was reduced to a duumvirate. It soon became apparent that in the circumstances then existing there could not be room in the dying Republic for both Caesar and Pompey, and Caesar's passage of the Rubicon marked the final breach which had been so long threatening. At Rome, Caesar's step created great consternation, and the confusion was increased by the hosts of fugitives that hurried to Rome and the crowds that were leaving Rome. Pompey realized very shortly that Rome could not be defended and that the only course left to him was to abandon the capital. This step he took on January 17, 49 B. C., having beforehand ordered the government to follow him. On the next day the consuls and the majority of the senators, accompanied by their wives and families, left the city and fled to Pompey.[1] Compelled by the rapidity of Caesar's movements Pompey decided to leave Italy. This he did in March; he crossed to Epirus by way of Brundisium, and thereby foiled Caesar's attempt to cut off his withdrawal from Italy.

In a letter addressed to Atticus on March 18, 49 B. C.,[2] Cicero refers to his meeting with Pompey on the memorable day, January 17, 49 B. C., when Pompey gave Rome up; Cicero declares that Pompey was *plenus formidinis*. Plutarch gives similar testimony: he declares that no one suffered Pompey to use his own judgment, but everyone infected Pompey's mind with his own fears and perplexities.[3] Pompey's perturbation is

---

[1]For the panic at Rome see Caesar, B. C. 1.14 (compare 1.33.2); Plutarch, Pompey 61, Caesar 34.2, 33.1–2; Appian 2.36–37; Dio 41.6.6, 41.7–9. See also Holmes, 3.6, 362, 377.

[2]9.10.2; compare also Att. 7.10.

[3]Pompey 61.1, Caesar 33.3–5. Dio also speaks (41.6.1) of Pompey's fear before his retreat from Rome; compare Appian 2.36.

easy to understand; besides the desperate political and military situation[4] he had to think of the safety of his own family.[5]

We have evidence that Pompey removed his wife Cornelia and his younger son Sextus from the war area, but our authorities do not agree concerning the date of this event. Velleius maintains[6] that after the Battle of Pharsalus Pompey fled with several companions, including his son Sextus. According to Lucan,[7] however, when Pompey saw before the Battle of Dyrrachium that the conflict was inevitable and that his army must soon face the decisive test, he decided to send Cornelia to Lesbos in order to keep her from the tumult of war. Lucan speaks of Sextus as being in Thessaly before the Battle of Pharsalus was fought, and as there consulting the witch Erichtho. Lucan's story is as follows. When Sextus heard of the witch, he hastened to her and asked her to reveal to him the issue of the war and the course of destiny.[8] She consented,[9] and after certain gruesome necromantic *diableries* informed him that the dead expected his father and family *in parte serena;*[10] of his own destiny she would tell him nothing.[11] Then both the witch and Sextus went to Pompey's camp.[12] This last statement surely implies that Sextus took part in the Battle of Pharsalus and in the events that followed it. But in Book 8, in which are described the events after the Battle of Pharsalus, Lucan says that among those who came to meet Pompey after his defeat Sextus was the first, arriving from the shore of Lesbos.[13] We should expect some information as to how Sextus got to Lesbos from Pharsalus, but Lucan does not enlighten us on this point.

---

[4]Plutarch, Caesar 34.2, compares Rome of these days with a storm-tossed ship abandoned by its helmsman.

[5]We have seen (page 19) that the older son Gnaeus had been dispatched to the East in 49 to raise a fleet. He commanded the Egyptian squadron. Compare also Plutarch, Antony 25; Caesar, B. C. 3.4.4, 3.5.3; Drumann 4. 562.

[6]2.53.1.   [7]5.722–727; compare 5.743–744, 786, 804–805, 8.40–43.
[8]6.413–430, 569–572.   [9]6.588–603.
[10]6.803–805. For a discussion of these *diableries* see H. J. Rose, The Witch Scene in Lucan (*Pharsalia*, VI, 419 sqq.), Transactions and Proceedings of the American Philological Association, 44 (1913), l–lii.
[11]6.812.   [12]6.827–828.
[13]8.204–205: primusque a litore Lesbi occurrit natus, procerum mox turba fidelis. That Sextus was at Lesbos will be seen from the testimony of the Greek historians, which is discussed below (pages 24–25).

There is apparently some inconsistency in Lucan's statements, for according to these statements Sextus would have to be at Pharsalus and at Lesbos almost simultaneously.

These two authors comprise our only Roman testimony for the whereabouts of Sextus during the Battle of Pharsalus. Velleius need not detain us long, for we have seen above (pages 16–17) that frequently his testimony can be accepted only *cum grano salis*.[14] Of Lucan's testimony one statement coincides with evidence supplied by certain Greek historians and therefore has historical value—the statement that Pompey sent Cornelia (and Sextus) away.[15] The episode of Sextus and the witch is nothing more than a poetic fiction.[16] Lucan was far from writing history; although the Pharsalia ventures into the field of history, it is by no means always a reliable source for the historian.[17] As Postgate says,[18]

Anything therefore in his account which is poetically or rhetorically effective, and is at the same time intrinsically improbable and unconfirmed by independent testimony, may safely be ascribed to the invention of the rhetorical poet.

The witch-episode fits very neatly into this category.

But what of Lucan's statement regarding Sextus's presence at Lesbos? If Lucan had not represented Sextus as having been in Thessaly, his statement about Sextus's presence at Lesbos might be explained as a poetic modification of another historic fact; we might assume that, instead of Pompey coming to

[14]Professor J. P. Postgate, commenting on this passage of Velleius, shared this view. In his edition of Lucan VIII (Cambridge, 1917; cited here as Postgate VIII), in the Historical Introduction, xxix, he says: "It might be thought from Velleius 2.53.1...that Sextus accompanied his father from the first, but the implication is not necessary, nor can Velleius be wholly trusted." For another error of Velleius see Postgate VIII, Introduction, lxiv, note 3. Professor Postgate did not observe that Velleius mentions the fact that Cornelia was at Mitylene (2.53.2), which is recorded also by the Greek historians (see below, page 24). Compare also Drumann, 3.432, note 10: "Velleius spricht von der Flucht des Vaters im allgemeinen, ohne die Zeit vor und nach dessen Ankunft bei Mitylene zu unterscheiden." Holmes (3.174, note 2) also rejects Velleius's testimony.

[15]Compare Drumann, 3.432, note 10. See below, pages 25–32.

[16]Postgate VIII, Introduction xxix, note 4.

[17]See Heitland's Introduction to Haskins's edition of the Pharsalia, 34 (London, 1887). Compare also Postgate's edition of Pharsalia VII (Cambridge, 1913; quoted as Postgate VII), Introduction, ix, and Duff, 319–321.

[18]Postgate VII, Introduction, ix.

Lesbos to fetch Sextus (and Cornelia), Sextus left Lesbos[19] to meet his father. But the inconsistency may be readily explained. Rhetoricians preoccupied with the beauty of their language are liable to lapses of memory. Lucan was poet as well as rhetorician, and therefore the more likely to be inconsistent,[20] though, to be sure, many of his statements are historically accurate.[21] Therefore the implication of Lucan, Book VI, that Sextus was in Thessaly immediately before the Battle of Pharsalus need not trouble us, for it is clear that he cannot have been in Thessaly and in Lesbos at the same time.

Let us now turn to the Greek writers, whose evidence is somewhat fuller. Three of them, Appian, Dio, and Plutarch, inform us that Pompey sent Cornelia and Sextus to the city of Mitylene in Lesbos for safety. The passages are as follows:

(1) Appian 5.133: ἔνθα ⟨in Mitylene⟩ αὐτὸν ἔτι παῖδα μετὰ τῆς μητρὸς[22] ὑπεξέθετο ὁ πατήρ, Γαΐῳ Καίσαρι πολεμῶν, καὶ ἡττηθεὶς ἀνέλαβεν.

(2) Appian 2.83: Ὁ δὲ Πομπήιος ἐκ Λαρίσσης . . . ἐς Μιτυλήνην διέπλευσεν· ὅθεν τὴν γυναῖκα Κορνηλίαν ἀναλαβὼν . . . .

(3) Dio 42.2.3–4: . . . ἐπὶ τὴν θάλασσαν καταβὰς ἐς Λέσβον ὁλκάδι πρός τε τὴν γυναῖκα τὴν Κορνηλίαν καὶ πρὸς τὸν υἱὸν τὸν Σέξτον ἔπλευσε. καὶ αὐτοὺς παραλαβὼν καὶ μηδὲ ἐς τὴν Μιτυλήνην ἐσελθὼν ἐς Αἴγυπτον ἀπῆρε. . . .

(4) Plutarch, Pompey 66.3: ⟨After the Battle of Dyrrachium⟩ ἐθελονταὶ δὲ πολλοὶ πρὸς Κορνηλίαν ἔπλεον εἰς Λέσβον εὐαγγελιζόμενοι πέρας ἔχειν τὸν πόλεμον· ἐκεῖ γὰρ αὐτὴν ὑπεξέπεμψεν ὁ Πομπήιος.

(5) Plutarch, Pompey 74.1: Οὕτω δὲ παραπλεύσας ⟨Pompey the Great⟩ ἐπ᾽ Ἀμφιπόλεως ἐκεῖθεν εἰς Μιτυλήνην ἐπεραιοῦτο, βουλόμενος τὴν Κορνηλίαν ἀναλαβεῖν καὶ τὸν υἱόν.

(6) Plutarch, Pompey 76.1: ⟨Pompey the Great⟩ Ἀναλαβὼν δὲ τὴν γυναῖκα καὶ τοὺς φίλους ἐκομίζετο. . . .

---

[19]Compare Haskins's note to 8.205 (page 279): ". . . Sextus had probably been in Lesbos all the time, though Lucan had in Book VI introduced him as consulting the witch in Thessaly." The word "probably" is not necessary.

[20]For inconsistencies in Lucan see Postgate VIII, Introduction, xiii–xiv; the present passage also is discussed there.

[21]Postgate VII, Introduction, xi, lists some accurate statements of Lucan. Compare also Postgate VIII, Introduction, x–xi. I shall quote Lucan as a source only when the information given by him concurs with that supplied by professed historians.

[22]Cornelia was his step-mother.

These historians are at one with Lucan in saying that Cornelia was at Lesbos, and, if we disregard the witch-episode, that Sextus was there also. There is a corroborative statement in Velleius 2.53.2:[23] ⟨Pompeius⟩ . . . a Mytilenis Corneliam uxorem receptam in navem fugae comitem habere coeperat. . . .

The testimony of the Greek writers is accepted by all modern scholars who have written about the life of Sextus.[24] Yet a careful examination of the several modern interpretations of the Greek accounts reveals disagreements concerning the time at which Sextus was sent with Cornelia to Lesbos.

(1) Doijer, speaking of Cornelia, says (97): "Quando vero eam dimiserit ⟨to Lesbos⟩ nescimus. . . ."[25]

(2) Drumann, speaking of the 'senate' that was constituted at Thessalonica after Pompey and the Senate left Italy in 49 B. C., says (3.432): ". . . die Vorsicht des Pompeius, welcher seine Gemahlin Cornelia mit dem jüngeren Sohne Sextus nach Lesbos schickte, machte einen ungünstigen Eindruck auf die Armee."[26]

Drumann, 2.40: "Im Jahre 49 *nach dem Rückzuge aus Italien*[27] schickte er Cornelia mit seinem jüngsten Sohne Sextus nach Lesbos. . . ."

Drumann, 4.564: ". . . der Vater schickte ihn im J. 49 mit der Stiefmutter Cornelia nach Mitylene. . . ."

(3) Postgate VIII, Introduction, xxix: " ⟨From Amphipolis⟩ . . . he ⟨Pompey⟩ at once weighed anchor for Lesbos, where were his wife Cornelia and Sextus, his younger son. *At the beginning of the war*[28] Pompey had placed Cornelia in Lesbos

[23]D. Doijer, in his dissertation, De Lucani Fontibus ac Fide Commentatio, 97 (Leyden, 1884) says: "Pompeium Corneliam uxorem Lesbum misisse apud historicos non invenimus; eam Lesbi fuisse quum bella in Graecia gererentur colligitur e vita Pompeiana, a Plutarcho descripta. . ." Here he quotes Plutarch, Pompey 66.3, and Appian 2.83. Since he had not read the other passages cited above in the text, it is small wonder that he arrived at such a conclusion, though Plutarch's very words, which Doijer quotes, ἐκεῖ γὰρ <i. e. to Lesbos> αὐτὴν <i. e. Cornelia> ὑπεξέπεμψεν ὁ Πομπήιος, indicate explicitly that Pompey sent her. There is, therefore, neither need nor room for 'conjecture' (*"colligitur"*). I observe also that Velleius's testimony is not quoted by Risse (1); Risse also omits Dio 42.2.4 and Plutarch 66.3 and 76.1. Instead, he quotes Plutarch 55, a chapter which makes no mention of the events in question.

[24]Drumann, 2.40, 4.564 (compare also 3.432); Risse, 1; Dorn Seiffen, 35; Postgate VIII, Introduction, xxix; Holmes, 3.174.

[25]Doijer does not include Sextus; the reasons are made clear in note 23.

[26]This statement of Drumann will be analyzed on page 32. There the question of the 'senate' and Pompey at Thessalonica will be discussed.

[27]The italics are mine. [28]The italics are mine.

. . . That Sextus was in Lesbos we know from Plutarch:[29] but when or why he went there we do not know."

(4) Holmes, 3.173–174: ". . . as it was rumoured that Caesar and his cavalry were approaching, the ship ⟨Pompey's⟩ sailed to Mytilene, where Pompey's wife Cornelia and his younger son Sextus had been staying *since the war began.*"[30]

The discrepancies are apparent enough. Doijer does not know when Cornelia and Sextus were sent to Lesbos. Drumann (in his second statement) places the event after Pompey's retreat from Italy; if I understand him correctly, he means that Pompey sent them away on or after March 17, 49, the date on which he left Brundisium.[31] Postgate and Holmes agree that the event took place at the beginning of the war.[32] Again, Drumann and Holmes agree that Pompey dispatched both Cornelia and Sextus to Lesbos.[33] Postgate admits that Cornelia and Sextus were together at Lesbos, but does not know why and when Sextus came to Lesbos. The ancient evidence (supported by the authority of Drumann and Holmes) would indicate that both Cornelia and Sextus were sent to Lesbos together. Pompey the Great was an affectionate father as well as a devoted husband,[34] and he would therefore take especial thought for his younger son, in view of the fact that the elder son was exposed to danger in his capacity of commander of a naval squadron.[35] The objection may be raised that Sextus was now old enough to be a *legatus* with his father: would he be likely to leave the war area for a place of safety? We shall see[36] that Cornelia

---

[29]And others, it may be added, whom Postgate quotes.

[30]The italics are mine. To this may be added the remark of Dittenberger, 2.758: "Vere anni 49 a. Ch. priusquam ipse Italia cederet Pompeius uxorem Mytilenas miserat. . . ." Sextus is not mentioned here, since the inscription deals with Cornelia exclusively; compare page 15 above, and note 34.

[31]Cicero, Att. 9.15.6; compare Holmes, 3.379.

[32]So does Risse, 1.

[33]So does Risse; see also Dorn Seiffen, 35: "Omnes enim reliqui hac de re scriptores consentiunt, filium a patre extra belli tumultum clam una cum Cornelia matre in Lesbon ablegatos fuisse." Why *clam?* There is no authority for that word, and its implications. The fact that Plutarch reports (Pompey 66.3) that many sailed to Cornelia with the news of the victory at Dyrrachium shows that her place of refuge was well known. See below, note 79.

[34]See above, page 15.

[35]In 48 he destroyed Caesar's ships at Oricum and Lissus.   [36]Page 19.

(and Sextus) spent almost a year near Pompey in Thessalonica before they were sent to Lesbos. They were not sent to Lesbos until danger was imminent; with danger imminent it is altogether possible that Pompey sent his son (at least ostensibly) to provide for the safety of Cornelia.

Drumann's expression, 'after the retreat from Italy,' and those of Postgate and Holmes, "at the beginning of the war" and "since the war began," are not as precise as they might be, and it may be in place to attempt the derivation from the testimony of the Greek historians of a more specific date. Of the authors cited above (page 24) only Appian indicates a date for Pompey's sending of Cornelia and Sextus away; he states that this happened *when Pompey was at war with Caesar* (Γαίῳ Καίσαρι πολεμῶν). Otherwise we have in the ancient authors only the three facts: (1) Cornelia and Sextus were sent to Lesbos; (2) they were sent there for their safety; and (3) Pompey joined them after the Battle of Pharsalus. Thus, with the exception of Appian's correct but broad statement, there is nothing to justify the views of the scholars mentioned above, that Cornelia and Sextus were sent to Lesbos at the beginning of the war or after the retreat from Italy.

In order to fix more precisely the date of the departure of Cornelia and Sextus from Italy and their arrival in Lesbos it will be necessary to review briefly the movements of Pompey the Great during the period involved. It has been mentioned (page 21) that Pompey abandoned Rome on January 17, 49, and that the consuls and the senators and their families followed him the next day. Pompey went to Capua and Teanum Sidicinum;[37] the latter place he left on January 25, and proceeded to Larinum[38] in Apulia. Here, as well as at Luceria and at Teanum Apulum, cohorts were concentrated.[39] From Larinum he went to Luceria, where he established his headquarters.[40] Caesar had been advancing steadily in the meantime, and, after occupying Firmum, Castrum Truentinum, and Aternum,

---

[37]Caesar, B. C. 1.14.4; Cicero, Att. 7.13b, 7.14.1, 8.11b. 2; Appian 2.37. Teanum Sidicinum was near Capua; see Strabo 5.4.10, 11.

[38]See Tyrrell and Purser, 4, Introduction, xiii, xv, and note to Att. 7.13 b. 3 (4.29); compare also Att. 7.12.2, 8.11b.2.

[39]Cicero, Att. 7.12.2.

[40]Cicero, Att. 8.11a; Appian 2.38. Compare also Tyrrell and Purser, 4, Introduction, xix; and Veith, Caesar, 101.

he marched against Corfinium, the most important concentration point of the Pompeian forces, 130 miles distant from Luceria. The defense of Corfinium was in the hands of Domitius Ahenobarbus.[41]

A delicate situation now developed. Pompey had already decided to quit Italy,[42] demonstrating thereby his foresight.[43] Desiring to concentrate the largest possible force, he urged Domitius to join him at Luceria;[44] a combination of his forces and Domitius's might still offer Caesar resistance on Italian soil.[45] Domitius at first agreed, but soon changed his mind, and, when Caesar reached Corfinium on February 14, he requested Pompey to rush to his assistance.[46] This message hastened Pompey's decision; he refused assistance to Domitius,[47] left Luceria on February 19, and arrived at Brundisium (via Canusium, where he remained a day) on February 25, 49.[48] Because of Caesar's continued advance,[49] Pompey sent part of his army to Epirus on March 4.[50] He himself remained in Brundisium and defended it against Caesar until his transports returned from Dyrrachium. He left Brundisium, on March 17;[51] Caesar entered the city on the next day.[52] Within 65 days, then, Caesar had accomplished his almost bloodless conquest of Italy.[53]

From this account of Pompey's movements certain deductions may be drawn. Since the senators and other officers of State evacuated the city only one day after Pompey's departure, we may infer that Pompey sent his own family away before

---

[41]Compare Holmes, 3.11–12; Tyrrell and Purser, 4, Introduction, xviii–xix.

[42]Holmes 3.12. For Pompey's reasons compare Dio 41.10.3–4.

[43]Compare Plutarch, Pompey 63.1; Veith, Caesar, 101; Parker, 49.

[44]Cicero, Att. 8.12c, 8.12a. 1, 8.12b. 2, 8.12d; Caesar, B. C. 1.19.4; Dio 41.11.1.

[45]Veith, Caesar, 102.   [46]Caesar, B. C. 1.17.

[47]Cicero, Att. 8.12d, 8.12 a.2–3.

[48]Cicero, Att. 8.9.4, 8.14.1, 9.1.1, 9.10.8.

[49]He reached the walls of Brundisium on March 9; compare Cicero, Att. 9.13a. 1.

[50]Cicero, Att. 9.6.3; but see Att. 9.15.6. Compare Caesar, B. C. 1.25.2; Appian 2.39–40; Dio 41.12.1; Plutarch, Pompey 62.2.

[51]Cicero, Att. 9.15.6.   [52]Ibidem.

[53]60, according to Plutarch, Pompey 63.2, but 65, according to Holmes, 3.32. Holmes's computation is correct.

January 17, perhaps as soon as the news of Caesar's crossing of the Rubicon reached the metropolis (January 14). Pompey must have realized that, from the military point of view, Caesar had the initiative; naturally, then, he would be prompted to act quickly, and not postpone the removal of his family until the last moment. January 14–16 would, then, be the possible dates for the removal of Cornelia and Sextus from Rome or its vicinity, for they may well have been sojourning on one of Pompey's estates near Rome.

Since Pompey was constantly on the move, it is hardly likely that his family joined him, though they may have been with him at Luceria, where he established his headquarters temporarily.[54] If so, they may have remained there until the arrival of Domitius's request for assistance, February 17.[55] But on February 19 Pompey "turned his back on Domitius"[56] and marched to Brundisium, which he reached on February 25. If Cornelia and Sextus were at Luceria, they left that place on February 17–19. February 19 is the preferable date. That they did in fact leave on that day (if they were at Luceria at all) may be inferred from Cicero's statement that Pompey left Luceria (for Brundisium) without his baggage and before his legions.[57] The latter arrived (at Brundisium) from Luceria about the end of February.[58]

Further, the duration of the stay of Cornelia and Sextus in Brundisium can not have been very long. The evacuation of the Pompeian forces was effected in two divisions, as has been stated (page 28). The first division sailed on March 4, and included, besides part of the army, the consuls, senators, and tribunes, with their wives and children.[59] Caesar reached Brundisium on March 9.[60] It is again hard to believe that,

---

[54]Temporarily, because, as was mentioned above (page 21), he had decided to quit Italy: compare Cicero, Att. 8.2.3: *Vagamus egentes cum coniugibus et liberis.* It is clear that the wives and children of senators accompanied them on their wanderings.

[55]That Luceria was a safe place, at least temporarily, is plain from Pompey's dispatch to Cicero (Att. 8.11a), wherein he invited him thither because he (Pompey) considered Luceria a safe refuge.

[56]Tyrrell and Purser, 4, Introduction, xxv; compare Cicero, Att. 8.9.4.
[57]Cicero, Att. 8.9.4.   [58]Holmes, 3.25.

[59]Cicero, Att. 9.6.3. Compare Velleius 2.50.1–2; Plutarch, Caesar 35.1, Pompey 62.2–3.   [60]See note 49.

while the senators, consuls, and others sailed on March 4, Pompey waited to the last minute (i. e. until March 17, the date of his own sailing) to send his family away and that he exposed his wife and his son to the dangers of the blockade which Caesar established shortly after he reached Brundisium. We are therefore led to the conclusion that, since Pompey arrived at Brundisium ahead of his army, he either dispatched Cornelia and Sextus thence to a place of safety immediately on his arrival (after February 25; see above, page 29), or included them in the first division, which sailed for Dyrrachium on March 4, and carried the wives and dependents of the members of the government. If this conclusion is correct, Cornelia and Sextus left Brundisium between February 26 and March 4, 49.

We may now sum up. When news of the crossing of the Rubicon reached the metropolis on January 14, Pompey dispatched Cornelia and Sextus from Rome or its vicinity before he himself left the city (January 17). There is a possibility that they were with him at Luceria, and that they left Luceria for Brundisium on February 19. They sailed from Brundisium on March 4, at the latest. The date of the departure of Cornelia and Sextus from Italian soil would, therefore, be between January 14 and March 4, 49 B. C.

To those who find the reasoning set forth above unsatisfactory and maintain that Pompey definitely decided to remove Cornelia and Sextus to Lesbos either immediately after Caesar crossed the Rubicon or after Pompey determined to leave Italy[61] the following questions may be addressed: (1) Does leaving Italian soil necessarily mean going to Lesbos', (2) Was it imperative that Cornelia and Sextus be sent to Lesbos immediately?, (3) If so, by what route did Cornelia and Sextus reach Lesbos?

In the first place, it is important to remember that both divisions of Pompey's forces which left Brundisium landed at Dyrrachium, and that the season of the year was unfavorable for the circumnavigation of the Peloponnese to Lesbos. Circumnavigation not being feasible, the only alternative was the land route, through Macedonia. We must realize that (a) Pompey knew very well that Caesar would be unable to follow him, because he had no ships available at Brundisium for the

---

[61]In February 49; see Heitland, 3.284.

purpose, and because he could be threatened from the rear by Pompey's veteran legions in Spain.[62] The truth of the latter statement is demonstrated by the fact that from Brundisium Caesar proceeded at once to the conquest of Spain. It was not until January 4, 48, that Caesar, upon his return to Italy from Spain, attempted to cross from Brundisium to Epirus, where he did in fact land on the following day.[63] Thus, from the time of Pompey's departure from Italy to Caesar's crossing over to Epirus nine months elapsed,[64] during which Pompey could proceed undisturbed with the preparations which he actually commenced before leaving Italy.[65]

Upon reaching Dyrrachium after leaving Brundisium, Pompey marched along the Via Egnatia to Thessalonica (modern Saloniki), the spot where Cicero had spent his exile. The city had a good harbor and *navalia* (docks), and, because of its central position, was an important trading-post.[66] Here Pompey established a 'senate,' composed of the senators who had followed him, on the ground that Rome was occupied by the rebellious Caesarians;[67] this 'senate' Cicero recognized as legitimate.[68] According to Dio, Pompey even wintered at Thessalonica, at the same time keeping an eye upon the Adriatic coast.[69] Here he was appointed commander-in-chief of the Republican armies. The concentration point of Pompey's army, however, was Berrhoea, about forty miles west of Thessalonica; there Pompey drilled his levies.[70]

From these facts it is clear that, until Caesar crossed to Epirus, there was no pressing need for Pompey to send his family to Lesbos, especially since the seat of government was

---

[62]Caesar, B. C. 1.29; Velleius 2.50.2; Plutarch, Pompey 63.2, Caesar 35.2; Appian 2.52; Dio 41.15.1.

[63]Caesar, B. C. 3.6.3.

[64]Or, as Caesar reckons it, a whole year: see B. C. 3.3.1.

[65]He was gathering together the resources of the East, as may be seen from Cicero, Att. 9.9.2; compare 9.10.3 and Caesar, B. C. 3.3. See also Orosius 6.15.18.

[66]Lübker, 1039. Compare also Lehmann-Hartleben, 285.

[67]Dio 41.18.6. Compare also 41.43; Plutarch, Pompey 64.3, 65.1, 66.4, Cato Minor 53.4. See Holmes, 3.113.

[68]Att. 10.1.2, Fam. 4.1.1. Cicero's attitude was legally justified since the consuls and many senators were with Pompey.

[69]Dio 41.44.1; but see Holmes, 3.431.

[70]Plutarch, Pompey 64.1; see also Holmes, 3.431.

established at Thessalonica. Not only in respect to government and administration did the city become a replica of Rome,[71] but intrigues and jealousies flourished among the senators quite as if they had been at home. Only in one respect was there unanimity in Pompey's camp, and that was in hatred of Caesar.[72] It is but natural to suppose that the wives and the children of the members of the government who had accompanied their husbands and fathers settled there, and, since Pompey also spent some time in Thessalonica, we may reasonably assume that Cornelia and Sextus too were there. So long as the military situation was safe, it was certainly better for them to remain among Romans and in contact with Roman society than to go to Mitylene in Lesbos. The 'many' whom Plutarch speaks of as sailing to Cornelia of their own accord with news of the battle at Dyrrachium could only be friends and acquaintances; they could only have sailed from Thessalonica, since Pompey must have notified the 'senate' there of his victory at Dyrrachium.[73] It must also be kept in mind that Berrhoea was no great distance away, and that Pompey could keep in constant communication with his family; his deep attachment to Cornelia must not be forgotten. Furthermore, even when he marched toward Dyrrachium, the Via Egnatia provided an excellent means of communication with Thessalonica.

The passage in Plutarch (Pompey 66.3), however, makes it clear that, when the battle at Dyrrachium was fought, Cornelia was at Lesbos. The question then arises, When did Pompey send Cornelia and Sextus from Thessalonica to Lesbos? A consideration of the military situation shows that there were two significant moments when this might have taken place. The shocking news that Caesar had successfully crossed to Epirus, had taken several cities, and was pushing on to lay siege to Dyrrachium reached Pompey as he was moving along the Via Egnatia, near Scampa (modern Elbassan), about forty miles east of Dyrrachium. Pompey succeeded in anticipating Caesar and secured Dyrrachium, but his army was in a panic-

---

[71]Dio 41.43. Compare Meyer, 313.   [72]Meyer, 312.

[73]If he sent messengers to all quarters of the globe announcing his victory (Caesar, B. C. 3.79.4 [compare 3.72.4]; Appian 2.63; Plutarch, Pompey 66.1), the Senate was surely the first to be notified.

stricken condition, and did not recover its spirits even when Caesar withdrew and encamped on the Apsus.[74] At this juncture Pompey may well have sent instructions to Thessalonica that Cornelia and Sextus should sail to Lesbos. For all its numerical superiority Pompey's army could not compare with Caesar's army of veterans. Aside from the Roman levies brought from Italy Pompey's army consisted of a multilingual rabble, re-cruited the world over, and inexperienced in warfare;[75] and for all Pompey's efforts to mold it into a fighting unit it remained ". . . a heterogeneous aggregate . . . which could not act in harmony . . ."[76] If such a feeble military critic as Cicero sensed the sad state of Pompey's army,[77] how could Pompey himself not be aware of it?

The second significant moment—much the more significant of the two—was Antony's successful crossing to Epirus at the end of March, 48. His junction with Caesar was accomplished on April 3, 48,[78] and strengthened Caesar's forces greatly. Pompey certainly did not underestimate the importance of this step, which he had tried to prevent, and, since he could not foresee Caesar's defeat at Dyrrachium and was careful by nature,[79] he may well have dispatched Cornelia and Sextus at that time to Lesbos; for, as has been said (page 32), at the time of the Battle of Dyrrachium they were at Lesbos. He is far more likely to have sent them to Lesbos at this time than at the time considered in the preceding paragraph. Between January, 48 (after Caesar's landing), therefore, and April, 48 (after Antony's junction with Caesar), Pompey sent Cornelia and Sextus to Mitylene in Lesbos; until that time he clearly had no absolutely compelling reason to do so. The route by

---

[74]Caesar, B. C. 3.11.2, 13.1. See also Holmes, 3.121–122; Heitland, 3. 298–299.

[75]Caesar, B. C. 3.4; Velleius 2.51.1; Appian 2.70-71; Dio 41.55.2–4; Plutarch, Pompey 71.5. Compare also Plutarch, Caesar 39.2, 40; Orosius 6.15.18.

[76]Holmes, 3.115; compare also Heitland, 3. 295–296.

[77]Fam. 7.32; Caesar's legions, on the other hand, he calls *robustissimae*. Pharsalus proved him right. Compare also Plutarch, Cicero 38.2.

[78]See Veith, Geschichte, 314. Compare also Holmes, 3.126–132; Heit-land, 3.301; Drumann, 3.440–441.

[79]In respect to Pompey's carefulness I agree with Drumann. Although there is no evidence that the sending away of Cornelia and Sextus de-pressed the army, the deduction is safe. Drumann's statement serves further to refute Dorn Seiffen's *clam;* see above, note 33.

which they reached Mitylene from Italy would be as follows: from Brundisium to Dyrrachium by sea, thence to Thessalonica by the Via Egnatia, and, after a stay at Thessalonica, by sea to Mitylene.

The question next arises, Why was Lesbos selected as a place of safety, and not, let us say, Lemnos, which was much nearer? We have already spoken of the strong influence which Theophanes of Mitylene exercised upon Pompey. It was in honor of this Greek that Pompey bestowed autonomy on Mitylene, on his return from the East.[80] Theophanes accompanied Pompey on campaigns, on his departure from Italy as well as after his defeat at Pharsalus.[81] The city of Mitylene honored Pompey as her benefactor and savior.[82] The selection of Mitylene, therefore, was natural. On the one hand, it was due probably to the influence of Theophanes, and, on the other, to Pompey's reliance on the city, which subsequently proved its loyalty by offering him shelter when he was in flight, a thing which many other cities refused to do.[83] It may be added that for a person of Cornelia's literary tastes[84] the country of Sappho and Alcaeus would possess a peculiar appeal, especially since traditional poetic contests were still being held there.[85]

Let us now revert to Drumann's first statement (page 25, above). It occurs in his discussion of the establishment of the 'senate' at Thessalonica, which was constituted soon after Pompey and the senators reached that city from Dyrrachium, approximately at the end of January, 49. If I understand Drumann correctly, he thinks that Pompey sent his family off shortly after he arrived in Thessalonica. How can this be reconciled with Drumann's second and third statements (page 25)? But, perhaps, by "nach dem Rückzuge" (in the second statement) Drumann means to signify the whole period of time until Pompey's arrival in Thessalonica. Even so, the statement is very obscure and not acceptable, because one may not speak

---

[80]Velleius 2.18.3; Plutarch, Pompey 42.4.

[81]Compare Caesar, B. C. 3.18.3; Cicero, Att. 9.11.4; Plutarch, Pompey 76.5, 78.2.

[82]Drumann, 4.555, note 6. For the relations between the people of Mitylene and the house of Pompey see C. Cichorius, Rom und Mitylene, 8–9 (Leipzig, 1888).

[83]Plutarch, Pompey 75.2.   [84]Ibidem 55.1. See also above, page 15.

[85]Plutarch, Pompey 42.2.

of a 'retreat' when there is no possibility of pursuit; Caesar did not and could not pursue. But the foregoing argument makes it sufficiently clear that Pompey was most unlikely to send his family away shortly after he arrived in Thessalonica, since there was no occasion for such haste. If Sextus was indeed a *tribunus* or a *legatus* in the army (page 26), there would be an element of disgrace involved in sending him away in such unseemly haste. Sextus's departure would quite likely have been pictured in derogatory light in the summary of his character in Velleius 2.73, or even in Appian 5.143.

Appian, therefore, in his statement that the departure of Cornelia and Sextus happened when Pompey was (actually) at war with Caesar comes nearer the truth than does any of the other historians. The same may be said for Lucan, who, for all his misstatements on other matters, rightly says (5.722–727):

> Undique conlatis in robur Caesaris armis
> summa videns duri Magnus discrimina Martis
> iam castris instare suis seponere tutum
> coniugii decrevit onus Lesboque remota
> te procul a saevi strepitu, Cornelia, belli
> occulere. . . .

It was only when his army was to face the supreme test, in this case the struggle at Dyrrachium, that Pompey decided to send his family away. As has been shown above (page 32), the decision may have been made at either of two important moments. In both instances Pompey himself was away from Thessalonica, and the touching farewell between Pompey and Cornelia pictured in Lucan 5.727–729 must, therefore, be a poetic fiction, a further instance of Lucan's interweaving of fact and fancy (see above, page 23).

The above outline of Pompey's movements should permit the substitution of the approximately precise dates here offered for the vague expressions of time employed by the scholars whose views I have discussed.

V. PHARSALUS TO THE IDES OF MARCH

Lucan closes his account of the farewell scene between Pompey and Cornelia with the line:[1]

Instabat miserae Magnum quae redderet hora.

The hour was indeed approaching which was to restore Pompey to his unhappy wife.

The joy after the victory at Dyrrachium was short-lived. Pompey dispatched messengers to all quarters to report his victory and to paint it in the fairest colors,[2] but he must himself have felt misgivings concerning the final result. Certainly he could not have been encouraged by the preposterous attitude of the leading members of his party, in whom the victory had engendered over-confidence.[3] Pompey intended to wear Caesar out by famine and delays, and, although he followed Caesar to Thessaly after the Battle of Dyrrachium, he avoided the risk of a decisive contest.[4] But with the Roman nobles personal interests played a more important part than military necessity, and they proceeded to divide the spoils and offices and even to plan proscriptions before the final victory had been won; these nobles forced Pompey to give battle at Pharsalus against his will and better judgment,[5] and ἐπὶ κακῷ τε αὐτοῦ, as Appian says.[6] No wonder Cicero shuddered to contemplate the victory of his own party. With good reason did he write,[7] Ex eo tempore vir ille summus ⟨Pompeius⟩ nullus imperator fuit. Appian, indeed, believed that Caesar's defeat at Dyrrachium turned out to be a godsend to him.[8]

In the Battle of Pharsalus, which was fought on August 9,

---

[1]Lucan 5.815.

[2]Caesar, B. C. 3.79.4; compare also 3.72.4. See also Appian 2.63; Plutarch, Pompey 66.1.

[3]Caesar, B. C. 3.72.1; compare 3.96.1. See also Plutarch, Pompey 66.2, Caesar 40.1, 42.1; Appian 2.69.

[4]Appian 2.63, 66; Plutarch, Pompey 66.1-2, 67.1, Caesar, 40.1, 41.1. Cicero was of the opinion that the war ought to be prolonged: see Fam. 7.3.2.

[5]Cicero, Fam. 7.3.2, Att. 11.6.2; Caesar, B. C. 3.82.4-5, 83. But see Velleius 2.52.1; Appian 2.67, 69; Plutarch, Pompey 67, Caesar 41.1-2, 42.

[6]2.67; compare also 2.71, at the end.   [7]Fam. 7.3.2.

[8]2.71 θεοβλαβεία... ἐν καιρῷ... τῷ Καίσαρι γενομένη; 2.67 θεοῦ βλάπτοντος. ...

48 B. C., the efficiency of Caesar triumphed over the numbers of Pompey.[9] Pompey did not wait until the very last moment, but left his camp, and with only a few companions fled to Larissa, where he embarked for Amphipolis.[10] After a short stay there he sailed to Mitylene, in order to take Cornelia and Sextus on board.[11] Sailing from Mitylene toward Egypt, he touched at several cities and islands on his way, among them Chios and Cyprus. The humiliation of his defeat was brought home to him by the refusal of certain cities, for example Rhodes and Antioch, to admit him.[12] Nevertheless he did succeed in gathering a little force, with which he sailed from Cyprus.[13] He reached Egypt[14] on September 27, 48,[15] but, instead of finding there a place of refuge, he met his miserable death before the eyes of Cornelia and Sextus,[16] on September 28, 48 B. C.

Even before Pompey was stabbed in the skiff that was taking him ashore, Cornelia and Sextus and the others on board

[9]Heitland, 3.308.

[10]Caesar, B. C. 3.96.3–4, 102.4; Orosius 6.15.27–28; Dio 42.2.2–4; Plutarch, Pompey 73.1–3, 74.1.

[11]See the evidence cited above, pages 22–25, and compare Caesar, B. C. 3.102.4. Pompey's flight is in a way parallel to the flight of Antony after Actium. Antony's land army was intact, and he might have joined it and have offered further resistance; similarly Pompey's navy was intact, and he had forces also in Africa. Both failed to make use of these resources, and in their flight thought only of the women they loved.

[12]Compare Caesar, B. C. 3.102.6–7. I do not aim to mention all the places at which Pompey touched. An excellent discussion and itinerary may be found in Postgate VIII, Introduction, xxv–xlii, lxxi–lxxvii; compare also Holmes, 3.174–178.

[13]Compare Plutarch, Pompey 76.3; Caesar, B. C. 3.103.1.

[14]The exact spot was Pelusium, at the easternmost mouth of the Nile: see Caesar, B.C. 3.103. Holmes's expression (3.176), "failing to make the harbour of Alexandria", is misleading. Pompey meant to go to Pelusium, for the king and his followers were there.

[15]Postgate VIII, Introduction, lxxvii.

[16]Caesar, B. C. 3.103.3–5, 104.3; Florus 2.13.52; Livy, Periocha 112; Lucan 8.536–636; Martial 5.74.1–2 (compare 3.66.1, 5.69.1); Velleius 2.53. 2; Appian 2.83–87; Dio 42.3–6; Plutarch, Pompey 77.1, 78.4, 79 (compare Plutarch, Caesar 48.1). Orosius says (6.15.28): *Pompei uxor filiique fugerunt.* This statement would imply that the older son was also present, but this cannot be true, inasmuch as he was with the fleet, which was concentrated at Corcyra (Plutarch, Cicero 39.1, Cato Minor 55.3). A statement similar to that of Orosius is made by Pseudo-Victor 77. The tragic pity of Pompey's death impressed itself on ancient writers, and became a stock example for the wretched end of a great character.

Pompey's vessels had seen that Egyptian galleys and men of war were taking their crews aboard, and that an army was drawn up on the shore;[17] and they quickly realized that the Egyptians were up to mischief. They therefore immediately turned their ships out to sea, and, assisted by a favorable breeze, escaped the pursuing Egyptians. They reached Tyre and then the island of Cyprus, from which they had sailed for Egypt.[18]

We must now turn back to the events after the Battle of Pharsalus. When Cato, who was in command at Dyrrachium, received the startling news of the defeat at Pharsalus, he decided to join the fleet, which was still intact and was concentrated at Corcyra; other Pompeian leaders sailed to Africa. Gnaeus Pompey was among those present at Corcyra, and was barely restrained from murdering Cicero when, at the council of war held in that place, Cicero refused to take further part in the war and to accept the command tendered him by Cato. Cato was as yet ignorant of the fate of Pompey, but guessed that he would try to escape to Egypt or to Libya; being eager to join his chief he sailed off, with Gnaeus Pompey.[19] Sailing along the coast of Laconia and Crete, Cato and Gnaeus met Cornelia and Sextus, who were continuing their flight from Cyprus. From the fugitives they learned of the death of Pompey. Their only remaining course was to make for Africa; thither Scipio, Labienus, and others had gone, and there they had commenced preparations for continuing the war against Caesar. Cato and his companions then coasted to Cyrene; they wintered in Libya. In the spring of 47 Cato joined his forces to those which were already gathered in Africa.[20] The surviving relatives

---

[17]Plutarch, Pompey 78.3; Appian 2.84.

[18]Cicero, Tusc. Disp. 3.66; Livy, Periocha 112; Lucan 9.117; Appian 2.85; Dio 42.49.2; Plutarch, Pompey 70.1.

[19]Appian 2.87; Dio 42.10 (compare 42.12.4); Plutarch, Cato Minor 55–56.1, Cicero 39.1–2 (compare Plutarch, Pompey 76.2). Cicero was saved from Gnaeus's wrath by Cato, and then sailed off to Brundisium. Compare also Livy, Periocha 111, and Lucan 9.121.

[20]Plutarch, Cato Minor 56; Lucan 9.36–50 (compare 9.120, and 297). Dio's statement (42.13.3; compare 42.57) that Cato and Gnaeus learned of Pompey's death at Cyrene is misleading; compare Drumann, 3.513 and note 4, 4.562, 564, and Blok, 6. Risse (2, note 5) believes that they met Cornelia and Sextus at Paliurus, a harbor situated in Cyrene, mentioned by

of Pompey, therefore, found refuge in Africa, but even this was destined to be only temporary.

The advent of Cato added considerable strength to the Republicans, or, as Cicero calls them, the patriots.[21] These leaders had had a respite of about a year and a half in which to recover from the defeat at Pharsalus,[22] and during this period their army had reached a high state of preparedness;[23] nor must we lose sight of the fact that Africa was hostile to Caesar.[24] Yet all these advantages were rendered void, chiefly through the ill-assorted leadership, which included the high-minded Cato on the one hand, and the conscienceless extortioner

---

Lucan (9.42). I follow Drumann and Blok, for the following reasons. Since Cornelia and Sextus fled to Cyprus via Tyre, as has been stated (page 38), it is clear that they followed the coast, and from the direction of their voyage we may assume that their objective was the fleet of Pompey; they surely knew that this fleet was intact, for Pompey in his flight to Egypt had bewailed the fact that he had made no use of his powerful navy, from which, in his infatuation after Pharsalus, he had run away (Appian 2.87; Plutarch, Pompey 76.2). Furthermore, they could travel quite safely, for Caesar was on his way to Egypt. When Cato (with Gnaeus) left Corcyra, he started to sail round the Peloponnese. On the way he seized Patrae, from which he was soon driven off (Dio 42.13.2–3, 14); hence it is seen that, on his way to join Pompey in Egypt or Libya, Cato sailed around Greece and Crete. He therefore probably met Cornelia and Sextus and received the sad news somewhere between Crete and Cyprus. Had he known of Pompey's death earlier (Dio 42.13.2 admits that after he sailed to the Peloponnese he did not know of it), he would doubtless have sailed to Africa straightway to join Scipio. The isonomy of Cape Palinurus in Italy and Paliurus in Cyrene (compare Strabo 17.3.22: κώμη Παλίουρος) must have appealed to Lucan's fancy, and he therefore changed the location of the meeting; compare C. M. Francken, M. Annaei Lucani Pharsalia (Leyden, 1896), note ad locum: "Merito dubitatur an deceptus sit Lucanus similitudine *Palinurus* et Paliurus." It may be added that, at Patrae, Cato and Gnaeus were joined by Faustus Sulla, son of the dictator and son-in-law of Pompey the Great, doubtless accompanied by his wife Pompeia, who was later captured by Caesar at Utica (see below, page 40). Nor must we forget that Q. Metellus Scipio, who commanded in Africa, was the father-in-law of Pompey the Great.   [21]Att. 11.7.3.

[22]Heitland, 3.327; Veith, Geschichte, 397. The most recent account of events in Africa between 49 and 46 B. C. is in Stephane Gsell, Histoire de l'Afrique du Nord, 8.27–155 (Paris, 1928). This book came into my hands after the present chapter was composed, but I have found nothing in it that would cause me to alter anything I have written.

[23]Dio 42.56.5; compare Appian 2.87.

[24]Velleius 2.54.2–3; Dio 42.56.2. Compare Plutarch, Caesar 52.1.

Scipio on the other; this combination is very suggestive of the
partnership of Brutus and Cassius. Instead of fostering and
capitalizing hostility to Caesar on the part of the provincials,
instead of profiting by the dearly purchased lesson of Pharsalus
and striving for a unity of counsel, instead of heeding the
moderating influence of Cato, the leaders repeated the mistakes
that had been committed in Thessaly. They quarreled about
the command, and vied with one another in gratifying the
wishes of Juba.[25] Scipio in particular, by his atrocious policy
of harshness, cruelty, extortion, and even devastation, soon
made himself and the army which followed his example almost
more feared than was Caesar.[26] Small wonder, then, that Cato
despaired of victory.[27]

The survivors of Pompey the Great established their quarters
in Utica;[28] after the differences between the leaders were
settled, Cato became governor of the city,[29] and it was protected by a strong garrison and fleet. It might be expected
that to the sons of that Pompey who had been a central figure
in Roman history for a generation, and in particular to the
elder son Gnaeus, who had seen service with the fleet, important
rôles would be given at this juncture. But this was not the
case, nor are the reasons far to seek. Pompey the Great had
never been a real favorite, either with the people, or with the
nobles; the latter had been estranged in part by the influence
which his freedmen exerted over Pompey. The nobles had
desired to destroy Caesar by senatorial decrees, and they found
that they required the prestige and the army of Pompey to
give weight to their decrees.[30] It was only their common

[25]Dio 42.57.1; Plutarch, Cato Minor 57.1–2, 58.5.

[26]For an account of Scipio see Drumann, 2.36–40; compare also 3.517–
518.

[27]Plutarch, Cato Minor 58.6–7.

[28]This may be inferred from Bellum Africanum 22.1, M. Cato interim,
qui Uticae praeerat, Cn. Pompeium filium multis verbis adsidueque obiur-
gare non desistebat, and from Appian 2.100, who reports that Caesar
captured at Utica the daughter of Pompey the Great (Pompeia) with her
two children. Her husband Faustus Sulla was captured after Thapsus and
was killed by the Caesarians. See Bellum Africanum 95.2–3; Eutropius
6.23; Livy, Periocha 114; Orosius 6.16.1–5; Pseudo-Victor 78.9; Dio 42.13.3,
43.12.2. Compare also Risse, 2, note 9.

[29]Dio 42.57.4. See also Plutarch, Cato Minor 58.2–3; Livy, Periocha 113
(compare 114); Bellum Africanum 22.1.   [30]Drumann, 4.548.

hostility to Caesar that induced the Senate and Pompey to combine against him; neither, however, realized that "mere military skill was not enough for civil war."[31] In the situation then prevailing elevation of the sons of Pompey in Africa would have meant the acknowledgment of the tradition of Pompey, which his sons represented. But it was not the Pompeian tradition[32] for which the Republicans were fighting. They had no desire that Gnaeus or Sextus should play in Roman politics the rôle of their late father, with the result that, in case of victory, a Pompey would again be the indispensable First Citizen of Rome. They were fighting rather for the Republic, or, to be more precise, for the oligarchy.[33] The sons of Pompey, in their opinion, were needed not even as instruments, and the union between them and the Republican leaders had inevitably to be dissolved. Policy dictated that the break should not be too apparent, for, as Velleius puts it,[34] *Nusquam erat Pompeius corpore, adhuc ubique vivebat nomine.* In this sense the sons of Pompey were still an asset. Furthermore, the passionate character of Gnaeus made him objectionable to the Republican leaders. They could not forget that at Corcyra he had in his anger almost killed Cicero, that he breathed violent threats against those who wished to sail away, that he was obstinate and haughty[35] and considered cruelty a virtue, that he suffered from what is now called an inferiority complex, being always supicious and afraid that he was being laughed at. General opinion was to the effect that in case of victory a man of such violent temper would vent his rage not only on the Caesarians who opposed him openly, but also on the Republi-

---

[31]Heitland, 3.311.

[32]Mommsen says (4.400): "To the newly founded hereditary monarchy the hereditary pretendership attached itself at once like a parasite." Marsh says (63): "...in spite of good intentions he <Pompey> struck deadly blows at the republic without realizing it, and set invaluable precedents for an empire of which he did not dream." Compare Veith, Geschichte, 440; Drumann, 3.567. Gaston Boissier, Cicero and his Friends (in the translation by Adnah David Jones, London [undated]) says (330): "If they <the Republicans> had wished to continue the traditions of the preceding war, their leader was already at hand. Sextus, a son of Pompey ....remained. But men no longer desired to be of a Pompeian party." We shall see that some did so desire.

[33]Veith, Geschichte, 398.   [34]2.54.2; compare also 2.55.2.

[35]Plutarch, Cicero 39.1-2, Cato Minor 55.2-3.

cans whose loyalty he should suspect.[36]   An opportunity soon
offered of ridding themselves of the undesirable, if we may call
him that, without the unpleasantness that an open breach
would involve, and even with certain definite advantages to
their own party.   News came that Southern Spain was in revolt
against its outrageously unjust governor, Q. Cassius, and against
his master Caesar.[37]   It was thought that the insurgents would
welcome a son of Pompey, and so Gnaeus was sent to Spain.[38]
The purpose of his mission was not only to organize the opposition to Caesar, but also to provide a refuge in case things should
go badly with the Republicans in Africa.   Cato, who had some
influence over Gnaeus,[39] was made spokesman to advise Gnaeus
to go to Spain *ad paternas clientelas.*[40]   Gnaeus went, accordingly, in the early part of the African campaign (in the middle
of 47 B. C.).[41]

For Gnaeus, then, a task was found; but Sextus, it follows
from the discussion above, could hope for nothing better from
the Republicans in Africa than being tolerated in their midst.
As a matter of fact we hear nothing of him during this period
except that he was in Africa.   Veith,[42] Bernoulli,[43] and Butler
and Cary[44] state that he took part in the various battles fought
in Africa.   The assumption is quite reasonable, though there is

---

[36]Cicero, Fam. 15.19.4, and Tyrrell's note (4.553); compare also Fam.
6.18.2.   For Gnaeus's cruelty see Bellum Hispaniense 20–21.

[37]For Q. Cassius see below, page 45.

[38]Dio 42.56.4 (compare 43.29.1–2); Velleius 2.55.2.

[39]This is shown by the fact that Cato calmed Gnaeus at Corcyra, thus
saving Cicero's life.   See Plutarch, Cato Minor 55.3, Cicero 39.1–2.

[40]Bellum Africanum 22.

[41]Ibidem, 22–23; Dio 42.56.4, 43.29.2; Livy, Periocha 113.   Compare also
Klotz, 35, 37; Holmes, 3.295; Heitland, 3.331; Drumann, 3.518, 4.562.
Appian's statement on this point is absurd.   He seems to think (2.87)
that Gnaeus and Labienus sailed from Corcyra to Spain.   This is impossible
for the reason that Labienus fought in Africa and escaped to Spain with
Sextus after the battle of Thapsus: compare Bellum Africanum, *passim.*
That Gnaeus and Labienus were in Africa is clear also from Dio 42.5.7,
43.30.4.

[42]Geschichte, 398.   [43]Römische Ikonographie, 1.225 (Stuttgart, 1882).

[44]H. E. Butler and M. Cary, C. Suetonii Tranquilli Divus Iulius, 89
(Oxford, 1927).   These editors base their statement on Dio 42.5.7, but the
passage reads, ... ὁ δὲ Σέξτος ἐς τὴν Ἀφρικὴν πρὸς τὸν ἀδελφὸν τὸν Γναῖον
ἐκομίσθη.... I fail to see here any hint that Sextus participated in the
Battle of Thapsus.

no authority for it in the ancient literature. Later, in Spain, he was in charge of the garrison at Corduba;[45] perhaps this implies that he had had a certain amount of military experience.

Veith is correct, then, in saying[46] that Sextus was a nonentity in Africa, but I cannot see his reasons for saying ". . . er diente vielmehr als Geisel." For whom should he be held as hostage? Surely the Republicans apprehended no defection on the part of Gnaeus, for he went off to Spain with a wretched armament:[47]

. . . cum naviculis cuiusquemodi generis XXX, inibi paucis rostratis, profectus ab Utica . . . expeditoque exercitu numero servorum, libertorum II milium, cuius partem . . . armatam habuerat. . . .

The poverty of his equipment and the uncertainty of conditions in Spain made Gnaeus too dependent on the Republicans in Africa to think of defection. That Sextus was being held as hostage is therefore hardly a probable statement; the ancient authors do not suggest the idea. In any case Sextus did not distinguish himself, or perhaps was not suffered to distinguish himself, during his sojourn in Africa.

After Caesar crossed into Africa,[48] the Republicans at first gained a few successes. It was the same story of the initial success at Dyrrachium, and, later, at Philippi. But Caesar forced his opponents to give battle, and on April 6, 46 B. C., the Battle of Thapsus was fought.[49] The battle was a second but bloodier Pharsalus; the second army which tried to stem the onrush of monarchy was destroyed. Cato's worst fears were realized.[50] Events after the battle were a foretaste of what was to happen after Philippi.[51] Some of the leaders, Scipio, Cato, Petreius, committed suicide; others were executed;[52] still others, Attius Varus and the renegade Labienus, succeeded in making their way to Gnaeus in Spain. With the

---

[45]See below, page 49. [46]Geschichte, 398.

[47]Bellum Africanum 23.1.

[48]He landed at Hadrumentum on December 28, 47 B. C. Compare Bellum Africanum 2.4–5, 3.1; Appian 2.95.

[49]Drumann, 3.535, and notes; Holmes, 3.267.

[50]Plutarch, Cato Minor 58.6–7. [51]Appian 4.135.

[52]Bellum Africanum 94–96; Eutropius 6.23; Florus 2.13.68–72; Livy, Periocha 114; Orosius 6.16.4–6; Pseudo-Victor 80; Appian 2.100; Dio 43.8.4, 9.5, 12.2–3; Plutarch, Caesar 53.3, 54.1, Cato Minor 58.7, 70.

latter fled Sextus,[53] and from this time until the Battle of Munda
his fate is closely bound with that of his brother Gnaeus.

Let us look back for a moment upon the events of Sextus's
life since his departure from Italian soil. Flight and exile are
at best unpleasant, but, so long as Sextus remained in Thessalonica and Lesbos, so long as his father lived and had power,
his lot was bearable. But the defeat at Pharsalus put an end
to his comfort and safety, and he was forced to flee for his very
life. From August 21, 48 B. C., when Pompey the Great left
Lesbos, until September 28, 48 B. C.,[54] the day Pompey was
murdered, Sextus experienced real suffering and humiliation.
He saw how cities upon which his father had showered bene-
factions now refused to admit him, how Deiotarus left him in
the lurch in order to transfer his allegiance to Caesar betimes.[55]
Even the little hope that remained so long as his father was
alive was shattered by the crime at Pelusium. Flight was again
his only resource, and, when he had met Cato and his brother
Gnaeus and with them sailed to Africa, he received no very
cordial welcome from the Republicans there. From the time
he left Lesbos, therefore, until his flight, after the defeat at
Thapsus, to Spain, which he reached about the middle of
August, 46 B. C.,[56] his life was one of privation and humiliation.
He endured, to use the words of Horace,[57]

> dura navis,
> dura fugae mala, dura belli.

When Gnaeus was sent off by the Republicans with the forces
mentioned above (page 42), he did not proceed directly to
Spain. From Utica he went to Mauretania and there assaulted

---

[53]Dio 43.30.4; compare Orosius 6.16.6. His stepmother Cornelia was
pardoned by Caesar and returned to Rome (Dio 42.5.7). His sister Pompeia (see above, note 28) and his two nephews Caesar sent to Spain after he
took Utica (Appian 2.100). Orosius 6.16.5 and Florus 2.13.90 are wrong in
stating that Caesar ordered Pompeia's execution; he did order the execution
of her husband (see above, page 40). The author of the Bellum Africanum
was an eyewitness of this campaign, and is therefore more to be trusted
than Orosius and Florus, especially in this case, where he is supported by
Appian. In Bellum Africanum 95.3 we read: Pompeiae cum Fausti liberis
Caesar incolumitatem suaque omnia concessit. See also Drumann, 4.592.

[54]For these dates see Postgate VIII, Introduction, lxvii.

[55]Cicero, De Divinatione 2.78–79 (compare also 1.26–27, and Pro Rege
Deiotaro 13); Plutarch, Pompey 73.6.

[56]Risse, 2.   [57]Carmina 2.13.26–27.

the town of Ascurum, but was repelled by the inhabitants. Thence he turned his course to the Balearic Islands and occupied them, but his progress was interrupted by an illness which almost cost him Spain. In Spain atrocious mismanagement by Caesar's lieutenant, Q. Cassius, who had proved himself worse than Verres, had rendered the name of Caesar hated and the country ready to welcome political changes.[58] Revolution spread. The disaffected legions in Spain had, before the Battle of Thapsus, secretly sent ambassadors to Scipio in Africa, and were expecting Pompey; but, when they heard that the Battle of Thapsus had been fought and lost, and that Caesar had dispatched C. Didius with a fleet against them, they became alarmed lest they be destroyed before Gnaeus Pompey should reach them. Without awaiting his arrival, therefore, they appointed as their leaders two knights, Titus Quinctius Scapula and Quintus Aponius, drove out Trebonius, who had succeeded Cassius, and caused the province of Baetica to revolt.[59]

In the meantime Gnaeus recovered from his illness, and crossed to Spain. The name he bore proved a decided asset; some cities received him voluntarily, others he took by force. New Carthage he was compelled to besiege. There he was met by Scapula and his followers and was made commander-in-chief. Thus, when Sextus arrived in Spain, he found his brother in control of a considerable army. This army was continually increased by increments consisting of the survivors of Pharsalus and the African War, and by contingents of Spaniards and Celtiberians, to say nothing of large numbers of emancipated slaves. With this larger force at his disposal Gnaeus continued the conquest of Spain. His army had grown to thirteen legions, and so, although Caesarian forces under Q. Pedius and Q. Fabius Maximus were on the scene, they dared undertake no action against him,[60] but could only avoid open warfare and

---

[58]For Cassius see Drumann, 2.129, 133; Holmes, 3.293–295. Heitland observes (3.319): ". . . in the far West events were illustrating the boundless mischief that could be caused by the misdeeds of an ill-chosen subordinate out of reach of his master's control."

[59]Dio 43.14.2, 43.29; compare also Cicero, Fam. 9.13.1, and Bellum Hispaniense 33.3.

[60]Bellum Hispaniense 1; Livy, Periocha 113; Velleius 2.55.2; Appian 2. 87; Dio 43.30–31.1.

urge upon Caesar the necessity of coming to Spain.[61] Spanish communities which were *contrariae Pompeio* also kept sending messengers to Caesar petitioning for assistance.[62]

It may now be well to pause and consider the question of the ideals and the aims for which the sons of Pompey struggled. It has been said that they received only slight consideration in Africa; such treatment was not likely to be agreeable to the sons of the great general of the Republican cause, who considered himself the first citizen of his generation. The Republican leaders were not interested in the persistence of the Pompeian tradition, and, so long as they and not the sons of Pompey held the balance of power, there was little chance for that tradition to assert itself. From these considerations and from what we know of the upbringing and the character of the two young men we need not attribute their struggles against the incipient Empire to chauvinistic devotion to the cause of Republicanism. At their age, and under the stimulus of the anti-Caesarians with whom they associated, they may have been impelled—or they may have convinced themselves that they were impelled—by an idealistic determination to overthrow the 'tyrant.' Other motives are not difficult to surmise. There was in the first place *pietas* of much the same sort as that which later led Octavian to hound the assassins of his adoptive father. The sons of Pompey wished to exact a reckoning from Caesar and his adherents, and also from those Republicans who had fallen short of their duty to the house of Pompey. Closely bound up with this motive was the desire for rehabilitation in the esteem of the world. We have said that these young men had been brought up in a household which considered itself the first in Rome; it was difficult for them to submit to being reduced to the common level. The palpable aspect of this second motive was the question of the property of their late father. Caesar had caused it to be sold, and it had passed into the possession of Antony and Dolabella. The young men were faced with destitution, and great wealth was to such a degree a

---

[61]Bellum Hispaniense 7.4–5 (compare 30.1); Dio 43.31.1; Plutarch, Caesar 56.1. Cicero, Fam. 6.18.2, speaks of eleven legions; but to this number two that were stationed at Corduba must be added. Compare Bellum Hispaniense 34.2; Holmes, 3.542–543.

[62]Bellum Hispaniense 1.5 (compare 2.1).

necessity of the position they were used to maintain that one may easily think of them as going to war for no other reason than to recover what they believed to be, in matters of money and property, their due. But, aside from considerations of property and vengeance, there is the simple instinct of self-preservation; Caesar's famous clemency might be a doubtful quantity in the case of the sons of his late enemy.

Dr. T. Rice Holmes says (3.297):

The ⟨Spanish⟩ war was one which even the most embittered partisan who gave a thought to his country's welfare would never have begun. The duty of all Pompeians was now to desist from useless rebellion and to support the head of the state; and no excuse can be imagined for Gnaeus except that he despaired of receiving the pardon which even to him, if he had frankly appealed to the magnanimity of the conqueror, would not have been denied. . . .

On the following page, however, Dr. Holmes says:

Even Caesar could hardly be expected to forgive the obstinate rebel who forced him to abandon his reconstructive work. . . .

Theoretically Dr. Holmes is doubtless right in his general condemnation of Gnaeus, but practically there are extenuating circumstances which we must keep in mind before we proceed to condemn Gnaeus unreservedly. About the question of pardon Dr. Holmes's self-contradiction is patent. It is only in the light of later events that Caesar may be spoken of as the head of the State to whom it was the duty of all to submit, and there were many who, for a long time, maintained the opposite view. The best proof that republican feeling persisted in Rome even after Octavian gained the ascendancy was Octavian's insistence that he had 'restored the republic.'[62a] The reconstructive work which, says Dr. Holmes, Caesar was then engaged in Caesar undertook chiefly for his own benefit. In the sight of Gnaeus, Caesar was only the head of one party, and he himself had as good right to head another. Caesar's party happened to be in the ascendant, and Caesar had made himself head of the State, but there was no reason why the Pompeians should acknowledge his headship as legal, or should give up the struggle.

[62a]Monumentum Ancyranum 35. I shall cite other evidence below (pages 90–92) to illustrate the persistence of republican sentiment in Rome.

What would Gnaeus (and Sextus) have gained if they had appealed for pardon and had received it? Nothing more than sufferance again, and destitution which their haughty spirits could not brook. To Caesar himself is attributed the famous saying:[63] . . . δύο τε εἶναι τὰ τὰς δυναστείας παρασκευάζοντα καὶ φυλάσσοντα καὶ ἐπαύξοντα, στρατιώτας καὶ χρήματα, καὶ ταῦτα δ' ἀλλήλων συνεστηκέναι. Caesar and the Pompeys were alike entitled to strive for δυναστεία; the significant difference was that genius and efficiency were on the side of Caesar.[64] The moral basis of the behavior of Gnaeus was no lower, in short, than that of Caesar, or of the Republicans who fought in Africa, or, later, of Octavian himself, when he appeared to claim his heritage; all were primarily concerned with their own interests and their own advancement. The public life of the age can show but one Cato, with sufficient moral integrity and pertinacity to rise above the level of the selfishness that was prevalent.

At first Caesar ignored the existence of Gnaeus, but, when he learned that his new opponent was making headway,[65] he decided to take a hand in matters in person, and reached Spain on December 2, 46 B. C.[66].

We must now try to discover the rôle that Sextus played in the war in Spain. The available evidence on the subject is not entirely satisfactory. It is as follows.

(1) Eutropius 6.24: . . . Caesar . . . ad Hispanias est profectus, ubi Pompei filii, Cn. Pompeius et Sex. Pompeius, ingens bellum praeparaverant.

(2) Florus 2.13.74: plurimum quantum favoris partibus dabat fraternitas ducum et pro uno duo stare Pompeios.

(3) Orosius 6.16.6: ⟨Caesar⟩ . . . continuo in Hispanias contra Pompeios, Pompei filios, profectus . . . adversus Pompeios duos et Labienum atque Attium Varum multa bella et varia sorte gessit.

---

[63]Dio 42.49.4.

[64]Compare also Marsh, 150: "The history of Rome, since the military reforms of Marius, had made it clear to all that only a government which held the sword could hope to stand..." Pompey's sons simply followed the trend of their time. If they are to be condemned, so are the others. The principle on which hero-worshippers have whitewashed the career of Caesar is that subsequent success atones for illicit beginnings. Professor Marsh does not belong with the hero-worshippers.

[65]Dio 43.28.2.   [66]Holmes, 3.296, 541–542.

(4) Suetonius, Iulius 35.2: Dehinc Scipionem ac Iubam reliquias partium in Africa refoventis devicit, Pompei liberos in Hispania.

(5) Suetonius, Augustus 8.1: Profectum mox avunculum in Hispania adversus Cn. Pompei liberos . . . subsecutus.

(6) Plutarch, Caesar 56.1: ⟨Caesar⟩ . . . εἰς ᾽Ιβηρίαν ἐστράτευσεν ἐπὶ τοὺς Πομπηίου παῖδας, νέους μὲν ὄντας ἔτι, θαυμαστὴν δὲ τῷ πλήθει στρατιὰν συνειλοχότας καὶ τόλμαν ἀποδεικνυμένους ἀξιόχρεων πρὸς ἡγεμονίαν. . . .

Taken at face value these passages would indicate that both Gnaeus and Sextus were instrumental in collecting forces, that they had equal powers, that both participated in the various operations and in the final battle at Munda.[67] But in connection with the available evidence certain observations must be made. In the first place, Gnaeus had been in control of a considerable army and had been made commander-in-chief before Sextus reached Spain.[68] Moreover, all the passages cited exhibit a certain sketchiness and a tendency to generalize; all mention the brothers together. Fortunately, however, we possess a contemporary work, written by a military man, which throws light on the movements of Sextus, in which we are here chiefly interested and of which the 'civil' historians cited above do not speak at all. This contemporary work is the Bellum Hispaniense, which is without merit as literature, but of high value for the historian, because its author evidently shared in the campaign he describes.[69]

One of Gnaeus's first tasks as commander-in-chief was the selection of some central spot that would serve as a depot for his army in the field; this depot had to be entrusted to a person in whose good faith he could have no doubt. He selected Corduba[70] for his depot, and he put his brother Sextus in charge, perhaps because there was no one else whom he could trust so fully. When Caesar reached Spain and joined his lieutenants

---

[67]Compare also Plutarch, Caesar 56.3. After giving a sketchy account of the battle of Munda, Plutarch says: τῶν δὲ Πομπηίου παίδων ὁ μὲν νεώτερος διέφυγε. . . .

[68]See above, page 45; compare Drumann, 3.567.

[69]For a characterization of the author of this work see Holmes, 3.298; Klotz, 3–4.

[70]Bellum Hispaniense 11.1. . .commeatus ad castra Pompei ex oppido ⟨Corduba⟩ portabant. Compare Holmes, 3.299, 546; Klotz, 15.

Q. Pedius and Q. Fabius Maximus, Sextus was already in
Corduba, as may be seen from Bellum Hispaniense 3.1:

Erat idem temporis Sex. Pompeius frater qui cum praesidiis
Cordubam tenebat, quod eius provinciae caput esse existima-
batur; ipse autem Cn. Pompeius adulescens Uliam oppidum
oppugnabat et fere iam aliquot mensibus ibi detinebatur.[71]

This passage makes it clear that Sextus did not share the
command in the field with Gnaeus, but remained in charge of
the supplies at Corduba. This town Caesar then proceeded to
assault, in order to draw Gnaeus from the siege of Ulia, the
inhabitants of which were Caesarians.[72] Hence,

. . . timore adductus Sex. Pompeius litteras fratri misit ut
celeriter sibi subsidio veniret, ne prius Cordubam caperet
⟨Caesar⟩ quam ipse ⟨Gnaeus⟩ illo venisset.[73]

Gnaeus thereupon hastened to relieve his brother at Corduba,[74]
and Caesar withdrew without effecting its capture.

Sextus then did not, properly speaking, share the command
in Spain. Yet it is not hard to see why the historians mention
the brothers together. They were the only surviving male
members of the house of Pompey the Great, and their cause
was the same, though the one served it by commanding, the
other by obeying. Nay, Caesar himself thought of them as a
unity, if we may judge from the words which he is reported to
have spoken to his soldiers during the Battle of Munda:[75]
ἐβόα . . . εἰ μηδὲν αἰδοῦνται λαβόντες αὐτὸν ἐγχειρίσαι τοῖς
παιδαρίοις.[76]

But fate was still unkind to Sextus. On March 17, 45 B. C.,
Munda saw the bloodiest battle of Roman history, which ended

---

[71]Dio (43.32.4; compare 43.33.2) indicates that Sextus was in charge of
Corduba; his account lacks clearness, however. Compare also Bellum
Hispaniense 32.4.

[72]Bellum Hispaniense 4.2; Dio 43.31.4, 32. 2–4.

[73]Bellum Hispaniense 4.3.

[74]Bellum Hispaniense 4.4. The importance that Gnaeus attached to
Corduba may be judged from the fact that, after his failure to relieve
Ategna, which Caesar besieged and subsequently captured, Gnaeus marched
to Corduba to protect his supplies. See Bellum Hispaniense 11.1, and
compare Klotz, 23.

[75]Sextus did not take part in the Battle of Munda; see below, page 51.

[76]Plutarch, Caesar 56.2. Compare Eutropius 6.24:. . .in quo proelio
⟨apud Mundam⟩ adeo Caesar paene victus est ut fugientibus suis se
voluerit occidere, ne. . .in potestatem adulescentium. . .veniret.

in the decisive defeat of Gnaeus.[77] Gnaeus was himself badly wounded, but he succeeded in reaching his fleet at Carteia. The fleet was overtaken and destroyed by Didius. But, though Gnaeus's condition was aggravated by fresh wounds, he succeeded in reaching land. He was pursued and killed, after a desperate defense, near Lauron in Hispania Tarraconensis, and his head was brought to Caesar.[78]

On the death of his brother Sextus was left to carry on the Pompeian tradition alone. However much his subsequent conduct may prejudice us against him, his plight after Munda is such as to arouse our sympathy. Hitherto, since his father's death he had still had his fiery older brother to lean on, and he had had in Spain the confidence derived from an active army in the field waging war on behalf of his cause. Now at one blow both were destroyed, and Sextus was left without a firm shoulder to lean upon, alone, the enemy of organized civilization. From this time forward the chronicler of Sextus's life finds his task changed. Sextus is now the leader of whatever cause he may be said to represent, and as such begins to receive due notice from the ancient authorities. There is no further need for conjecture; the evidence becomes relatively abundant, and needs only to be pieced together with proper consideration for chronology, proportion, and significance.

After the Battle of Munda a certain young Valerius who had escaped with a few horsemen brought the first report of the disaster to Corduba, and Sex. Pompeio, qui Cordubae fuisset, rem gestam refert;[79] the remnants of Gnaeus's army that fled to Corduba made clear the extent of the debacle.[80] Sextus, obviously, could not have taken part in the Battle of Munda, the specific statement of Pseudo-Victor to the contrary notwithstanding: Sextus Pompeius in Hispania apud Mundam victus. . . .[81] It was evident that Corduba would be Caesar's immediate objective, and as a matter of fact he proceeded thither straightway.[82]

---

[77]Bellum Hispaniense 31.8; compare Plutarch, Caesar 56.3.

[78]For a graphic description of his death see Appian 2.105. Compare also Bellum Hispaniense 32.6–8, 37–39; Plutarch, Caesar 56.3; Florus 2. 13.86; Velleius 2.55.4; Eutropius 6.24; Dio 43.40.1; Strabo 3.2.2.

[79]Bellum Hispaniense 32.4.   [80]Appian 2.105.

[81]Liber De Viris Illustribus 84.1 (compare 78.8).

[82]Bellum Hispaniense 33.1; Appian 2.105; Dio 43.39.1.

Accordingly, Sextus left Corduba[83] on March 18[84] with a detachment of horsemen to whom he had distributed money.[85] To the inhabitants of the town he indicated that his errand was for the purpose of negotiating peace with Caesar. He left behind two legions composed of fugitives and of slaves whom he had himself manumitted; these were subsequently massacred by the Caesarians.[86] Sextus himself was pursued, but he succeeded in effecting his escape.[87]

The name of Pompey the Great had not lost its magic in Spain, and the natives were well disposed toward his son. Sextus found refuge first in the country of the Laeetani, on the eastern coast of Spain (in the neighborhood of Barcelona), in whose territory his father had waged war against Sertorius.[88] Here he gathered a small following and practised robbery and piracy on a minor scale, keeping his own identity secret. Soon elements of dubious morals and quality were attracted to him, and his numerical strength was increased.[89] A word of caution may be in place against the harshness of the ugly words "robbery" and "piracy" used above. Although the Romanization of Spain had begun in the earlier Republic,[90] it was only by Caesar that the work was prosecuted with energy and on a large scale.[91] Furthermore, the character of the country and

---

[83]Cicero, Att. 12.37.4; Dio 45.10.1 (compare 43.39.1); Strabo 3.2.2. Compare also Eutropius 6.24; Livy, Periocha 115; Florus 2.13.87.

[84]Klotz, 108.

[85]Bellum Hispaniense 32.5. Orosius 6.16.9 confuses the names of Gnaeus and Sextus.

[86]Bellum Hispaniense 32.5, 34. Dio 43.39.1 is confusing. He says: "the natives came over to his <Caesar's> side, although their slaves, since they had been made free, resisted them." Dio probably has in mind the legions to which the author of Bellum Hispaniense 34 refers. These legions were recruited *ex perfugis . . . partim oppidanorum servi* (34.2). Dio and the author of Bellum Hispaniense agree on the massacre. But see Holmes, 3.309, note 1.

[87]See references in note 83, and Plutarch, Caesar 56.3; Florus 2.18.1.

[88]Strabo (3.4.10) calls these people 'Ιακκητανοί and their country 'Ιακκητανία. For the different spellings of the name see A. Schulten, in Pauly-Wissowa, 12.399. I use the form Laeetani, which, Schulten declares, is the correct form. Compare also Meyer, 467, note 2. Florus (2.13.87) says: Sextum fortuna in Celtiberia interim abscondit. Compare also Strabo 3.2.2; Appian 2.103.

[89]Appian 4.83, 5.143; compare Florus 2.18.1.

[90]T. Mommsen, The Provinces of the Roman Empire, 1.74 (in the translation by W. P. Dickson, New York, 1887).   [91]See note 94, below.

of its population was such that, as Livy says,[92] it was the first province which Rome attempted to win and the last that it completely subdued. The career of Sextus at this time should therefore suggest to us some such picture as that of a warrior chief in a backward country where there is no constitutional authority, where, in effect, there is no authority other than that embodied in the persons of the successful chieftains. We should not think of Sextus as a robber chief carrying on open war against the constituted authorities, and contrary to the will of the majority of the population.

Meanwhile Caesar remained in Spain. That so shrewd a general ignored the existence of the surviving son of Pompey immediately after he had paid a high price for ignoring the older son may occasion some surprise. Appian[93] says that Caesar ignored Sextus on account of his youth and want of experience. The whole world at the time was at the feet of Caesar, and it might seem to him that he could well afford to ignore an enemy that was reduced to insignificance, and whose operations, moreover, were on a petty scale. But in ignoring Sextus Caesar committed a grave error, as the sequel was to show.

After the Battle of Munda Caesar devoted six months to the reorganization of affairs in Spain.[94] Near Carteia he was met by his heir Octavius,[95] who, in the later war against Sextus, was destined to reap the fruits of Caesar's mistake in ignoring Sextus. Caesar remained in Spain from March until his return to Rome in September;[96] during all this period Sextus was practically unmolested and was free to organize his forces. As Florus aptly puts it,[97] Sextum fortuna ... aliis ... post Caesarem bellis reservavit.

After Caesar's departure to Rome, the situation in Spain assumed new aspects. Caesar had left only a small garrison in Baetica (modern Andalusia).[98] This fact emboldened Sextus to more overt activity. His confidence grew and he revealed his

---

[92]28.12: ... prima Romanis inita provinciarum, quae quidem continentis sint, postrema omnium nostra demum aetate, ductu auspicioque Augusti Caesaris perdomita est.

[93]4.83.

[94]Dio 43.39; Nicolaus of Damascus 12, as edited by Clayton Morris Hall (Smith College Classical Studies IV, 1923).

[95]Nicolaus of Damascus 11, and note.

[96]Holmes, 3.312.   [97]2.13.87.   [98]Dio 45.10.2.

identity, whereupon greater numbers flocked to his standard, and he was enabled to venture on more daring enterprises.[99] The topography of this part of Spain suited his type of warfare.[100] As news of his activity and of his identity spread, he was joined not only by natives, but also by soldiers who had served under his father and under his brother,[101] by all, in short, who escaped from Munda.[102] These men considered him their natural leader. Even with his augmented forces he avoided an open engagement with the lieutenants of Caesar, but his acts of 'robbery' and 'piracy' became more numerous and were prosecuted on a larger scale.[103] He had to change his position frequently, but this only spread his fame and brought him new adherents. He received an important accession from Africa in the person of the African king Arabio, son of Masinissa. During his African campaign Caesar had taken Arabio's territory from him and had assigned it to Sittius, who had helped him destroy Juba's general Saburra, and to Bocchus, King of Mauretania. Deprived of his country, Arabio fled to Spain, and continued to support Sextus even after the death of Caesar.[104]

At length Caesar sent C. Carrinas,[104a] whom he had appointed propraetor of Spain, against Sextus. This is itself sufficient indication that the forces Caesar had left in Baetica had proved ineffective. Sextus continued warily to avoid an open encounter with his enemies. He preferred to wear them out by guerrilla fighting; this type of warfare had been employed against Sextus's father by Sertorius, who had been essentially in the situation in which Sextus now found himself.[105] In this way

---

[99] Appian 4.83, 5.143; compare Florus 2.18.1. See also Seneca, Ad Paulinum 5.2: ... iam victo patre Pompeio adhuc filio in Hispania fracta arma refovente....   [100] Dio 45.10.2.   [101] Appian 4.83.

[102] Appian 2.105; Dio 45.10.2–3; Florus 2.18.1.

[103] He could not have practised piracy on a large scale, for his ships cannot have been numerous. See Ormerod, 250.

[104] Appian 4.54, 4.83. Arabio finally transferred his allegiance to Octavian and was pardoned. See Appian 4.56.

[104a] For Carrinas see F. Münzer, in Pauly-Wissowa, 3.1612, Number 2.

[105] In this connection the following remark must be made. Sextus cannot have failed to note the parallelism between his own situation and that of Sertorius. Sertorius had considered himself and had been considered not a rebel, but a Roman leader fighting against a faction; his courage, integrity, and idealism were acknowledged even by his enemies: see Schulten, 159–165. Probably the thought of Sertorius helped to justify Sextus in his own mind.

numerous cities were won over to Sextus's side. So ended for him the year 45.[106]

The year 44 began with a fresh prosecution of the war against Sextus. Carrinas having proved a failure, Caesar entrusted the command to Asinius Pollio,[107] to whom he assigned Hispania Ulterior as a province. But Pollio was no match for Sextus. Although Appian says (4.84) that Pollio and Sextus waged war on equal terms, and Velleius says (2.73.2) that Pollio distinguished himself against Sextus,[108] yet Sextus succeeded in taking the city of Carteia.[109] On the day on which he took the city of Barea the news of Caesar's death reached him. It is easy to see how this news must have changed Spanish sentiment toward Pompey and must have strengthened his hands. Cicero says that after the capture of Barea Sextus returned to the six legions which he had left in Hispania Ulterior;[110] his strength must therefore have been very considerable even before the capture of Barea. Except from the moral point of view (in regard to which much may be said on both sides) Sextus's accomplishments since his brother's death thus far are very creditable. Particularly shrewd was his avoidance of open battle with the lieutenants of Caesar until such time as he was prepared to face them on favorable terms.

---

[106]Appian 4.83; Dio 45.10.3. Carrinas became governor of Spain in 41. He commanded three legions against Sextus in 36; see below, page 136.

[107]Appian 4.84; compare Dio 45.10.3. For a recent discussion of Pollio see Elizabeth D. Pierce, Gaius Asinius Pollio, A Roman Man of Letters (Columbia University Dissertation, Privately Printed, Poughkeepsie, 1922).

[108]See above, page 17.

[109]Cicero, Att. 15.20.3, and Tyrrell and Purser's note there (5.348). Compare also Drumann, 4.565; Blok, 11.

[110]Cicero, Att. 16.4.2. Pollio had three legions: see Cicero, Fam. 10.32.

VI. THE IDES OF MARCH UNTIL THE PEACE OF MISENUM

If the conspirators thought that after the assassination of Caesar the Republic would be restored peaceably, they had less foresight than Julius Caesar, who knew, according to Suetonius,[1] rem publicam, si quid sibi eveniret, neque quietam fore et aliquanto deteriore condicione civilia bella subituram. Florus[2] puts the situation neatly:

Populus Romanus Caesare et Pompeio trucidatis redisse in statum pristinum libertatis videbatur. Et redierat, nisi aut Pompeius liberos aut Caesar heredem reliquisset, vel, quod utroque perniciosius fuit, si non collega quondam, mox aemulus Caesarianae potentiae, fax et turbo sequentis saeculi superfuisset Antonius. Quippe dum Sextus paterna repetit, trepidatum toto mari. . . .

For tracing the intricate pattern of the events which followed the assassination of Caesar we have plentiful evidence from ancient sources, but the evidence is frequently of a strongly partizan character.[3] The conspirators had no plan of action and no military force to carry out the restoration of the Republic, or, indeed, to protect their own persons; apparently they relied on rousing the mob to their support. But Lepidus had a legion on the spot, and to Antony all the Caesarian veterans looked for guidance. Furthermore, Calpurnia, Caesar's widow, delivered to Antony Caesar's memoranda and ready money, and thus confirmed his position as the representative of Caesar's interests. The Senate as a whole was cowed by the superior power of the Caesarians; many senators, moreover, being designated appointees of Caesar, had a personal interest in the fulfilment of his plans. The senatorial decrees of March 17 granted amnesty to the conspirators, but validated the acts of the dictator.

The passions of the Caesarian mob and the power of Antony were heightened by the reading of Caesar's will, in which

---

[1] Iulius 86.2.   [2] 2.14.1–3.

[3] For a discussion of the value of the authorities for this period and of their relation to one another see Schwartz, Vertheilung, 196–223. Schwartz is the author of the articles in Pauly-Wissowa on Appian (3.216–237) and Dio Cassius (3.1684–1722).

Caesar had dealt so generously with the Roman populace and had put such faith in the men who proved to be his murderers. Antony acted with great shrewdness. Lepidus he made sure of by promising him the succession to Caesar as Pontifex Maximus; Dolabella he won over by withdrawing opposition to his effort to enter the consulship. He succeeded also in partially conciliating the nobles by asking their advice, abolishing the dictatorship 'perpetually,' and restoring order in Rome. Meanwhile he made unscrupulous use of Caesar's papers, real and supposititious, for his own financial and personal aggrandizement. The need for quieting the mob, which clamored for vengeance for Caesar's murder, provided him with an excuse for enlisting a personal body-guard, which he gradually increased to 6000 picked soldiers. Antony next proceeded to carry a law by which Dolabella was to have the province of Syria (as Caesar had arranged), while he himself should have Caesar's old province of Gaul (with the exception of Narbonese Gaul); the conspirator Decimus Brutus was to be transferred from Gaul to Macedonia, but the army in Macedonia was to be recalled to Italy. Of these posts the tenure was to be six years, not two, as Caesar had intended. Marcus Brutus and Cassius were sent by the Senate to organize the grain supply in Italy and in Sicily; they were to have, after their praetorships, the unimportant provinces of Crete and Cyrene.

But Antony's plans did not work out as smoothly as he wished. Brutus and Cassius made their way to the East, won over part of the army in Macedonia, overcame all opposition in Asia Minor, and put an end to Dolabella. In Italy Antony found an unexpected rival in the person of Gaius Octavius, who reached Rome toward the end of April, demanded that Antony should repay the money of Caesar which he had seized, and that he himself should receive a share in the government. Antony refused, and Octavius began to discharge the obligations of his adoptive father's will with his own and borrowed moneys. Large bodies of Caesar's veterans rallied to Octavius, and two of the four legions recalled by Antony from Macedonia went over to his side. To the Senate Octavius offered his support in the war against Antony, who was trying to expel Decimus Brutus from Northern Italy. Cicero favored this arrangement, and the imperium of a propraetor was conferred on Octavius.

Octavius cooperated with the consuls Hirtius and Pansa in defeating Antony at Mutina. But the two consuls fell at the battles of Mutina (April 15 and 21, 43 B. C.), and most of their soldiers went over to Octavius.[4]

We have seen that the news of the death of Caesar reached Sextus in Spain on the day that he captured the city of Barea.[5] With the death of Caesar the emergence of Sextus as a full-fledged general was complete. He need no longer confine himself to guerrilla warfare; indeed, the power which had made him an outlaw existed no longer. Asinius Pollio carried on his campaign against Sextus, but with little heart and less success. Once, when Sextus was reported far distant, Pollio plundered some of the cities that had gone over to him, but, when Sextus returned unexpectedly, Pollio fled, leaving behind him his general's cloak that he might not be recognized. It so happened that a knight also bearing the name of Pollio had been killed in the encounter; the soldiers, hearing that Pollio was dead, and finding the general's cloak, surrendered to Sextus.[6] It was after this victory that Sextus was first hailed as Imperator, and he struck coins so styling himself.[7]

---

[4]Good accounts of these stirring events are to be found in many places; see especially Holmes, Architect, 1–71, Heitland, 3.372–425, Domaszewski, 1.11–80. Drumann's standard scholarly work on the period is made difficult to use by its extraordinary plan of giving individual lives of the leading characters, with no sort of connection between the lives. For a compact, chronological summary of the events as related in the ancient authors (with references to these authors, though not to the modern subdivisions of their work) the supplement to Livy worked out on the basis of the Periochae, by Johann Freinshemius, is very useful; apparently Freinshemius was Drumann's starting point. In Drakenborch's edition of Livy (Amsterdam, 1744) Freinshemius's supplements of Periochae 116–124, which deal with this period, are to be found, in 6.680–798; for an appreciation of Freinshemius see Sandys, 2.367. Tyrrell and Purser's essay, Antony Succeeds Caesar, 5.xlviii–xciii, is a neat summary of events, chiefly from the point of view of Cicero's correspondence. The article on Augustus by K. Fitzler and O. Seeck in Pauly-Wissowa, 10.275–381 (1917), especially 279–295, summarizes the events from the point of view of Octavian.

[5]See above, page 55.   [6]Dio 45.10.4–5.

[7]The fact is not mentioned in our authorities, but is proven by a lead bullet inscribed Mag<nus> Imp<erator>: see Drumann, 4.565, note 5. The coins of Sextus Pompey are discussed in H. Cohen, Description Historiques des Monnaies Frappées sous l'Empire Romain, 1².30–32 (Paris, 1880), and, better, in Babelon, 348–353. On page 341 Babelon gives the criteria for differentiating the coins of the three Pompeys. Coins of

In Rome the rise of Sextus was looked upon with some misgivings by the nobles who had deserted the Pompeian cause. Yet they could not but feel satisfaction in the thought that his power would constitute from the West a check on Antony and Octavius. How splendid a source for the history of the period is comprised in the correspondence of Cicero is sufficiently well known; for our particular problem this correspondence is useful in that it enables us to follow the attitude of its author, and consequently of a large body of aristocratic opinion in Rome, toward Sextus Pompey. On April 7, 44 B. C., Cicero is rather indifferent about Pompey's attempts.[8] Three days later he is fearful about them; vereor ipse, he says, Sextus quo evadat;[9] and five days later he is most anxious to know what Sextus is doing, being concerned as to what deleterious effects his actions may have on the peace of Italy.[10] Ten days later he is sure Sextus will remain under arms, sure that there will be civil war, and only doubtful as to what his own course is to be; he is considering the advisability of taking refuge in Sextus's camp.[11] A fortnight later he is still puzzled. He cannot go over to the Caesarians, for he had exulted openly in the assassination of Caesar, and had proven himself an ingrate to the memory of Caesar. The only alternative seems to be the camp of Sextus, though

---

Sextus that bear simply *Imp* or *Imp Sal* or *Sal Imp* were coined after he won the victory over Pollio (in the summer of 44), and before he obtained the command of the fleet (in the beginning of 43); in Babelon these comprise numbers 16–40, pages 350–351. Coins minted after the spring of 43 make some reference to Pompey's command of the fleet. These are Numbers 21–28 in Babelon, 351–354. Harold Mattingly, Roman Coins (London and New York, 1928), in Plate XIX, Coin 12, gives an excellent example of the first type of Sextus's coinage. M. Rostovtzeff, A History of the Ancient World, 2.151, Plate XXVII, d (Oxford, 1927), figures a coin of the second type. The Civil War lead to a great increase in the coinage, which provides a running commentary on the course of events. See Mattingly, 82–85.

[8]Att. 14.1.2. In the dating of these letters and in their interpretation generally I follow Tyrrell and Purser.

[9]Att. 14.4.1 (April 9 or 10, 44).

[10]Att. 14.8.2 (April 15, 44): Quid Sextus agat vehementer exspecto.

[11]Att. 14.13.2 (April 26, 44): ... si est bellum civile futurum, quod certe erit si Sextus in armis permanebit, quem permansurum esse certo scio, quid nobis faciendum sit ignoro. Neque enim iam licebit, quod Caesaris bello licuit, neque huc neque illuc.... Restat ut in castra Sexti aut, si forte, Bruti nos conferamus....

the whole situation is extremely distasteful to him: Miliens mori melius, huic praesertim aetati.[12] By June 17–20 Cicero has heard of the capture of Carteia by Sextus, and supposes that Sextus will carry the war into Italy (compare the next letter, Att. 14.23). He still wonders with which of the two presumably anti-Caesarian commanders (Sextus or Brutus) he should seek refuge, though he considers Sextus's cause unholy: Utra ergo castra? Media ⟨i. e. 'neutrality'⟩ enim tollit Antonius. Illa infirma, haec nefaria.[13]

A day or so later he decides to depart at once, before Sextus, who is reported *en route*, should come: Ego propero, ne ante Sextus, quem adventare aiunt.[14] Again he writes: Ego autem scripsi Sextum adventare, non quo iam adesset, sed quia certe id ageret ab armisque nullus discederet. Certe, si pergit, bellum paratum est.[15] Between June 21 and July 6 Cicero must have heard that Sextus meant to give up the struggle, for on the latter day he expresses his regret at this decision to withdraw: Sextum scutum abicere nolebam.[16] This latest attitude on the part of Cicero is easily intelligible. Some counterweight to Antony must be found, and the Liberators were still showing themselves as inffective as they had been from the day following their deed.[17] Hence, when Cicero heard that Sextus would lay aside his arms, he anticipated servitude without even the alternative of civil war: Quod si verum est ⟨that Sextus is giving up his arms⟩, sine bello civili video serviendum.[18]

During the first days of July a letter of Sextus addressed to the consuls was shown to Cicero by Sextus's father-in-law, Scribonius Libo.[19] The bearers of this letter had reported the capture of Barea and the size of Sextus's army. To Libo himself Sextus had written his ultimatum. The *sine qua non* of further negotiations was that his family mansion be restored; the gist of his demands was that all armies be disbanded; Ad ipsum Libonem scripsit nihil esse nisi ad larem suum liceret.

---

[12]Att. 14.22.2.   [13]Att. 15.20.3 (June 17–20).
[14]Att. 15.21.3 (June 21).   [15]Att. 15.22 (June 22 or 23).
[16]Att. 15.29 (July 6).

[17]They had themselves in fact thought of the camp of Sextus in Spain as a place of refuge. See the letter (Fam. 11.1.4) of Decimus Brutus written to M. Brutus and C. Cassius on the morning of March 17; compare Tyrrell and Purser there (5.241).   [18]Att. 16.1.4 (July 8, 44).

[19]Att. 16.4.2. For a discussion of this letter see above, page 18.

Summa postulatorum, ut omnes exercitus dimittantur qui ubique sint.[20]

As a matter of fact Sextus was but little concerned with aspirations for dominion over the Roman world. His great desire was to regain the wealth and position due him as the son of his father. The death of Julius Caesar had seemed to remove the great obstacle to the realization of this hope. It is conceivable that Sextus believed that the Republic would automatically be restored if the armies concentrated in Northern Italy should be disbanded. But, more probably, he believed that war or the threat of war was the only way to render effective his hope of restoration to his former position. It is hard to believe that Octavius's motives when he appeared in Rome to claim the heritage of Julius were any loftier. It happened that Julius Caesar had left a greater heritage than Pompey the Great had left, and that Octavius was shrewder and more persistent in getting his 'rights' than was Sextus in getting his.

It may be suggested that in this juncture, as in the war at Perusia and after his two great naval victories, the dilatoriness of Sextus and his failure to follow up advantages seem to be an inherited trait. The Elder Pompey had frequently hesitated at the crucial moment and had failed to deliver the decisive blow that would make all power his; he always contented himself with being, in the apt expression which Heitland frequently uses, the Indispensable Man. So Sextus neglected numerous opportunities to deliver telling blows when circumstances had put it into his power to do so, and contented himself with being a source of dread to others. He seemed to believe that his successes were due somehow to supernatural intervention, and was genuinely surprised when they did not continue. With the Senate and Antony and Octavius and their respective followings jostling one another for position, it would seem that Sextus and his fighting organization might have turned the scales in one direction or the other. It is a sad commentary on the public figures of the late Republic that a student of the period should find it a cause for blame that an

[20]The translation in my text is suggested by the notes ad loc. of Tyrrell and Purser, 5.381. Compare Phil. 2.75. The plural *liberi* is used in the latter passage merely for rhetorical reasons; of course Cicero means Sextus only.

armed young man was content not to take something to which
he had no legitimate claim, and yet, under the circumstances,
Sextus hardly deserves to be praised (as his father possibly
deserves to be) for his abstinence.

The greater part of the property which Sextus claimed had
been bought up by Antony (and Dolabella) at a sham auction,
and it was politic for Antony to see that Sextus formed no
compact for mutual protection either with the Senate or with
Octavius, with whom Antony was then at odds. Lepidus, who
as governor of Gaul could most easily communicate with Sextus,
was commissioned to effect an understanding with him, of such
a nature as to deceive both him and the Senate.[21] On the date
of the offer of restitution to Sextus there is no satisfactory
information in our ancient sources; there is decided disagreement
on the subject among modern scholars. T. Rice Holmes[22] says
that Antony arranged that Lepidus should be commissioned to
offer restitution to Sextus early in April. Antony's motive, he
says, was to conciliate the republicans and influential senators
whose feelings he had offended by his funeral oration for
Caesar. For the same purpose and at the same time Antony
offered the motion to abolish the office of dictator, and supported
the proposal of Servius Sulpicius that no decree of Caesar
should thenceforth be published.[23] Holmes cites as his authority
Appian 3.4 and Dio 45.10.6. The passage in Dio reads:

When he ⟨Sextus⟩ had thus become powerful ⟨after the victory
over Asinius Pollio⟩, Lepidus arrived to govern the adjoining
portion of Spain, and persuaded him to enter into an agreement
on the condition of recovering his father's estate. And Antony,
influenced by his friendship for Lepidus and by his hostility
towards Caesar, caused such a decree to be passed. So Sextus,
in this way and on these conditions, departed from Spain.

The fact that Dio mentions this offer of restitution immediately after his report of the successes of Sextus in Spain is of
little help in establishing a date, for the passage is meant to
give the outstanding events in the career of Sextus without

---

[21]Sextus could properly be restored to his former status because Caesar
had pardoned all his adversaries of the Civil War and restored them to
their rights: see Suetonius, Iulius 75. Compare Brueggemann, 29.

[22]Architect, 5.

[23]The abolition of the dictatorship and the motion of Sulpicius took
place on March 20, 41. See Groebe, Quaestiones, 45.

regard to specific dating, and in Sextus's career the offer of restitution is the next significant event after his successes.

The passage in Appian (3.4) is much more specific as to date:

Antony also moved that Sextus Pompey (the son of Pompey the Great who was still much beloved by all) should be recalled from Spain, *where he was still attacked by Caesar's lieutenants,* and that he should be paid 50 millions of Attic drachmas out of the public treasury[25] for his father's confiscated property and be appointed commander of the sea, as his father had been, with charge of all the Roman ships, wherever situated, which were needed for immediate service. The astonished Senate accepted each of these decrees with alacrity and applauded Antony the whole day; for nobody, in their estimation, was more devoted to the republic than the elder Pompey, and hence nobody was more regretted.

The line which I have italicized in this passage gives a date, but our suspicions are aroused by the statement that Sextus received a command of the Roman fleets at the same time as restitution of his property was granted to him. Schwartz, in his article on Appian,[26] gives a very incisive criticism of this passage:

Antonius wäre ein Narr gewesen, wenn er im Mai 44 S. Pompeius zurückberufen, entschädigt und zum Admiral gemacht hätte (III 4), nur um den damals wehrlosen und in beständiger Angst vor den Veteranen schwebenden Senat sich gefällig zu machen; nicht einmal die republicanische Partei liess sich derartiges traümen, sondern noch um 23. Juni (ad Att. XV 22, vgl. Ruete 26) fürchtete Cicero, dass Sextus den Krieg brächte: erst am 6. Juli (ad Att. XV 22) hörte er dass diese Gefahr beseitigt sei, und am 10. Juli (ad Att. XVI 4) erfuhr er Sextus Vorschläge. Die *restitutio* durch Lepidus dürfte erheblich

---

[25]Attic drachmas are equivalent to denarii. Compare also Appian 3.57, 4.94. Cicero gives (Phil. 13.12) the sum as 700 million sesterces. The suggestion has been offered that for *septiens miliens* we should read *bis miliens,* which would = 200 million sesterces, the equivalent of 50 million denarii. But Cicero (in Phil. 13.12) refers to the Temple of Ops which, before it was plundered by Antony, was supposed to contain 700 million sesterces: Cicero, Phil. 2.93, 5.11, 8.26, 12.12, 13.12. It was to the wealth of this temple, therefore, that Sextus was referred, i. e., to the consuls. The treaty of Misenum granted Sextus only 17½ million denarii (Dio 48.36.5); Appian is therefore probably mistaken in the sum he mentions in the present passage. See Drumann 4.566, note 7. In any case, as Dorn Seiffen says, 58, note 1, Utut est, neutrum umquam solutum fuit.

[26]In Pauly-Wissowa, 3.230–231. Compare also Tyrrell and Purser, 5.371.

später, aber noch vor den 28. November (Cic. Phil III 23. V 39) anzusetzen sein; die Entschädigungssumme erhielt er erst während des Krieges mit Antonius, zwischen dem 1. Januar und dem 20. März 43 (Cic. Phil. XIII 10) durch ein SC zugebilligt und das Flottencommando gar erst nach der Schlacht bei Mutina (Vell. II 73.2. Dio XLVI 40. XLVIII 17).

In another article[27] Schwartz sets the date for the negotiations between Sextus and Lepidus in September:

Sextus forderte Wiedereinsetzung in seine Güter (*ad Att.* 16, 4); dies hat ihm offenbar Lepidus bewilligt, und der Senat wollte diesem schon am 28. November dafür besondere Ehren decretiren (Cic. *Phil.* 5, 39 vgl. 13, 8 ff.). Der lange Zwischenraum zwischen dem 5. Juli und dem 28. November erklärt sich zum guten Theil durch die weite Entfernung von Spanien nach Rom; der Vertrag mit Lepidus wird in den September 44 zu setzen sein.

These arguments of Schwartz seem forceful enough to discredit the early date offered by Holmes. It is possible, however, that Schwartz himself sets the date somewhat late. He does not cite the very careful dissertation of Paul Groebe,[28] which suggests, with great probability, after searching criticism of the sources, that August 1 was the date for the recall: "Quae cum ita sint, Kal. Sext. Pompeium a senatu revocatum esse resque familiares ei restitutas, mihi quidem verisimillimum videtur."

In any case, we see that it was decreed by the Senate that Pompey was to receive a very considerable sum from the public treasury as recompense for his property, and that, on the motion of Antony, a *supplicatio* was to be granted to Lepidus, the intermediary of this pacific arrangement.[29]

At the end of November, 44, Antony led his army off to Cisalpine Gaul to take the province that had been transferred to him from Decimus Brutus. He left behind him in Italy Octavius, with the troops Octavius had raised or had won over from Antony, and Cicero, by this time irrevocably committed to hostility to Antony and determined to use every available resource against him. Cicero was in constant communication with the governors of the various provinces, endeavoring to confirm their loyalty to the 'Republic.' With the accession of

---

[27]Vertheilung, 205, note 1.

[28]See especially Caput IV, De Restitutione Sex. Pompei, 27–31.

[29]Dio 45.9.4, 45.10.6, 48.17.1; Appian 3.12, 3.36, 3.57, 4.94; Cicero, Phil. 5.40, 13.8; Velleius 2.73.2.

the new magistrates of 43 the 'Republic' was ostensibly restored, with Cicero as its guiding spirit. Cicero realized what power Lepidus possessed in spite of his seeming insignificance, and so, apparently with the purpose of conciliating both Lepidus and Sextus, he brought it about in the early days of 43 that the Senate should honor the one with a gilded equestrian statue in recognition of his services in reconciling the other to the 'Republic.'[30]

As the army of Decimus Brutus fell back before the superior forces of Antony, the latter was inclined to attach less importance to the good will of Sextus and to ignore him and his claim. Sextus therefore proceeded to Massilia with his army and his fleet in order to observe developments in Italy more closely and to be able to act as circumstances should dictate.[31] As Antony seemed more and more successful in his military operations, and more and more recalcitrant in his relations with the Senate, the importance of attaching Sextus to the senatorial cause seemed to Cicero more and more pressing. At the close of his Thirteenth Philippic[32] (delivered at the end of March, 43) he read to the Senate a letter sent by Antony to Hirtius and Octavius and provided it with a commentary to the effect that accommodation with Antony was impossible. Immediately after the reading of the letter he proposed a decree honoring Sextus in the most fulsome terms. He desired, furthermore, to have him coopted into the college of augurs.[33] Cicero's purpose, patently, was to summon Sextus to the relief of Mutina. A delegation composed of L. Aemilius Paullus (the brother of Lepidus), Q. Minucius Thermus, and Gaius Fannius met Sextus at Massilia, doubtless at Cicero's suggestion, and tried to induce him to undertake the relief of Mutina, but he feared the veterans of Caesar, so he said,[34] and doubtless also the intentions

[30]Cicero, Phil. 5.41: eique <Lepido> statuam equestrem inauratam in rostris aut quo alio loco in foro vellet ex huius ordinis sententia statui placere, Phil. 13.9: statuam in rostris cum inscriptione praeclara. Compare Ad Brut. 1.15.9.

[31]Appian 4.84; Dio 45.10.6, 48.17.1; Cicero, Phil. 13.13.

[32]13.50: Magnum Pompeium, Gnaei filium, pro patris maiorumque suorum animo studioque in rem publicam suaque pristina virtute, industria, voluntate fecisse, quod suam eorumque quos secum haberet operam senatui populoque Romano pollicitus esset, eamque rem senatui populoque Romano gratam acceptamque esse, eique honori dignitatique eam rem fore.

[33]Cicero, Phil. 13.12.   [34]Ibidem 13.13.

of the Senate. But Sextus must be won over at all costs, not only as an active opponent of Antony, but also as a make-weight against Octavius, and so to him was given the chief command of the Roman fleets and of the maritime coasts, the same sort of command which his father had had.[35] But Antony was defeated at Mutina (toward the end of April, 43) with no sort of cooperation from Sextus, and now the Senate desired to be rid of Octavius, the troublesome young man who had checked Antony; to this end it was doubtless ready to use the help of Sextus, if Sextus could be made to give any help.

How the young heir of Caesar outwitted his enemies who thought they were handling him so shrewdly, how he hastened to Rome and had himself made consul (August 19, 43 B. C.) is a familiar story.[36] Whether Sextus meant to make some use of his grand title we cannot tell; apparently he was proud enough of it.[37] But he delayed and hesitated, and his hesitation brought him no favor from either side. Octavian's colleague in the consulship, Q. Pedius, another great-nephew of Julius Caesar, carried a law to set up a special court for the trial of all concerned in the murder of Julius Caesar. Under the terms of the Lex Pedia defendants were prosecuted in their absence, their goods were confiscated, and they were 'interdicted from fire and water.'[38] Although Sextus could have had noth-

---

[35]Appian 3.4, 4.84; Dio 46.40; Velleius 2.73.1. From this time Sextus's coins bear the legend PRAEFECTUS CLASSIS ET ORAE MARITIMAE, or some variation of that legend: see Babelon, 352–354. Kromayer states (Entwicklung, 442) that this *imperium* gave Sextus immediate control of all shipping in the harbors of the Western Mediterranean. The greater part of this shipping consisted of vessels which had belonged to Caesar; these now constituted the larger part of Sextus's fleet. Kromayer calculates that the fleet of Caesar in the West at the time of his assassination comprised 150 vessels. The weakness of the Triumvirate in naval matters indicates that Sextus must have taken all these vessels. In addition he had gathered many pirate vessels. Appian (4.117) quotes Brutus as saying that Pompeius and Murcus and Ahenobarbus together had 260 ships blocking the sea. Kromayer shows (441) that Murcus and Ahenobarbus had 130, which leaves 130, he says, for Sextus. Kromayer's figure is conservative.

[36]Drumann, 1.470, and references; Gardthausen, 1.124, and references.

[37]His coins show this. Sextus had been brought up from childhood under the shadow of his father's greatness, and that greatness had to do chiefly with naval commands; Pompey's house was decorated with the beaks of ships (Cicero, Phil. 2.68).

[38]Dio 46.48.4, 47.12.2, 48.12.2; Appian 5.61; Velleius 2.69; Suetonius, Iulius 87; Livy, Periocha 120.

ing to do with the assassination, since he was in Spain at the time, he was included among the condemned, so that, like Brutus and Cassius, he became an outlaw whom any man might kill at any moment. His name alone, quite apart from his activities in Spain, was sufficient, it was held, to prove his enmity toward Julius Caesar, and Octavian was thoroughly intent on exterminating those who had the remotest connection with his 'father's' death. On the side of expediency, Sextus had received an extraordinary naval command on the same day that their transmarine provinces had been granted to Brutus and Cassius, and he had been summoned with them to defend the 'Republic;' he would therefore seem to be committed to the policy of Octavian's enemies.[39] That Sextus had not entered whole-heartedly on this policy did not matter to Octavian.[40]

After Octavian had made himself master of Rome, his forces were still inferior to those which Brutus and Cassius had collected in the East. He therefore entered upon a course of action which led to the formation of the Triumvirate, composed of Octavian, Antony, and Lepidus; this arrangement was legalized by the Lex Titia of November 27, 43. The members were to assume office formally in January, 42, but their arrangements for the government of Italy and the provinces and concerning other matters, with one important exception, were published to their armies at once.[41] Sicily and Sardinia were given to Octavian. The exception was the list of the proscribed, which included the name of Sextus Pompey.[42]

[39]Dio 46.51; compare Appian 3.85; Livy, Periocha 118; Cicero, Fam. 11.14.　　　[40]Dio 46.51; Appian 4.84.

[41]Heitland, 3.411–416; Gardthausen, 1.127–130. An excellent monograph on the proscriptions, analyzing the motives for them and listing the proscripts, is the book of Kloevekorn.

[42]Dio 47.12.2, 48.17.3; Appian 4.96; Zonaras 10.16, 17, 21; Orosius 6.18. Groebe, in Drumann 1.247, note 7, admits that Sextus was condemned, but denies that he was proscribed. In 4.567 Groebe seems less certain. The ancient authorities are explicit enough on the point. Holmes accepts (Architect, 81, note 4) the testimony of the ancients. Kloevekorn (93) includes Sextus among the proscribed. On pages 24–25 Kloevekorn shows that the proscripts were chiefly men of the old aristocracy, who would resent an upstart régime, whereas the followers of the Triumvirs were, with very few exceptions, nonentities. This would in itself be a sufficient reason for believing that Sextus was included among the proscripts, and would also help to explain the popularity of Sextus, which persisted long after his ignominious death: see below, page 160.

Now again Sextus found himself cast down from whatever
high hopes he had cherished. He had been courted by the
leading statesman of the restored 'Republic,' and had been
constitutionally clothed with a great naval command. He may
have entertained the hope that, when Antony and Octavian had
weakened each other, he would be called in to play the rôle of
the Indispensable Man (the rôle his father had always chosen)
and restore the government, with himself in some important
position.[43] Even when he had been condemned by the Lex
Pedia he may still have hoped for pardon from Octavian,
inasmuch as he had had no actual part in the murder of Caesar.
He retained his fleet, sailed around the islands of the Western
Mediterranean, kept away from the mainland, and refrained
from committing any injury. But, when he learned that his
name was among the proscribed, no hope was left to him.
Furthermore, the provinces which were actually under the
control of the Triumvirate were adequately protected, and it
was difficult to get such another foothold as he had had in
Spain. The extraordinary command bestowed upon him by
the Senate had given him legitimate control of all the shipping
in western waters.[44] In view of the greatly altered circumstances
in which he now found himself he gathered all the vessels he
could, and, at first without any base for his operations, plundered the seas. His motives are easy to understand. First
there was necessity, then hereditary hatred, and, finally, a
desire for revenge against a treatment that seemed the more
unfair as it came after a period of hope. Other resources he
had none; a fleet he possessed, and 'piracy' was the time-
honored refuge of men in despair.[45] From Sextus's own point

---

[43]Appian (3.75–76) has a story to the effect that Pansa on his death bed
told Octavian that the Senate hoped, after he and Antony had fought,
to be able to get the better of the survivor, and then to crush the whole
Caesarian party and restore that of Pompey.

[44]See note 35, above. Sextus may have believed that his command had
not been revoked, since he did not recognize Octavian's power as constitutional. Similarly Sulla retained the proconsulship which he held against
Mithridates, and did not recognize the validity of the government which
pronounced him a public enemy. See Appian 1.81.

[45]Thucydides's classic passage on the history of piracy (1.5) indicates
that in his day it was still considered respectable in some backward countries, and it is not unlikely that the same thing was true four centuries later.
One thinks of the Odyssey, which was favorite Roman reading. See
Ormerod, Chapter II, 59–73.

of view, moreover, it was not piracy he was engaged in, but legitimate warfare. We must not forget that his naval command had not been revoked by an authority that he would consider constitutional.

The most widely heralded of his father's achievements had been his exploits on the sea, though *against* pirates,[46] and the high water mark of his own career had been the extraordinary command of the sea. It may be mentioned that, despite Pompey the Great's diligence in bringing the pirates to book, he had felt a real sympathy for them, as is shown by his leniency to those who survived the war. Instead of executing them he settled them on the land, though in regions, to be sure, where they would not be tempted to relapse into piracy.[47] Certainly Sextus was familiar with a saying of his father which must have become famous, a saying which Plutarch (Pompey 50.2) cites in Greek: πλεῖν ἀνάγκη, ζῆν οὐκ ἀνάγκη. Probably also he had laid to heart the lament of his father that he had made no use of his fleet, the arm of warfare in which he was so much superior; this remark he doubtless overheard on the fateful voyage to Egypt.[48] For his dubious conduct he may have found justification in his own eyes and in the eyes of his fellow-men in one very humane use to which he put his fleet, the deliverance of proscribed Romans. In as harrowing thirty-five pages of Greek as have come down from antiquity Appian describes selected horrors of the proscription (4.8–52). One is grateful to Sextus and willing to condone much in his conduct when one comes upon the frequently recurring statement that this person or the other found refuge with Sextus Pompey. In 4.36 Appian says (he is borne out by other writers): ὁ δὲ πολὺς ἐς Σικελίαν ἤει . . . Πομπηίου σφᾶς προθύμως ὑποδεχομένου. That Sextus himself esteemed his own service in this regard is shown by the fact that he figured an oak crown on his coins.[49] Besides the proscribed, he gave welcome also to debtors and runaway slaves, acts for which less credit is due him.

---

[46]Compare Florus 2.18.1: O quam diversus a patre! Ille Cilicas extinxerat, hic se piratica tuebatur; Manilius, Astronomica 1.920–921: Cum patrios armis imitatus filius hostes aequora Pompeius cepit defensa parenti.
[47]Plutarch, Pompey 28.3–4.
[48]Ibidem 76.2: ὠδύρετο πρὸς τοὺς φίλους, καταμεμφόμενος ἑαυτὸν ἐκβιασθέντα τῷ πεζῷ συμβαλεῖν, τῇ δὲ κρείττονι ἀδηρίτως δυνάμει πρὸς μηδὲν ἀποχρήσασθαι . . . .
[49]See Babelon, 353 (No. 24). This coin shows a bare and bearded head of

But, humane as the deliverance of the victims of the proscription was, the fact remains that Sextus's tactics differed little if at all from those of the Cilician pirates whom his father had suppressed.[50] His leading admirals were in all probability ex-pirates. The most skilful of them, Menas and Menecrates, whose names indicate an Anatolian origin, are said to have been freedmen of Pompey the Great.[51] They may have been enslaved and freed by him, because of their special ability, in the course of the war with the pirates.[52] Furthermore, the ancient authorities, beginning with Augustus himself,[53] are unanimous in regarding the war with Sextus as a pirate war.[54] It must be remembered, however, that every statement on this subject in our ancient authorities is itself official or was derived

---

Sextus, surrounded by a crown of oak, with the legend MAG. PIVS IMP. ITER. The reverse bears the legend PRAEF. CLAS. ET ORAE MARIT. EX S. C., and shows confronting heads of Pompey the Great and his son Gnaeus; to the right the *lituus* is shown, to the left a tripod.

[50]Ormerod, 251. On the other hand accusations were made that Pompey the Great himself caused a shortage of grain in Rome in 57 B. C., in order to obtain a command: see Plutarch, Pompey 49.4.

[51]Velleius (2.73) calls them both *paternos* libertos; Dorn Seiffen objects (7), saying that only Menas is mentioned (by Appian 5.79, 96) as being a slave of Pompey the Great, and that Menecrates is described in the passages of Dio and Appian as Sextus's own freedman. I am inclined to think that both had the same status. The extreme hatred they cherished for each other (see below, page 100) seems to indicate a rivalry of many years' standing. In any case they were both in the service of Sextus and thus might fairly, if somewhat inaccurately, be called the freedmen of Sextus, even if they were in truth his father's. Dio indeed speaks of both alike, in 48.30.4... Μηνᾷ δὲ ἐξελευθέρῳ οἱ, ᾧ πάνυ προσέκειτο...., and in 48.46.1 ἔπεμψε Μενεκράτην... ἐξελεύθερον καὶ αὐτὸν ἑαυτοῦ ὄντα. Appian regularly calls Menas Menodorus; Menas is simply the ὄνομα ὑποκοριστικόν for the longer form.

[52]Niebuhr, Römische Geschichte, 3.152, long ago suggested that the conquered and partly rehabilitated pirates over whom Pompey the Great had won his victory had become the clients of the Elder Pompey, and now continued this relationship to the son of their original patron. One may imagine that the traditional service to the patron was undertaken with great alacrity in this instance, since its form was congenial to the tastes of the ex-pirates.

[53]Monumentum Ancyranum 25: Mare pacavi a praedonibus.

[54]Strabo 5.4.4: ἐνταῦθα δὴ λῃστήρια συνεστήσαντο οἱ Πομπηΐου Σέξτου ναύαρχοι ....; Velleius 2.73.2: latrociniis ac praedationibus...utebatur; Lucan 6.421: Siculus pirata; Florus 2.18.1: hic se piratica tuebatur.

from an official source.[55] In the sequel Sextus proved unsuccessful, and was therefore technically a rebel, though he could at almost every point establish the legitimacy of his conduct.[56] In the present instance he could claim the right to continue in the command which the Senate had given him. He would naturally not acknowledge the authority which had condemned and proscribed him.

In any case such a movement as Sextus's, undertaken at such a time, was bound to grow by its own momentum. Fugitives came flocking in, ships were seized or built, Sextus's power grew rapidly, and with it his audacity in plundering ships and harbors.[57] Octavian was much too preoccupied with more pressing cares to check the progress of Sextus. Dio gives two reasons for his neglect of Pompey's rise: "both because he despised him and because the business in hand kept him fully occupied." The second cause is undoubtedly the preponderant cause, but the first may have operated more than is generally admitted. In military matters the judgment of Julius Caesar had been regarded as impeccable, and no one was more apt to respect that judgment than Octavian. Octavian's first lessons in the art of war under the tuition of his adoptive father were in connection with that very campaign after which the great Julius was willing to leave Sextus at large as being a person of no potential danger to Caesar's cause.[58]

For the widened scope of his activities Sextus had to have a base on shore able to sustain him, preferably in a region not open to attack by land. The position and the resources of Sicily made it ideal for his purposes. His father had been sent by Sulla to wrest Sicily from the Marians in 82, and had taken

---

[55]For a discussion of the prejudice shown by the ancient sources, see my last chapter, especially pages 163–166.

[56]See below, page 100.

[57]Dio 48.19.1; Appian 4.84, 85; Zonaras 10.17; Orosius 6.18.19. Livy, Periocha 123, reads: Sex. Pompeius Magni filius, collectis ex Epiro proscriptis ac fugitivis.... On this passage Blok (16, note 3) is worth quoting: "...pro lectis ex *Epiro* etc., legendum censeo 'ex continenti.' Livius in Graeco fonte legerat ἐκ τῆς ἠπείρου quod male vertit 'ex Epiro:' hoc tempore autem nihil audimus de fugitivis et proscriptis in Epiro..." The emendation seems certain. It is not mentioned in Rossbach's Teubner text of the Periochae (Leipzig, 1910).

[58]See above, page 53.

the island.[59] He had established a great reputation in Sicily for disinterested and impartial justice.[60] The aristocratic Roman leaders had always counted on their personal following to form the nucleus of their power.[61] Now there was such a nucleus ready to hand for Sextus in Sicily, as there had been such a nucleus for him in Spain.[62]

In December, 43,[63] Sextus took Mylae,[64] near Messana, and Tyndaris,[65] on the north coast of Sicily. This act seems to have gone unnoticed in the general tumult; at any event Aulus Pompeius Bithynicus[66] (also a Pompey, it will be observed), whom Caesar shortly before his death had made propraetor of Sicily, could do nothing to stop it.[66a] Pompey then proceeded

[59]Cicero, De Imp. Cn. Pomp. 30: quam multis undique cinctam periculis non terrore belli, sed consilii celeritate explicavit.

[60]For Pompey's government of Sicily see Cicero, Verres 3.42. Compare Holm, 3. 123: "Pompeius selbst hinterliess bei den Sikelioten den Ruf grosser Rechtschaffenheit und Uneigennützigkeit und einer Klugheit, die bei dem erst 22 jährigen Manne um so mehr anerkannt wurde..." In Raccolta, 1.5–15, Casagrandi, under the caption Sui Possessi della Gens Pompeia in Sicilia, indicates the extent of Pompeian influence in Sicily. Holm gives (3.401) a shorter list of persons and places in Sicily which bore 'Pompey' as part of their name; the length of the list, nevertheless, indicates the enduring influence of the Elder Pompey in the island. Compare also Elsie S. Jenison, The History of the Province of Sicily, 59 (Columbia University Dissertation, Privately Printed, Boston, 1919).

[61]See below, pages 152–154.   [62]See above, page 52.

[63]Cicero, Fam. 12.28 (latter part of March 43) speaks of an attack on Lilybaeum without specifying who made it. Gardthausen suggests (2.60) the possibility that it was Sextus, but he is surely wrong. The Lex Pedia had not yet been passed, and we have seen above (page 68) that Sextus refrained from antagonizing the powers in Italy until after the passage of the Lex Titia. Tyrrell and Purser ad loc. say (6.78): "It would appear that certain mercenaries of Antony had started from Africa to seize Lilybaeum."

[64]Modern Milazzo, the site of Agrippa's victory over Sextus in 36, for which see below, page 131.

[65]Modern St. Maria di Tindaro; Cicero, Verres 3.103 calls it *nobilissima civitas*.

[66]For Pompeius Bithynicus see Drumann, 4.322–323. When Sextus defeated Octavian's fleet for the first time, he put Bithynicus to death on the pretext that he was plotting against his life: Livy, Periocha 123; Dio 48.19.1; Appian 5.70. A letter of Bithynicus and its reply are to be found in Cicero, Fam. 6.16, 17. Compare Klein, 85–86.

[66a]A. Aiello, Il Nuovo Piano di Attacco alla Sicilia, in Raccolta 1.69–83, would have it that Bithynicus offered no real opposition to Sextus, but came into collusion with him from the first.

to besiege Bithynicus in Messana, but was repulsed; Bithynicus had become the more obdurate because of the loss of the two other cities. Sextus overran the country, prevented the importation of provisions, frightened off or ambushed those who tried to come to the relief of Bithynicus, and got possession of the quaestor of Bithynicus and a large sum of money. Finally the two leaders came to terms, with the understanding that they should enjoy equal authority on the island.[67] The understanding was effected through the mediation of two proscribed Roman nobles, Hirrus and Fannius.[67a]

The intervention of Lucilius Hirrus, in particular, is significant for the character of the support which Sextus attracted. Hirrus had been an ardent Pompeian all through his career, and his adherence to the cause of Sextus is an excellent example of the working of the doctrine of *Hausmachtpolitik* which, as I shall show in the sequel (pages 152–154), was for Sextus a source of strength and moral justification. Hirrus had campaigned for the tribunate in 54 for the purpose of having Pompey the Great named dictator. On the outbreak of the Civil War he recruited for Pompey in Picenum. During the campaign which ended in the Battle of Pharsalus he was absent on a mission to the Parthians on behalf of Pompey. He made his peace with Caesar, but rejoined his old party after the Ides, and was proscribed. Then he went to Bruttium and collected a great number of slaves and other dependents of the large estates of his family in that region, and crossed to Sicily with a consider-

---

[67]Pompeius Bithynicus had fought on Caesar's side during the Civil War, although he was related to Pompey. But his father had followed Pompey loyally and met his death with him in Egypt (Orosius 6.15.28). The present understanding was arrived at possibly on the basis of the relationship and of the Elder Bithynicus's service to the Elder Pompey.

[67a]For Fannius see Pauly-Wissowa, 6.1991, Number 7. He was a consistent Pompeian: Cicero (Phil. 13.13) mentions him as a member of the embassy to Sextus; see above, page 65. Hirrus is called "Ιρτιος in Appian 4.84. Gardthausen (1.131), Drumann (1.471, 3.74), and Münzer (Pauly-Wissowa 8.1962, Number 4) all follow Appian and give the name as *Hirtius*. But Cichorius (67–70) has identified this Hirtius with C. Lucilius C. f. Hirrus (the name is given in full in Cicero, Fam. 8.8.5). Cichorius explains the error of Appian as due to his habit of writing "Ιρτιος for the consul of 43; that name occurs fifteen times in 3.50–76. Münzer, in his article on Lucilius Hirrus, in Pauly-Wissowa, 13.1644–1645 (1927), accepts Cichorius's identification.

able force. There he (and Fannius) persuaded Pompeius Bithynicus to join Sextus.[68] In this way Sextus acquired rich stores of arms and money, as well as men. He now got control of Syracuse and other cities, adding many soldiers and ships to his forces. Finally, all Sicily was forced to acknowledge his supremacy.[68a]

Sextus now constituted the only armed opposition to the rule of the Triumvirs in the West. When it became known that Africa, Sicily, and Sardinia had fallen to Octavian as his share of the Empire, Q. Cornificius, the senatorial governor of Africa, sent strong reinforcements to Sextus, as a sort of outworks for himself.[69] The proscribed persons who had taken refuge with Cornificius also went over to Sextus. In addition, the cities which the Triumvirs had expropriated for bounties to their veterans also sent large contingents of men.[70]

Allusion has been made (page 69) to the service Sextus rendered to the victims of the proscription.[71] The Triumvirs had set a high price upon the head of each proscribed person, but the emissaries of Pompey went about offering twice the reward to anyone who should save a proscribed person, and the vessels of Sextus cruised about the waters convenient to the Italian harbors for the express purpose of picking up as many refugees as they could find. All these refugees Sextus received kindly, entertained, provided with money, and appointed to positions befitting their rank in his army and his navy. For example, Lentulus was made praetor by Sextus. We may fairly say that Sextus deserved his oaken wreath. In summarizing the

[68]See Cichorius, 70; Münzer, in Pauly-Wissowa, 13.1642–1645.

[68a]Dio 48.17.4–6 (compare 47.12); Appian 4.84; Livy, Periocha 123; Velleius 2.72.4, 73.3; Florus 2.18.1.

[69]Dio 48.17.6. Q. Cornificius is one of the most interesting figures of the period, an honest and highly cultured gentleman. Excellent accounts of him are to be found in Drumann, 2.531–535; F. Münzer, in Pauly-Wissowa, 4.1624–1628; Tyrrell and Purser, 4.ci–cvii. The governorship of Africa Vetus was given him shortly after the Ides, and he adhered to the senatorial cause from conviction. It was he that beat off Antony's (?) men from Lilybaeum: see note 63, above. He is the only correspondent with whom Cicero was intimate during the last year of his life; the letters are Fam. 12.17–30.   [70]Appian 4.85.

[71]Gardthausen collects (2.60) from Appian 4.36–48 and Valerius Maximus 6.1.3, 7.3.9, the names of those who are specifically mentioned as having been saved by Sextus.

life of Sextus, Appian writes:[72] "Of most importance was the aid he rendered in the proscriptions to Rome when exposed to utter destruction, rescuing many of the nobility who were, at this later time, safe at home by means of him." Even Velleius, who is consistently hostile to Pompey, grants him this merit:[73] id unum tantummodo salutare patriae Sextum attulisse, quod clarissimos viros rei publicae servasset ac restituisset. Naturally these acquisitions increased the numbers of Sextus, but to a greater extent they increased his prestige. His prestige was not enhanced, however, by the much more numerous slaves who found refuge with him. So great was the number of these runaways that formal prayers for the purpose of stopping the exodus were offered by the Vestal Virgins.[74] Skilful sailors came to Sextus from places as far distant as Africa and Spain. All the more ambitious pirates of the Mediterranean joined him, attracted by the large scale of his operations, and the semi-respectable air they bore.

Still Octavian made no move to check the growing power of Sextus. The shrewd master of men who at nineteen could befool the veteran politician Cicero surmised that, however troublesome Sextus might make himself, he would do nothing of real significance and could probably be brought to book by some means in due season. However, Brutus and Cassius were strengthening their hold on the East, and with Sextus holding Sicily and controlling the western Mediterranean, Rome began to feel the pinch of hunger and even of disease.[75] It was becoming imperative that some steps be taken. Q. Salvidienus Rufus[76] was therefore sent to Rhegium to free the coast of

---

[72]5.143.   [73]2.77.3.

[74]Dio implies (48.19.4) that these prayers were offered even before Philippi, and it is so related in the accounts of Drumann and Gardthausen. Dorn Seiffen (65) puts the event, with some probability, after Philippi.

[75]Dio 48.18.1; Appian 5.143; Orosius 6.18.19.

[76]Salvidienus Rufus was, with Agrippa, in Octavian's company when Octavian received the news of the death of Julius Caesar; like Agrippa he was put in command of a fleet. He was eventually accused of conspiracy against Octavian, and was put to death amid rejoicing for Octavian's deliverance; Dio 48.33. A conjecture of Lambinus identifies the Nasidienus Rufus of Horace, Sermones 2.8, with Salvidienus, but, as Wickham points out, in his Introduction to this Sermo, it was written long after the death of Salvidienus. In any case Nasidienus is a Roman name; it occurs in Martial 7.54.

Bruttium from the incursions of Sextus. Octavian himself was to march through Italy and join Salvidienus at Rhegium, whence Salvidienus was somehow to convoy his army across to Sicily. Octavian had no doubt that, once in Sicily, he could prevail over Sextus.[77] In the first part of his task Salvidienus was successful; he forced Sextus to evacuate his posts in the southern part of Italy.[78]

Octavian had ordered ships to be built, apparently in the Adriatic, for Sextus had made the western seaboard of Italy unsafe, but these ships were not ready. Wanting boats, therefore, Salvidienus attempted to make rafts of a kind by stretching uncured ox-hides over wooden frames. These rafts were probably meant as transports to be convoyed by the few ships at hand. But Salvidienus was only laughed at for his pains, and was constrained to give up the attempt.[79] In the meanwhile the new ships had arrived, and with them he engaged Sextus off the Scyllaean promontory, but, although his ships were more numerous[80] and larger, he could make no headway against Sextus's expert seamen. When the usual current rushed through the straits,[81] the latter were not in the least disturbed, but the landlubbers who had been willing to essay a crossing on ox-hide rafts had no sea legs and could manage neither their oars nor their rudders. The ships suffered equally on both sides, but it was Salvidienus who first gave the signal for retreat, and in view of his larger armament he may rightly be said to have lost the engagement.[82] It may be remarked that the loss by Salvidienus of an equal number of ships implies a much greater loss of men, stores, and material on his part (his ships were the larger).

---

[77]Appian 4.85; Dio 48.18.1.

[78]For inscriptions on lead bullets and a coin attesting his success see Drumann, 4.568, note 7; Gardthausen, 1.146.

[79]Dio 48.18.2.

[80]But only in this battle. In total number of ships the fleet of Sextus outnumbered the fleet of Octavian at this time. See Kromayer, Entwicklung, 449–450.

[81]For the Fretum Siculum, its currents and its extent, see Ziegler's article on Sicily in Pauly-Wissowa, Zweite Reihe 2.2461–2522, especially 2472–2474; Nissen, 1.105–106.

[82]Dio 48.18.3; Appian 4.85; Livy, Periocha 123; Orosius 6.18.19. The battle is described by Gardthausen, 1.147, but this account is criticized by Holm, 3.454. I do not believe that the sources are sufficiently detailed to justify a description of the battle.

Salvidienus took his ships into the port of Balarus[83] facing the straits, and there made what repairs he could.

Although the majority of his fleet was still intact, Octavian did not again venture to cross openly, but made many attempts to effect a crossing secretly, feeling that, if he should once set foot in the island, he would, with his superior infantry, soon settle matters. But the vigilant watch which Sextus kept on all sides rendered these attempts futile. Antony was urging his colleague to hasten to join him in the campaign against the Liberators in Macedonia, but it was essential for Octavian to secure the good will of the cities of Vibo and Rhegium[84] before leaving Italy; this he did by giving solemn promises that he would never distribute their fields and houses to the soldiers.[85] Then he left to join Antony, sailing 'with Sicily on his left,' according to Appian,[86] that is, he was forced by Sextus to circumnavigate Sicily in order to reach Brundisium. Dio reports that Octavian looked on at the battle between Salvidienus and Sextus, and that he was particularly chagrined at the result, since it was the first set-back he had suffered.[87] It was likewise the first real victory of Sextus over Octavian. It is perhaps significant—it is at least an interesting coincidence—that the

---

[83]Balarus probably corresponds to the modern harbor of Bagnara, nine kilometers northeast of the Scyllaean Promontory. See Nissen, 2.916; Baedeker, Southern Italy and Sicily (Sixteenth English edition, 1912), the map facing page 268, and the text, 280. The equation of Balarus and modern Bagnara is established by Axt, 19. Axt also makes Abalas (see below, page 136) refer to the same place.

[84]Strabo reports (6.1.6) that, when Sextus was finally ejected from Sicily, Rhegium suffered from a dearth of men, which Augustus then supplied out of his expeditionary force. Holmes says (Architect, 81): "Octavian, before he went to join Antony, was obliged to promise that Rhegium and Vibo, two of the towns that had supported Sextus, should be exempted..." My impression is that they had not actually supported Sextus, but that Octavian wished to assure himself of their good will. There was a large Greek element in the Calabrian cities until quite late in Roman history. In fact, folk-songs in a corrupt form of ancient Greek were supposed to be current there until the last century: see A. F. Pott, Altgriechisch in Heutigen Kalabrien, Philologus 11 (1856), 245–269. Compare Axt, 14–15. This Greek element may have been sympathetic to Sextus, and especially so to his lieutenants.

[85]Appian 4.86.

[86]Ibidem: καλοῦντος δ' αὐτὸν 'Αντωνίου κατὰ σπουδὴν διέπλει πρὸς αὐτὸν ἐς τὸ Βρεντέσιον, ἐν ἀριστερᾷ ἔχων Σικελίαν καὶ Πομπήιον καὶ Σικελίαν ὑπερθέμενος ἐν τῷ τότε·   [87]48.18.4.

battle was fought in the same waters in which C. Cassius Longinus, a lieutenant of Sextus's father, had won a decisive victory over the fleet of Octavian's 'father' in 48.[88]

It is characteristic, perhaps, of the mentality of Sextus, and of his following, that he proceeded to celebrate his victory with a sham battle in which wooden boats contended with boats of leather, so arranged that the objects of his ridicule must needs look on.[89] In his elation Sextus gave himself the title of Son of Neptune, and to his heavenly parent he is reported to have sacrificed oxen with gilded horns, horses, and, according to some, even human beings. He discarded his admiral's cloak, and assumed a sea-blue habit befitting his lineage.[90] But, as

[88]Caesar, B. C. 3.101.1–3. For this battle see F. Graefe, Studien zur Marinegeschichte, Hermes 57 (1922), 432–433.

[89]Dio 48.19.1.

[90]Dio 48.19.2; Pseudo-Victor 84.2: cum mari feliciter uteretur, Neptuni se filium professus est eumque bobus auratis et equo placavit. In Epod. 9.7–10 Horace calls Sextus *Neptunius dux:*

> ut nuper, actus cum freto Neptunius
> dux fugit ustis navibus,
> minatus Urbi vincla, quae detraxerat
> servis amicus perfidis.

While we are speaking of Horace, it may be worth mentioning that Acron says that the ship of Carmina 1.14 represents the fortunes of Sextus Pompey, whom Horace would dissuade from embarking again on war with Octavian after the treaty of Misenum, in 39 B. C. This interpretation is not generally accepted, however. See Wickham's introduction to the poem; see also the remarks of Professor Charles Knapp, in The Classical Weekly 15 (1922), 150–151, in connection with a review of Walter Leaf, Horace Carm. I 14, <The English> Journal of Philology, 34 (1918), 283–289. Wickham suggests that Horace's friend followed the fortunes of Sextus Pompey after the defeat at Philippi. Appian 5.100 thus describes the behavior of Sextus: "It is said he was so much puffed up by these circumstances that he exchanged the purple cloak customary to Rɩ ɩan commanders for a dark blue one, to signify that he was the adopted son of Neptune." But this is told in connection with the storms which wrecked the fleets of Octavian on July 3, 36, where, to be sure, it is more appropriate; Dio 48.31.5 makes it clear that Sextus had assumed the style of Son of Neptune before 40. Coins of Sextus figuring Neptune are to be found in Babelon, 352–355 (Numbers 21, 22, 25–31); Hill, 126–128, Plate XIII, Numbers 78 and 79; Drumann has (4.569, note 3) some interesting remarks on these coins. The opinion of scholars has tended to fix the date for coins bearing IMP. ITER. at this period; compare Blok 21, note 1. However, an inscription found near Lilybaeum in 1893 (see page 100) makes it clear that before July, 36 Sextus did not call himself *Imperator Iterum.* Compare

Merivale properly remarks,[91]
Such stories against an unpopular and vanquished chieftain
must of course be received with suspicion. If they were generally
credited at the time, we should expect to hear them mentioned
by Velleius and Horace.

A further indication of his increased self-confidence is his
murder of Pompeius Bithynicus,[92] an act of which historians
ancient and modern speak with righteous indignation.[93] The
execution of Bithynicus is cited as an extreme instance of
Sextus's high-handed behavior toward his associates. He frequently refused to heed their advice, and at times even went
to the lengths that this incident illustrates. But perhaps Sextus
remembered that his father's counsellors had brought ruin at
Pharsalus; perhaps he had heard also that the Liberators at
Philippi had been handicapped by too much advice. Risse[94]
suggests that Bithynicus may well have conspired with the
enemy. In any case clemency was a rare virtue in the Civil
Wars; one should think of the *Arae Perusinae*[95] of Octavian
and his repeated *moriendum esse*.

We have had occasion to remark on Sextus's neglect of the
opportunity for effective and profitable intervention while all
the remaining armed forces in the West were at one another's
throats at Mutina. But, now that the breach with the Triumvirs was complete, the neglect of his opportunities is nothing
short of astounding. He neither offered assistance to the
Liberators nor took advantage of the defenseless state of Italy
to seize cities and establish fortifications. Yet nothing was
more certain than that his fate no less than that of the con-

---

also note 68, page 140, below. Hill is probably also wrong in saying (128),
"The augurship of Pompeius the Great is alluded to by the *lituus* behind
his head..." If the coin is to be dated after 39, the symbols of augurship
refer to Sextus himself. This would serve to show how Sextus persisted in
regarding his position as constitutional, and in ignoring the change in the
attitude of Octavian.

[91]3.195, note 1. It should be remarked that Merivale is generally extremely hostile to Sextus; see for example 3.185–187.

[92]Dio 48.19.1; Appian 5.70; Livy, Periocha 123.

[93]Drumann, 4.569; Dorn Seiffen, 64; Appian 5.70.

[94]Page 12. Dio 48.19.1 may well justify such a view.

[95]Suetonius, Augustus 15.1; Dio 48.14; Seneca, De Clementia 1.1.3.
See Shuckburgh's note to the passage in Suetonius in his edition of Augustus, 29–30. Fitzler-Seeck, 10.302, accept the traditional story of the
butchery as true. Compare also Blumenthal, 284.

spirators was bound up with the outcome of Philippi. Perhaps the republican leaders were in a measure themselves to blame. They themselves possessed a considerable fleet in eastern waters under L. Staius Murcus and Cn. Domitius Ahenobarbus. An effective cooperation with Sextus would have enabled the combined anti-Caesarian forces to sweep the Caesarians from the sea and to harass them in other ways.

Of the results of Philippi Sextus was apprised by fugitives from the battle.[96] Although the defeat of the Liberators strengthened the enemies of Sextus immeasurably, yet by that same defeat his own position was now exalted to that of the chief opponent of the Triumvirs. On the report that Lepidus had been in communication with Sextus, Octavian and Antony resolved to make a fresh distribution of the provinces, of which the details are somewhat vague.[97] L. Staius Murcus,[98] who had been the principal naval commander under the Liberators, now joined Sextus with two legions, eighty vessels, and a large sum of money.[99] Appian[100] reports that the son of Cicero, among others, joined Murcus before Murcus joined Sextus; we may therefore suppose that the young Cicero was with Sextus. No other Roman name was as much revered by the Sicilians as was the name of the Elder Cicero, and the accession of a Cicero to Sextus's forces must have been a distinct gain for him. Cn. Domitius Ahenobarbus,[101] who was the leader of the

[96]Dio 48.19.3; Velleius 2.72.4; Zonaras 19.21; Eutropius 7.4.

[97]See Holmes, Architect, 89, 218–219.

[98]L. Staius (not Statius: see Lübker, 982) Murcus was an officer of Caesar (B. C. 3.15.2). He commanded an army in Syria, which he turned over to Cassius together with himself upon Cassius's invasion of the East (Cicero, Fam. 12.11.1). Sextus procured his death in 39 (Appian 5.70). See below, page 94. Compare also Kloevekorn, 54–56.

[99]Appian 5.25; compare Dio 48.19.3 and Velleius 2.72.4. Velleius states (2.77.3) that Murcus by his arrival *vires eius <Sexti> duplicaverat.* Kromayer, Entwicklung, 449, accepts this as literally true: "Es ist also im wörtlichen Sinne wahr, was Velleius sagt, dass durch die Ankunft der Flüchtlinge der republicanischen Partei des Pompeius Macht verdoppelt sei." This would imply that Murcus brought 130 vessels: see above, page 66. But the statement of Appian is quite explicit.   [100]5.2.

[101]Cn. Domitius Ahenobarbus was a nephew of Cato and a republican by strong conviction. Whether or not he was one of the Conspirators against Julius Caesar is disputed; there is a good discussion of the matter in Tyrrell and Purser, 4.lxix. He sailed East with Brutus and Cassius. When the breach between Antony and Octavian occurred, he went to

remainder of the fleet of the Liberators, would not join his former colleague in going over to Sextus, but continued to operate independently. For two years he was so successful that he became reconciled to Antony through the mediation of Asinius Pollio, and was included in the treaty made with Sextus in 39.[102]

Speaking of this period Blok[103] says:

Sextus bellum ipse non amplius gerebat sed classem mandabat libertinis, quorum Menecrates, Menodorus, Demochares, Apollophanes, notissimi sunt: jure Velleius Paterculus Sextum propterea nominat 'libertum libertorum suorum' (2.73).

I cannot believe that Sextus's career could have continued as long as it did unless Sextus *bellum ipse gerebat.* Of course operations such as he carried on required trusted and capable lieutenants. The use of freedmen he received, we have seen, as a tradition from his father. But Octavian, we may observe, did not scruple to use freedmen for similar operations. A coup in Sardinia, successful at first, was carried out by Helenus,[104] and Menas himself came over to Octavian's side, where he was welcomed and entrusted with a command.[105]

In view of his naval resources, but much more in view of his proven integrity and ardent republicanism, Domitius's cooperation would have been an enormous asset to Sextus. It would have justified Sextus's behavior by making it clear that his cause was honorable, and it would have paved the way for his restoration to an honorable position in Roman civil life in the event of ultimate victory. But, so far as evidence and probability indicate, Sextus made no attempt to form such a union. Neither in this nor in other ways, so far as we know, did he make any effort to spread the opinion abroad that his struggle was on behalf of the 'republic,' although as late as August, 36, there were people in Rome that favored his cause.[106] He might have continued in the position in which he found himself (without effort on his part) during the twenty months between the deaths of Caesar and Cicero. He might have lived

---

Antony to Ephesus, but was disgusted by Antony's amorousness. The ancient evidence is cited in Drumann, 3.24–28. Domitius is characterized by Shakespeare in Antony and Cleopatra.

[102]Appian 5.2; Velleius 2.72.3.

[103]Page 23.   [104]See below, page 105.   [105]See below, page 106:

[106]Appian 5.80, 92. See below, page 136.

up to the position which Cicero in the Philippics assumes for
him.[107]   He might have delivered telling blows on the cities of
Italy in the guise of saving them from monarchy, and might
otherwise have shown himself the steadfast defender of republicanism.   But it seemed plain that Sextus's war was a war
in his personal interest only.   Even his plan of campaign
suggested this interest.[108]   Sicily was his fortress, and he made
no effort to spread his dominion.   His blows were delivered
only to check his enemy; he made no effort to force the issue,
but considered that he himself was besieging Italy, and that
the pinch of hunger would lead Italy to demand of Octavian
the satisfaction of his claims.   Yet one *caveat* must be pronounced: if Sextus's motives were in any measure selfish, so
were the motives of the Triumvirs.   The difference was not in
ideals, but in resources and ability and good fortune.   In 36,
when it had become fairly obvious that true patriotism required
the unselfish support of Octavian, Lepidus was ready to start
a new and certainly bloody revolution to promote his own
interests.   Surely we can understand that Sextus (at this time
and in his situation) would not regard Octavian as the savior
of Rome.   Furthermore, a partial explanation of Sextus's com-
parative inactivity may be offered.   Sextus's camp was filled
with Roman nobles, who, we may be sure, were not sparing of
advice.   We have seen what the results of advice were even
with so experienced a general as the Elder Pompey at Pharsalus.

---

[107]5.39: Pompeio enim patre, quod imperii populi Romani lumen fuit,
extincto interfectus est patris simillimus filius.   Sed omnia mihi videntur
deorum immortalium iudicio expiata Sex.   Pompeio rei publicae con-
servato; 5.41: Sextusque Pompeius Cn. f. Magnus huius ordinis auctoritate
ab armis discesserit et...civitati restitutus sit; 13.8: Magnum Pompeium,
clarissimum adulescentem, praestantissimi viri filium, auctoritate adduxit
ad pacem....; 13.9: Cn. Pompei filium res publica aspiciet suoque sinu
complexuque recipiet neque solum illum, sed cum illo se ipsam sibi resti-
tutam putabit; 13.12: utrum populus Romanus libentius sanciet, Pom-
peiumne an Antonium?   <the implication of course is that Sextus is incomparably superior to Antony>; 13.34: paucis diebus et in domum et in
hortos paternos immigrabit; 13.50: Magnum Pompeium, Gnaei filium, pro
patris maiorumque suorum animo studioque in rem publicam suaque
pristina virtute, industria, voluntate fecisse, quod suam eorumque quos
secum haberet operam senatui populoque Romano pollicitus esset, eamque
rem senatui populoque Romano gratam acceptamque esse, eique honori
dignitatique eam rem fore.   [108]Drumann, 4.570 makes this point.

A crowd of the same sort of advisers as were in Sextus's camp had contributed largely to the disaster at Philippi. The presence of these nobles in the camp of Sextus may explain both the uncertainty of his movements and his greater trust in the judgment of his freedmen.

But to hope for the eventual success of such a campaign as Sextus was conducting was folly, murmur as the people might in Rome at a dear loaf. The resources of Rome were almost inexhaustible, so long, at least, as Octavian and Antony were willing to cooperate; and Italy is not an island to be shut off completely by a blockade. Octavian's land armament was incomparably superior to Sextus's, and, even though Sicily was an excellent fortress, the issue would eventually have to be settled by a battle on land. The wonder, then, is, not that Sextus was defeated but that he succeeded in maintaining himself for so long. That he did so maintain himself is a symptom of the contemporary chaos. As Dean Merivale put it,[109]

His eventful story gives ample evidence of the distracted state of the doomed republic in which so long a struggle could be maintained by a roving buccaneer against the great public interest of the Roman world.

But, however hopeless of ultimate success a modern may consider the cause of Sextus, there was much in the situation to encourage him. Despite his phenomenal preliminary successes and the astuteness which later ages may easily perceive, Octavian was still a youth of uncertain potentialities, with an uncertain hold on the Roman people. It was not hard to see, moreover, that a breach with Antony was inevitable. On the other hand, Sextus's seamen were as successful as they were daring. Of Menas and Menecrates we have already spoken. The two other chiefs of Sextus's forces were Demochares and Apollophanes; the Greek names of all four are likely to denote an eastern origin and freedman status.

With the advice and the cooperation of these worthies Sextus devoted himself to harassing the coasts of Italy, and, particularly, to raiding the shores of Bruttium. These raids Octavian tried to repel by patrols of cavalry along the shore, but without success.[110] It is very difficult for a land army to protect the coasts of Italy, and the situation which occasioned such a step

---

[109]Merivale, 3.205.   [110]Appian 5.19.

as Octavian took must have been serious. Gardthausen[111] indicates how these patrols of soldiery must have increased the misery of the people. He refers two hoards of coins to this particular period; these would show the troubled condition of Italy brought about by Sextus's raids and the defensive measures taken against them. But Sextus's especial efforts were and continued to be in the direction of cutting off Rome's grain supply. To this end Domitius Ahenobarbus was also operating, although independently of Sextus. The dear loaf threatened to dwindle to no loaf at all, and the resultant unrest assumed such alarming proportions that the very position of Octavian was threatened.[112]

The forces of Sextus continued to grow. As Appian says,[113]

Those who feared for their safety, or had been despoiled of their property, or who utterly abhorred the form of government, mostly went and joined him. Young men, also, eager for military service for the sake of gain, who thought that it made no difference under whom they served, since all service was Roman service, rather preferred to join Pompeius as representing the better cause.

In the popular opinion of Italy, therefore, Sextus was not simply a rebel against the constitutional authority of Octavian. His cause seemed as just as Octavian's and his means of carrying on warfare as honorable.

But, in spite of this, whether because his ex-slaves lacked imagination or because he himself lacked confidence, Sextus did not make as full use of the opportunities offered by the Perusian War (between Octavian and the brother and the wife of Antony, in 41–40 B. C.) as he might have made. Surely something more ambitious than blockades and raids was possible for a good general when his enemies were at one another's throats. After this war also (toward the end of February, 40),[114] many who had been on the wrong side went over to Sextus.[115] A significant accession was the Antonian cavalry, which had been under the command of Munatius Plancus.[116]

Among those who came to Sextus for refuge after the end of the Perusian War were Tiberius Claudius Nero and his wife

---

[111]1.198.   [112]See below, page 91.   [113]5.25.
[114]For the chronology of 40 B. C. see Kromayer, Kleine Forschungen, 556–563.
[115]Dio 48.15.2.   [116]Appian 5.61.

Livia, together with their child, the future Emperor Tiberius. Claudius had taken a prominent part in the war on the side of the Antonians, and his escape to Naples with his wife and wailing infant had been very thrilling.[117] But Sextus made the proud Claudius wait for an interview, and would not grant him the courtesy of permitting him to use his *fasces;*[118] Claudius was annoyed by this treatment and went off to join Antony.[119] More cordial was the reception Sextus gave to Julia, the mother of Antony; his reasons were obviously politic. When Antony left Cleopatra in 40 in order to verify for himself reports of the happenings in Italy, Sextus[120] sent his mother to meet him at Athens,

. . . with warships, and escorted by some of the optimates of his party, by Lucius ⟨Scribonius⟩ Libo, his father-in-law, by ⟨Sentius⟩ Saturninus and others, who being attracted by Antony's capacity for great deeds, sought to bring him into friendly relations with Pompeius and to form an alliance between them against Octavian. Antony replied that he thanked Pompeius for sending his mother and that he would requite him for the service in due time; that if there should be a war with Octavian he would ally himself with Pompeius, but if Octavian should adhere to their agreements he would endeavour to reconcile him with Pompeius.

Antony then sailed off to Italy with his admiral, Domitius

---

[117]Suetonius, Tiberius 6: Infantiam pueritiamque habuit laboriosam et exercitatam, comes usque quaque parentum fugae; quos quidem apud Neapolim sub inruptionem hostis navigium clam petentis vagitu suo paene bis prodidit,. . .per Siciliam quoque. . .circumductus. . . ⟨est⟩.

[118]Pompeia, the sister of Sextus, seems to have treated the future Emperor kindly. Compare Suetonius, Tiberius 6.3: Munera quibus a Pompeia Sex. Pompei sorore in Sicilia donatus est, chlamys et fibula, item bullae aureae, durant ostendunturque adhuc Baiis. We learn from this passage incidentally that Pompeia was with her brother in Sicily, and we see also something of the hospitality which the Pompeys offered their guests.

[119]Suetonius, Tiberius 4.3: deditione a ceteris facta, solus permansit in partibus ac. . .in Siciliam profugit. Sed indigne ferens nec statim se in conspectum Sexti Pompei admissum et fascium usu prohibitum, ad M. Antonium traiecit in Achaiam. Governors frequently granted to senators travelling in their provinces the use of lictors; see Mommsen, Staatsrecht, 1.370. Dio tells (48.15.3) the same story, with a remark on the waywardness of Fate.

[120]Appian 5.52 (compare 5.63, 122, 134); Dio 48.15, 16; Plutarch, Antony 32. Kromayer, Kleine Forschungen, 556–563, suggests May, 40 as the date of the understanding between Antony (and Domitius) and Sextus.

Ahenobarbus. After the Perusian War, Octavian left Agrippa to defend Italy against the attacks of Sextus, and himself marched toward the Alps with the legions of Salvidienus, which had been called for service in the Perusian War. At this extraordinarily favorable moment Antony's governor of Gaul mysteriously died, and Octavian took the provinces over from his son. This action shows that Octavian already had in view the inevitable break with Antony. Agrippa was praetor and as such had to officiate at the Ludi Apollinares.[121] While Agrippa was absent at Rome for this purpose, Sextus made an incursion into Italy. This incursion must have taken place July 6–13, the date of the Ludi Apollinares.[122] When Agrippa heard of this raid, he hastened in person to the threatened region.[123] This attack was only one of the ordinary raids of Sextus, not an attack in force. Previous students of these events,[124] with the exception of Kromayer,[125] assume that this attack is identical with the later ambitious effort undertaken in conjunction with Antony. Their argument is based on the statement of Appian 5.62: . . . ὁ δὲ Πομπήιος οὐ πρότερον, ἀλλὰ νῦν Ἀντωνίῳ θαρρῶν ἐπιβέβηκε τῆς παραλίου. But the fact that Appian is ignorant of the earlier attack shows simply that that attack was one of the usual raids, and not a serious effort planned in conjunction with Antony.

In due course news of the negotiations between Sextus and Antony reached Octavian. Octavian had forty legions, but hardly a ship, and no time to build any. If his adversaries should unite, they would have in all 500 ships, and so be able to enforce any demands they might choose to make. In Italy there was increasing bitterness because of the scarcity of grain, and also because of the confiscations that had been made for the purpose of settling the veterans.[126] With a view to opening the way for an accommodation with Sextus, Octavian therefore

---

[121]This was a function of the Praetor Urbanus; see Marquardt, Römische Staatsverwaltung, 3.384 (Leipzig, 1887).

[122]Marquardt, 3².578; W. W. Fowler, The Roman Festivals of the Period of the Republic, 179–181 (London, 1899).

[123]Dio 48.20.2.

[124]Dorn Seiffen, 38; Risse, 15; Blok, 25; Drumann, 4.570–571.

[125]Kleine Forschungen, 558.

[126]The most recent account of the complicated events of the spring and the summer of 40 is in Holmes, Architect, 101–105.

had a marriage arranged for himself with Scribonia,[127] the sister of the father-in-law of Sextus,[128] and a woman much older than Octavian.[129] Scribonius Libo was of the opinion that the understanding with Antony could not be relied upon. He was therefore eager for the match, both for his sister's sake, and because he hoped that his son-in-law might reach an accommodation with his new brother-in-law.[130] Octavian's motive, apparently, was not so much to settle the problem of Sextus as to provide for the inevitable conflict with Antony. The accession of Domitius had enormously strengthened Antony's sea-power. If Sextus should also join with Antony, their combined forces would constitute a great menace. If, on the other hand, Sextus could be induced to join Octavian, Octavian would have the dominant power on sea as on land.[131]

But Sextus refused to play into the hands of Octavian. Relying on his understanding with Antony for support, he sent Menas to take Sardinia.[132] Menas with his four legions was at

[127]Appian 5.53; Dio 48.16.3; Zonaras 10.21. Compare Tacitus, Annales 2.27; Propertius 4.11.55. Heitland has (3.406) an interesting remark on such marriages. Speaking of the fact that Lepidus and Cassius had married two half-sisters of Brutus, he says, "Among the Roman nobles these marriage connexions were generally a matter of careful calculation. In spite of frequent divorces and much marital infidelity, the fact of the connexion constituted a bond which social habit made it difficult to ignore. Cicero himself had found it hard to break finally with Dolabella, whose bad character he knew and loathed, and whose treatment of his beloved Tullia had been infamous." See also Münzer, Chapter 7.

[128]In a moment of oblivion Merivale (3.187) calls Libo "the father-in-law both of Sextus and Octavian."

[129]"As her son (P. Cornelius Scipio) by her second husband was consul in B. C. 16, he must have been at least in his 17th year at the time of her marriage to Augustus (B. C. 40, Dio 48.16) and she must have been many years older than her husband." So Shuckburgh, 121.

[130]A remark of Holmes seems fatuous. He says (Architect, 103): "Scribonius Libo, who had been an ardent follower of Pompey, was the father-in-law of Sextus; but he consented to give his sister in marriage to Octavian." He was eager for the match *because* he was a follower of Pompey.

[131]See Gardthausen, 1.214.

[132]On the importance of holding Sardinia, Bouchier has this to say (85): "The first seizure was due to strategic needs in the struggle with Carthage; its retention may have been dictated by the fear that a foreign power or piratical chief might make it a center from which to harry the shores of Italy." For Sardinia see H. Philipp in Pauly-Wissowa, Zweite Reihe, 1. 2480–2495. In his outline history of Sardinia (2491) Philipp makes no mention of the present disturbances.

first defeated by M. Lurius,[133] who, with two legions, was holding the island for Octavian. Later, however, Menas defeated Lurius and drove him from the island, and then besieged and took Caralis, the capital of the island, in which many of the fugitives had sought refuge.[134] It may be surmised that Octavian sent an expedition under Helenus to attempt the recovery of the island. Helenus, whom Appian (5.66) calls στρατηγὸς Καίσαρος, is mentioned as being defeated and captured by Menas. Helenus was not the governor of the island, however, for this post was occupied by M. Lurius.[135] Helenus must therefore have come with an independent force. Appian uses αὖθις ἐξέβαλε of Menas, which would indicate that he conquered the island twice. The date of the expedition of Helenus is doubtful. Kromayer is inclined to think that it took place *after* the Treaty of Brundisium.[136] Kromayer bases his view of the date on the situation of the various forces and on the chronology suggested by the order of the narrative in Dio.

When Antony and Domitius approached Brundisium, they found the harbor closed against them.[136a] Antony forthwith set about constructing siege works, and called upon Sextus to get into action.[137] Thereupon Sextus laid siege to Thurii in Lucania, but was driven off by a lieutenant of Octavian. Sextus stubbornly prosecuted an attack against Consentia in Bruttium, and with his cavalry pillaged the surrounding country. The persistence and scope of this effort indicate that it was part of a larger plan, agreed upon by Sextus with Antony. Over his connection with Octavian by marriage Sextus was but little concerned.[138] The date for this attack has been calculated by Kromayer to be August, 40.[139]

---

[133]For Lurius see Klein, 247–248.   [134]Appian 5.66; Dio 48.30.7–8.
[135]Dio 48.30.7; Klein, 247–248.

[136]Kleine Forschungen, 560, note 3. Fitzler-Seeck, 10.303, followed by Holmes, Architect, 106, alone of students of the period (besides Kromayer), accept the recapture by Helenus as a fact.   [136a]Compare Blumenthal, 84.

[137]Appian 5.56. Kromayer (Kleine Forschungen, 561) fixes the date for the Treaty of Brundisium at September, 40.

[138]Appian 5.56, 58, 63; Dio 48.20. This attack is independent of the one mentioned above (page 86), for this time Octavian was with his army before Brundisium, Agrippa was in Sipontum, and the attack of Sextus was made on orders from Antony (Appian 5.58); none of these circumstances would apply in the earlier attack, Dio 48.20.1, 2.

[139]Kleine Forschungen, 562.

In the meantime Fulvia, who had been the chief occasion for dissension between Octavian and Antony, died. Octavian hastened to join Agrippa, and marched his troops south, conveying to them the impression that they were to fight against Sextus. When the troops discovered that they were in fact to attack their old comrade, the victor of Philippi, they deserted in large numbers. Although this defection was not so serious as it might have been, in view of the preponderance of Octavian's forces, yet it was a plain indication of the state of feeling on the part of the veterans. Since fighting was alike contrary to the will of the soldiers and the interest of the leaders, and since Antony was hampered by want of adequate land forces and Octavian by want of a fleet, matters remained at a deadlock. The two came to an understanding, therefore, and divided the empire between them anew. Antony had requested Sextus to retire from Italy so as not to hinder the negotiations; but in his new agreement with Octavian he disregarded his previous promises to Sextus, and in fact entered upon a compact to prosecute the war against Sextus.[140]

But Italy had been better pleased if Sextus had been included in the understanding. With bases in Sicily, Sardinia, and Corsica,[141] Sextus renewed his activities with redoubled zeal. His vessels not only terrified Italian waters but penetrated also to Gaul[142] and Africa.[143] The blockade was growing so effective that no grain at all could reach Italy, except from Macedonia and Thrace, whose supplies were being rapidly exhausted. The populace was impatient of bickerings and agreements between

---

[140]Dio 48.29.1; Appian 5.63. Dio makes Antony's change of front particularly reprehensible; it may have been, but Dio's anti-Antonian bias is well known. Antony's agreement may have been 'provisional.' Niese also blames Antony (269): "Antonius liess den Sext. Pompeius ganz fallen. . ."

[141]When Corsica was taken is not mentioned; Appian 5.67 speaks of it as being in the power of Sextus.

[142]Dio 48.30. Marcus Titius, who had established himself as a freebooter in Narbonese Gaul, was taken by Menas and his men, but was pardoned for the sake of his father, who had been proscribed and was serving with Sextus. The case of Titius is important for our judgment of Sextus, for it serves to remove the stigma of piracy. Nor must it be forgotten that Domitius Ahenobarbus, whose moral qualities were never called into question, was following much the same career as was Sextus.

[143]Appian 5.67.

the leaders. The hardships of the past few years seemed all in vain if no bread was to be had. Dio well describes popular dissatisfaction with the exclusion of Sextus from the Treaty of Brundisium:[144]

Menas, then, was so employed; but as for the people in Rome, they would no longer hold their peace, inasmuch as Sardinia was in hostile hands, the coast was being pillaged, and they had had their corn supply cut off, while the famine, the great number of taxes of all sorts which were being imposed, and in addition contributions assessed upon such as possessed slaves, all irritated them greatly. Much as they were pleased with the reconciliation of Antony and Caesar,—for they thought that harmony between these men meant peace for themselves,— they were equally or even more displeased at the war which the two men were carrying on against Sextus. But a short time before they had brought the two rulers into the city mounted on horses as if at a triumph . . .; at the present time, however, they changed their behaviour to a remarkable degree. At first, when they met at various gatherings or came together to witness a spectacle, they would urge Antony and Caesar to secure peace, and at this they raised loud shouts of approval; and when these leaders would not heed them, they were alienated from them and favoured Sextus. They not only kept up a general talk to foster his interests, but also at the games in the Circus[145] honoured by loud applause the statute of Neptune carried in the procession, thus expressing their great delight in him.[146] And when on certain days it was not brought out, they took stones and drove the magistrates from the Forum, threw down the statues of Caesar and Antony, and finally, when they could not accomplish anything even in this way, they rushed violently upon those men as if to kill them. Caesar, although his followers were wounded, rent his garments and betook himself to supplicating them, whereas Antony bore himself with more violence toward them; and when, chiefly because of this, the people became angered and it was feared that they would even commit some act of violence in consequence, the two were forced against their will to make overtures to Sextus.

It may be interesting to compare with this the parallel account of Appian, which, in spite of its flourishes, gives the impression that Appian had more precise information:[147]

---

[144]Dio 48.31.

[145]These were the *ludi plebei*, which took place in the middle of November.

[146]This incident provides proof that Sextus assumed the title of son of Neptune even before the Treaty of Misenum.   [147]Appian 5.67–68.

Now famine fell upon Rome, since the merchants of the Orient could not put to sea for fear of Pompeius, who controlled Sicily, and those of the west were deterred by Sardinia and Corsica, which the lieutenants of Pompeius held, while those of Africa opposite were prevented by the same hostile fleets, which infested both shores. Thus there was a great rise in cost of provisions, and the people considered the cause of it to be the strife between the chiefs, and cried out against them and urged them to make peace with Pompeius. As Octavian would by no means yield, Antony advised him to hasten the war on account of the scarcity. As there was no money for this purpose, an edict was published that the owners of slaves should pay a tax for each one, equal to one-half of the twenty-five drachmas that had been ordained for the war against Brutus and Cassius, and that those who acquired property by legacies should contribute a share thereof. The people tore down the edict with fury. They were exasperated that, after exhausting the public treasury, stripping the provinces, burdening Italy itself with contributions, taxes, and confiscations, not for foreign war, not for extending the empire, but for private enmities and to add to their own power (for which reason the proscriptions and murders and this terrible famine had come about), the triumvirs should deprive them of the remainder of their property.

They banded together, with loud cries, and stoned those who did not join them, and threatened to plunder and burn their houses, until the whole populace was aroused, and Octavian with his friends and a few attendants came into the forum intending to intercede with the people and to show the unreasonableness of their complaints. As soon as he made his appearance they stoned him unmercifully, and they were not ashamed when they saw him enduring this treatment patiently, and offering himself to it, and even bleeding from wounds. When Antony learned what was going on he came with haste to his assistance. When the people saw him coming down the Via Sacra they did not throw stones at him, since he was in favour of a treaty with Pompeius, but they told him to go away. When he refused to do so they stoned him also. He called in a larger force of troops, who were outside the walls. As the people would not allow him even so to pass through, the soldiers divided right and left on either side of the street and the forum, and made their attack from the narrow lane, striking down those whom they met. The people could no longer find ready escape on account of the crowd, nor was there any way out of the forum. There was a scene of slaughter and wounds, while shrieks and groans sounded from the housetops. Antony made his way into the forum with difficulty, and snatched Octavian from the most manifest danger, in which he then was, and

brought him safe to his house. The mob having been dispersed,
the corpses were thrown into the river in order to avoid their
gruesome appearance. It was a fresh cause of lamentation to see
them floating down the stream, and the soldiers stripping them,
and certain miscreants, as well as the soldiers, carrying off the
clothing of the better class as their own property. This in-
surrection was suppressed, but with terror and hatred for the
triumvirs; the famine grew worse; the people groaned, but did
not stir.

Either because he believed that popular agitators were
exaggerating the seriousness of the situation, or because a
youthful stubbornness forbade him to negotiate with the
hereditary pretender, Octavian was reluctant to yield to the
popular demand. It was Antony that suggested to the relatives
of Scribonius Libo in Italy that Libo be invited to negotiate
for peace; and, when Libo had sailed, with the permission of
Sextus, and had landed at the island of Aenaria, it was the
populace that prevailed on Octavian, though with difficulty, to
give Libo a safe-conduct to Rome, that terms might be discussed. Furthermore, the populace, by threatening to burn
her house down over her, prevailed upon Mucia,[148] the mother
of Sextus, to go to her son and persuade him to accept terms.
Libo's assurance grew as he perceived the great distress prevalent at Rome, and he demanded that Octavian and Antony
meet Sextus to discuss terms of peace; to this request popular
pressure forced the triumvirs to accede.[149] The hesitancy of
Octavian must have sprung from some political reason, for, in
view of the existing popular feeling, it was manifestly dangerous
to attempt a serious war against Sextus. What these political
reasons were, and why he steadfastly refused to conciliate

[148]Mucia was the daughter of Q. Mucius Scaevola, consul in 95; she was
the third wife of Pompey the Great. During her husband's long absence
in the wars with the pirates and with Mithridates she proved unfaithful,
and was the occasion of Pompey's dubbing Caesar Aegisthus. Pompey
divorced her in 62, before he actually arrived in Rome; the divorce was
generally applauded. Mucia then married M. Aemilius Scaurus, the
brother of Pompey's second wife. She reached a high old age, surviving
Actium, and being kindly treated by Octavian. For references to her see
Drumann, 4.560–561.

[149]Appian 5.68, 69 Dio seems (48.16.3) to misunderstand the circumstances of Mucia's embassy to her son.

popular feeling by making some temporary concessions to Sextus it is difficult to understand.[150]

The conference was arranged to take place in the spring of 39 B. C., in the Bay of Naples. To Sextus it could not but seem that his policy had been justified and his efforts crowned with success. He had brought his adversaries to their knees, as it were; at least they were acknowledging him as a power to be negotiated with. So confident had he grown, indeed, that it required the persuasion of his friends to make him consent to the meeting. The Roman gentry among the followers of Sextus were all most eager for peace and for the opportunity peace would give them to return to their normal lives in Italy. We may guess that, aside from the necessary deprivations of military life, the camp of Sextus was not a congenial place for Roman gentlemen. Positions of trust, it would seem, and the entire confidence of the commander were given only to freedmen; the political refugees in the camp were always regarded with some suspicion. That, at least, is the impression the ancient accounts uniformly give. I have indicated above[151] that this course may have been dictated to Sextus by the requirements of efficient administration. Furthermore, we must always remember that the ancient accounts are themselves official or are based upon official sources; it turned out in the end that Sextus was not a party leader but a rebel, and any defamation of his character was therefore patriotic. Surely this may be said of such a statement as that of Velleius: ⟨Pompeius erat⟩ libertorum suorum libertus servorumque servus.[152]

The freedmen admirals, on the other hand, stood to lose all

---

[150]Ferrero says (3.268, note): "Historians have failed to observe that if Octavianus and Antony pursued a policy so obviously republican during these months, their action was dictated by public ill-feeling and by the popularity of Sextus Pompeius." I do not know why Octavian's policy should be called "obviously republican," but the expressions "public ill-feeling" and "the popularity of Sextus Pompeius" seem justified.

[151]Page 83.

[152]2.73.1. I do not mean to imply that the characterization is entirely without truth. Those interested in tracing in Sextus the traits inherited from the Elder Pompey may find another point here. Pompey the Great was notoriously devoted to his freedmen, frequently to the great annoyance of his peers.

if the war should be brought to a stop; they therefore urged its continuance with might and main. Menas, for example,[153]

wrote to him from Sardinia either to prosecute the war vigorously or still to procrastinate, because famine was fighting for them, and he would thus get better terms if he should decide to make peace. Menodorus ⟨Menas⟩ also advised him to distrust Murcus, who opposed these views, intimating that he was seeking power for himself. Pompeius, who had been vexed with Murcus lately on account of his high position and his stubbornness, became still more averse to him for this reason, and held no communication with him whatever, until, finally, Murcus retired in disgust to Syracuse. Here he saw some of Pompeius's guards following him, and he expressed his opinion of Pompeius to them freely. Then Pompeius bribed a tribune and a centurion of Murcus, and sent them to kill him and to say that he had been murdered by slaves. To give credibility to this falsehood he crucified the slaves. But he did not succeed in concealing this crime,—the next one committed by him after the murder of Bithynicus,—Murcus having been a man distinguished for his warlike deeds, who had been strongly attached to that party from the beginning, and had rendered great assistance to Pompeius himself in Spain, and had joined him in Sicily voluntarily.

After the death of Murcus the party whose spokesman he had been continued to urge peace in order to escape a similar fate and to secure a safe return to Italy. They charged Menas with desire to rule, saying that he counselled a continuance of the war not to advance his master's cause but to continue his own sway over an army and a province. Sextus followed their advice, and with many picked vessels crossed to Aenaria, an island on the Campanian coast. He himself sailed in a very large and splendid ship, and toward evening proudly paraded before his enemies at Puteoli.[154]

---

[153]Appian 5.70. For Murcus and a possible explanation of the murder see above, page 80. Compare Velleius 2.77.3: Statium autem Murcum, qui adventu suo classisque celeberrimae viris eius duplicaverat, insimulatum falsis criminationibus, quia talem virum collegam offici Mena et Menecrates fastidierant, Pompeius in Sicilia interfecerat. For *celeberrimae, celerrimae* has been suggested by P. Thomas, Notes Critiques sur Velleius Paterculus et sur Tacite (Bulletin l'Academie Royale de Belgique 1919, 305).

[154]The conference and the circumstances attendant on it are described in Appian 5.71 and Dio 48.36, with slight discrepancies. Dio, for example, says that the whole fleet of Sextus was present. This could not have been

Early in the morning two platforms were constructed on piles, one extending from the land, the other out in the sea, but separated by only a narrow space from the first, so that voices might be heard without being raised. On the landward platform Antony and Octavian took their places; Sextus Pompey and Scribonius Libo took their places on the other. But the expectations of Sextus were set at too high a pitch; he demanded nothing less than admission into the triumvirate, in the place of Lepidus, on an equality with Octavian and Antony. The Triumvirs also went to the extreme, and would offer Sextus nothing more than restoration to citizenship. Hence the groups separated with nothing accomplished.[155]

But friends of both parties were unwilling that the negotiations should be thus fruitlessly broken off, and proposals and counter-proposals were carried back and forth.

Pompeius ⟨probably equivalent to 'the party of Pompeius'⟩ demanded that, of the proscripts and the men with him, those who had participated in the murder of Gaius Caesar should be allowed a safe place of exile, and the rest restoration to their homes and citizenship, and that the property they had lost should be restored to them. Urged on by the famine and by the people to an agreement, Octavian and Antony reluctantly conceded a fourth part of this property, promising to buy it from the present holders. They wrote to this effect to the proscripts themselves, hoping this would satisfy them. The latter accepted all terms, for they already had apprehensions of Pompeius on account of his crime against Murcus. So they gathered around Pompeius and besought him to come to an agreement. Then Pompeius rent his garments, declaring that he was betrayed by those for whom he had fought, and he frequently invoked the name of Menodorus as one most competent to command and his only friend.[156]

---

the case, for Menas was holding Sicily with part of the fleet, and was by letter advising Sextus against peace (Dio 48.30, 31; Appian 5.66). Appian says (5.72) that the conference took place at Dicaearchia, that is, Puteoli. On the basis of Dio, Plutarch, and Velleius it has always been assumed that the place was Misenum, but none of these authors names Misenum specifically. The passages are as follows: Velleius 2.77.1: cum Pompeio quoque *circa Misenum* pax inita; Plutarch, Antony 32.2: κατὰ τὴν ἐν Μισηνοῖς ἄκραν; Dio 48.36.1: πρὸς Μισηνῷ ἐς λόγους ἦλθον·

[155]In general, in regard to the relative merits of the accounts by Dio and Appian of the events of this period the justice of the remark by Dorn Seiffen (18) is easily apparent: "Universe autem in iis, quae foedus Misenicum antecesserunt et subsecuta sunt, multo copiosior et verior est Appianus, acriterque sibi oppositae sunt huius cura et Dionis negligentia, ut cuique legenti facile patet."   [156]Appian 5.71.

But Sextus finally yielded to the combined entreaties of his friends, and in particular to the solicitations of his mother and his wife.[157] Thereupon the chiefs met again in full view of their several forces. One may safely infer, both from what preceded the conference and from the joy that followed the making of the treaty, that control of the situation had passed in a measure from the hands of the leaders, and that the insistence of their followers practically forced them to come to some amicable arrangement. Of the treaty that was concluded the following were the terms.[158] Arms were to be laid down, both on land and on sea, and neither party was to violate the treaty. Sextus was to draw off his garrisons from all parts of Italy, was not to receive fugitive slaves, and his vessels were never to attack Italian shores. To his tenure of provinces the *status quo* was to apply. He was to retain Sicily, Sardinia, Corsica,[159] and the other islands which he held, for as long a period as Antony and Octavian had extended their rule over their several provinces. In addition, Sextus was to obtain control of the Peloponnese. He was to hold the consulship *in absentia*, and it was provided that he should be permitted to fill his office with whomever of his friends he should designate.[160]

---

[157]Appian 5.72 says: Μουκίας δὲ αὐτὸν τῆς μητρὸς καὶ 'Ιουλίας τῆς γυναικὸς ἐναγουσῶν.... Why he calls the lady Julia is not clear; that was certainly not her name. "'Ιουλίας iure susp. Sch<weighäuser>, *Mucia ac Julia Antonii matre compellentibus* vertit C<obet> errorem correcturus. Desideramus Σκριβωνίας, sed fort. est mendum Appiani ipsius," says Viereck, 583. Following the authorities I place this petition *after* the first unsuccessful negotiation, rather than, as Gardthausen does (1.221), before the negotiations were undertaken.

[158]Risse (20–23) makes a detailed comparison of the provisions of the treaty as given in Appian 5.72 and Dio 48.36. From the almost verbal agreement of some sections and the great discrepancies in others he concludes that Appian and Dio followed separate authorities; the ultimate source of those authorities was, he assumes, Livy.

[159]There is no specific statement concerning the time at which Sextus took Corsica, but it is mentioned as being in his power in Appian 5.67, 78, 80. It would naturally have fallen into his possession. Velleius (2.77.2) omits both Sardinia and Corsica from the terms of the treaty. Dio (48.36) mentions Sardinia, but not Corsica.

[160]But since, in the Treaty of Brundisium, appointments had already been made as far ahead as 36 B. C., this would hold good only after 36. See Drumann, 1.315, and Mommsen, Staatsrecht, 1.567, note 3; compare Mommsen, Hermes 30 (1895), 460–461. See also Merivale, 3.188, note; Holmes, Architect, 107, note.

Furthermore, he was to be created augur.[161] As recompense for his patrimony he was to receive 17½ million sesterces.[162] The exiles were to be permitted to return to Rome, with the exception of those who had been publicly condemned as murderers of Caesar. Those who had fled only because of fear and had lost their goods through violence should have their real property restored to them. The proscripts were to receive a fourth of their property. Slaves who had fought with Sextus were to receive their freedom. The freedmen were to receive their pay, and in addition the same rewards as should be bestowed on the veterans of Antony and Octavian. Dio adds that Pompey agreed to discontinue building ships. Appian refers in a later passage[163] to this stipulation. This provision may well have been included. In return for all this, of course, Sextus was to refrain from molesting the transports of grain, and himself to forward the customary allotments of grain from the islands which he held.[164]

These conditions of peace were signed and sealed, and sent to Rome to be deposited with the Vestal Virgins.[165] Of the exuberant joy which followed the proclamation of peace Dio gives a remarkable description:

Upon this a great and mighty shout arose from the mainland and from the ships at the same moment. For many soldiers and many civilians who were present suddenly cried out all together, being terribly tired of the war and strongly desirous of peace, so that even the mountains resounded; and thereupon great panic and alarm came upon them, and many died of no other cause, while many others perished by being trampled under foot or suffocated. Those who were in the small boats did not wait to reach the land itself, but jumped out into the sea, and those on land rushed out into the water. Meanwhile they embraced one another while swimming and threw their arms around one another's necks as they dived, making a

---

[161]Appian says, τῆς μεγίστης ἱερωσύνης ἐς τοὺς ἱερέας ἐγγραφῆναι, which would mean that Sextus was made Pontifex Maximus, but this can hardly be true; see Mommsen, Hermes 30 (1895), 460–461. Dio, in fact, says οἰωνιστὴν ἀποδειχθῆναι, and Cicero had already proposed that Sextus be coopted into the College of Augurs. White (501) makes the correction tacitly, and says: "...and be inscribed as a member of the Augurs' College."

[162]For the sum involved in the compensation for Pompey's property see above, page 63. [163]5.77.

[164]Appian 5.72; Dio 48.36; Plutarch, Antony 32; Zonaras 10.22; Livy, Periocha 127; Velleius 2.77; Orosius 6.18; Tacitus, Annales 5.1.

[165]Appian and Dio, as cited in Note 164.

spectacle of varied sights and sounds. . . . Accordingly they
became neither sated with joy nor ashamed of grief, because
they were all affected in the same way, and they spent the entire
day as well as the greater part of the night in these demonstrations.

After this the leaders as well as the rest received and entertained one another, first Sextus on his ship and then Caesar
and Antony on the shore; for Sextus so far surpassed them in
military strength that he would not disembark to meet them
on the mainland until they had gone aboard his ship. And
although, by this arrangement he might have murdered them
both while they were in the small boat with only a few followers,
as Menas, in fact, advised, he was unwilling to do so.[166] Indeed
to Antony, who had possession of his father's house in the
Carinae (the name of a region in the city of Rome), he uttered
a jest in the happiest manner, saying that he was entertaining
them in the Carinae; for this is also the name for the keels of
ships.[167] Nevertheless, he did not act toward them in any way
as if he recalled the past with bitterness, and on the following
day he was not only feasted in turn but also betrothed his
daughter to Marcus Marcellus, Caesar's nephew.[168]

[166]This story can hardly be true, at any rate of Menas, for he was away in
Sardinia. It caught the imagination of the ancients, for both Appian (5.73)
and Plutarch (Antony 32) repeat it at greater length; Zonaras (10.22) also
recounts it. Plutarch says Menas actually whispered the advice into the
ear of Pompey. The report of Appian is more credible: "It is said that,
while the three were feasting in the ship, Menodorus sent a message to
Pompeius to entrap these men and avenge the wrongs of his father and his
brother, and to avail himself of this most favorable occasion to resume the
sway that his father had exercised, saying that he, with his own ships,
would take care that nobody should escape; but that Pompeius replied, in
a manner worthy of his family and his position, 'Would that Menodorus
had done this without my knowledge.' False swearing, that is, might suit
Menodorus, but not Pompeius." Domaszewski accepts (1.114) the story
at face value, and grants Sextus grudging praise for not following the
advice of Menas: ". . . entgingen dem tückischen Rate des Menodorus, die
kostbaren Vögel durch Kappen des Anker zu entführen, nur durch die Erin-
nerung des Pompeius, dass er nicht immer ein Räuber gewesen." Merivale
does not (3.189) accept the story as true. For us the compliment to the
honor of Sextus is the significant point in all the accounts.

[167]This witticism is also famous. It is repeated in Velleius 2.77.1 and in
Pseudo-Victor 84. Plutarch repeats (Antony 32) the story without under-
standing the point; the Latin pun was apparently too much for him.
Even Velleius admits that this repartee was *haud insulse*.

[168]The groom was only four years old, and his bride was younger; see
Drumann, 1.313–314. Risse says (23, note 7): "Propertio teste—III, 18—
tum Marcellus quatuor annos natus erat." The poem is about Marcellus,
to be sure, but does not yield the information here ascribed to it. It seems
as if Risse confused and then failed to verify the reference in Drumann.
The marriage was never consummated; see below, page 148, for a later
mention of Pompeia.

On the next day consuls for four years were designated. These were to be as follows: for the first year, Antony and Libo, Antony being privileged to exercise his office through any lieutenant he might choose; for the second year, Octavian and Pompey; for the third year, Ahenobarbus and Sosius; for the fourth year, Antony and Octavian. At the end of this period they hoped, so they said, that they could restore the government to the people.[169] The greater number of the exiles who were with Pompeius took their leave of him at Puteoli, and joyfully set out for Rome, where they were no less joyfully received.[170]

For the biographer of Sextus Pompey one point in regard to this peace is of supreme importance, and that is the eager unanimity with which all Italy sought it. The impression of popular feeling one gets is, not that a brigand and corsair must be pacified, but that a noble Roman of illustrious ancestry must receive his due. Octavian was much exercised later[171] to justify his resumption of the war. I cannot help thinking that this self-justification of Octavian, and the point of view he promulgated as official inspired our sources, directly or indirectly, and still colors the views of modern historians of the period.[172]

---

[169]Appian 5.73. Dio speaks (48.35.1) of consuls being appointed for eight years. For a reconciliation of the discrepancy see Mommsen, Staatsrecht, 1.586, note 4, and Drumann, 1.314.

[170]Appian 5.74. Velleius names (2.77.3) Claudius Nero, M. <Iunius> Silanus, <C.> Sentius Saturninus, <L.> Arruntius, and <M.> Titius. We have seen above, page 85, that Claudius Nero had already left Sextus.

[171]See page 104, below.

[172]Livy speaks (Periocha 127) of the peace as a *pax postulata*. Velleius says (2.77.1) the peace was arranged *expostulante consensu populi*. Velleius and Livy, we must remember, were the worst offenders against the reputation of Sextus. From Appian (5.70) also we get the impression that Octavian was much concerned over shifting the blame for the renewed hostilities. Here, surely, our authorities have drawn from the Commentaries of Octavian. This is the view of Blumenthal, who says (286), "Die kaiserliche Überlieferung hat S. Pompeius als mutwilligen Friedensstörer hingestellt." Henrica Malcovati, Caesaris Augusti Imperatoris Operum Fragmenta², ix (Corpus Scriptorum Latinorum Paravianum, 1928), speaks as follows of the Commentaries: "<commentarii> quos Augustus sui excusandi atque defendendi causa scripsit, quorum quae nobis servata sunt fragmenta satis ostendunt eum minime rerum veritati obsecutum esse, sed eas et exornasse et mutasse et auxisse, quasdam autem negasse, quasdam deformasse aut vario modo colorasse." For a fuller discussion of the prejudice of our authorities see pages 162–166, below.

VII. FROM THE PEACE OF MISENUM TO 36 B.C.

After the events described at the close of the preceding chapter Sextus sailed again for Sicily, no longer an outlaw, but a partner in the government and the lawful master of the realm he governed. An advocate of Sextus might well defend the legality of his behavior at each point in the last years of his career. After his father's defeat at Pharsalus he refused to acknowledge the usurpation of Caesar. When the 'Republic' showed life again for a moment after the Ides, he came into the possession of a proper naval command, which he refused to surrender when the government which had bestowed it collapsed. At Misenum he acknowledged the legality of the new order, and himself became a governor under that order and a consul elect. From this point until his death he insisted on the prerogatives of his position, resulting from the Treaty of Misenum, and to defend these prerogatives he was willing to wage war. When he was carrying on his war against Lepidus, who was cooperating with Octavian by besieging Lilybaeum, Sextus still insisted, and with right, that he himself was an augur and a consul designate.[1]

---

[1]In point here is an inscription found in 1894 near Lilybaeum and published by A. Salinas, in Notizie degli Scavi, 1894, page 389 (= Dessau, 8891. The inscription is preserved in the Museum at Palermo). It reads as follows:

MAG· POMPEIO: MAG· F· PIO· IMP: AVGVRE
COS· DESIG· PORtaM· ET· TVRRES
L· PLINIVS· L: F· RVFVS· LEG· PR· PR· DES· F· C

Salinas printed PORTVM. The correction into PORTAM was suggested by Mommsen, Hermes 30 (1895), 460–462. Mommsen points out that the use of the ablative indicates a normal and legal incumbency of office. The date of this inscription can be determined by AVGVRE, which indicates a period after the treaty of Misenum in 39, and by the absence of II after IMP, which indicates a period before 36. The name PLINIVS is therefore to be identified with the Πλένιος or Πλέννιος of Appian 5.97, 98, 122; see below, page 124. Mras (288–292) used this inscription to prove that *Magnus* was employed by Sextus as part of his cognomen. Mras suggests (289–290) that Octavian copied the device of Sextus by incorporating *Imperator* into his name. The *terminus post quem* of Octavian's change of name and the *terminus ante quem* of Sextus's change of name support Mras's contention. For a full discussion of the epigraphical questions relating to this inscription see V. Casagrandi-Orsini, Il Cursus Honorum di Sesto Pompeio Magno Pio sulla Lapide Lilibetana, in Raccolta, 2.158–180. Compare, for Plinius (Plennius), Klein, 139.

The new colleagues of Sextus returned together to Rome, to enjoy for a moment the popularity which came to them, partly, there can be no doubt, because they had at last given the son of Pompey the Great his deserts. Ferrero is as prone to bias against Octavian as Velleius is against Sextus, but there is more than a germ of truth in his statement that Sextus was

. . . the young man who was regarded by Italian opinion as the champion of the republic and its liberty.[2]

In any case Rome gave itself up to great rejoicing.

The civil wars, it was augured, were now finally at an end; the youth of Italy would no longer be torn from their fathers' hearths; the soldiers no longer permitted to live at free quarters; there would be no more confiscation of lands, agriculture would raise her drooping head, above all, plenty would be restored, and abundance extirpate the first cause of war.[3]

The so-called Messianic Eclogue of Vergil was written in the consulship of Pollio, toward the end of 40 B. C.[4] Perhaps there is significance, therefore, in the abrupt pause which interrupts the prophecy of the Golden Age:

. . . in men's hearts some lingering seed of ill
E'en yet shall bid them launch adventurous keels,
And brave the inviolate sea, and wall their towns,
And cut earth's face with furrows. . . .[5]

However, the joy which the Treaty of Misenum brought to the people of Italy was doomed to be short-lived. The accord which the contracting parties had reached was more apparent than real. In the first place, three men had made an agreement whereby one was to give something of value to a second for the benefit of the third. Little wonder that Antony was loath to yield the Peloponnese to Sextus. Antony claimed that the

---

[2]3.271. [3]Merivale, 3.189.

[4]R. S. Conway, in Virgil's Messianic Eclogue, Three Studies, by Joseph B. Mayor, W. Warde Fowler, R. S. Conway, 13 (London, 1907).

[5]I give the translation by R. S. Conway, on page 5 of the work named in note 4, of Vergil, Eclogae 4.31–33. The text of 4.31–36 is as follows:

pauca tamen suberunt priscae vestigia fraudis,
quae temptare Thetim ratibus, quae cingere muris
oppida, quae iubeant telluri infindere sulcos.
Alter erit tum Tiphys, et altera quae vehat Argo
delectos heroas; erunt etiam altera bella
atque iterum ad Troiam magnus mittetur Achilles.

province was in debt to him. Unless Sextus should discharge the obligations of the province, it would be necessary for Antony—so the latter maintained—to retain his rule until the debts should be paid.[6]

Octavian, on his side, divorced Scribonia, and thereby made it manifest how little he was concerned about the continuance of peace.[7] We need not agree with Ferrero,[8] who calls the divorce a "means for accelerating his rupture with the master of the islands," but we must see with him that Octavian was the aggressor in the war. Ferrero thinks that Octavian deliberately undertook the war to restore his military prestige, and to balance the reputation which Antony seemed sure of making for himself in the East.

Sextus in his turn intended to keep the peace no more faithfully than the other two planned to keep it, and so he sent his vessels out anew to scour the seas. The result was that the scarcity of grain in Rome was in no wise abated, and the populace was as little satisfied as before the signing of the Treaty of Misenum. Indeed, complaints were made that the

[6]Appian 5.77; Dio 48.46.1. Ferrero cites Plutarch, Antony 67. <3> to illustrate the rapacity of Antony in Achaia: "...to secure the property of the richest landowner in the Peloponnese, a certain Lachares <for whom see Pauly-Wissowa, s. v. Eurykles 5, 6.1330>, he ordered the man to be beheaded." Plutarch says nothing of the wealth of Lachares, and states that the execution was inflicted on a charge of robbery: ὁ δὲ Λαχάρης ὑπ' Ἀντωνίου λῃστείας αἰτίᾳ περιπεσὼν ἐπελεκίσθη. But G. Fougeres, Bulletin de Correspondance Hellenique 20 (1896), 155, to whom Ferrero refers, does show that the son of Lachares was wealthy and of good position. Fitzler-Seeck lay (308) the blame for the broken peace at the door of Antony.

[7]Dio 48.34.3; Suetonius, Augustus 62.2. The divorce took place on the day of the birth of Julia in 39: see Shuckburgh's note on the passage in Suetonius (page 121). Suetonius (62.2) quotes from Augustus himself the reason for the divorce: pertaesus, ut scribit, morum perversitatem eius. In Augustus 69.1 Suetonius quotes a charge of Antony regarding this divorce: dimissam Scroboniam, quia liberius doluisset nimiam potentiam paelicis <probably = Livia>. Dio says (48.34) the reason for the divorce was that Octavian was already in love with Livia, but, even so, if his policy had required it, Octavian would almost certainly have retained Scribonia. Fitzler-Seeck say (308): "...doch wäre er trotz seiner Verliebtheit kaum so entschieden vorgegangen, wenn er nicht schon zum Bruche mit Pompeius entschlossen gewesen wäre." The date of the marriage to Livia was January 17, 38: see C. Scaccia-Scarafoni, Notizie degli Scavi 20 (1923), 194.   [8]3.282.

peace had brought not plenty but merely a fourth member to the company of rulers. Gardthausen[9] cites Varro, whose treatise on agriculture was composed about 36,[10] as proving that Sicily had entirely passed out of the reckoning as a granary of Rome.[11]

Appian[12] tells us how the peace was broken:

While Antony was thus occupied the treaty existing between Octavian and Pompeius was broken for other reasons, as was suspected, than those avowed by Octavian, which were the following: Antony had ceded the Peloponnesus to Pompeius on condition that the tribute then due from the Peloponnesians should either be given over at once, or that it should be guaranteed by Pompeius to Antony, or that Pompeius should wait till the collection had been made. But Pompeius had not accepted it on these conditions. He thought that it had been given to him with the amount of tribute then due. Vexed, as Octavian said, whether at this state of things, or from his general faithlessness, or his jealousy because the others had large armies, or because Menodorus had prompted him to consider the agreement as a truce rather than a lasting peace, he began to build ships and recruit crews, and once harangued his soldiers, telling them they must be prepared for everything. Mysterious robbery again infested the sea; and there was little or no relief from the famine among the Romans, who cried out that the treaty had brought no deliverance from their sufferings, but only a fourth partner to the tyranny. Octavian having caught certain pirates and put them to torture, they said that Pompeius had sent them out, and Octavian proclaimed this to the people and wrote it to Pompeius himself, who disavowed it and made a counter complaint respecting the Peloponnesus.

[9]1.246, 2.127.

[10]De Re Rustica 1.1.1: Annus enim octogesimus admonet me ut sarcinas colligam antequam proficiscar e vita. He was born in 116. See Duff, Golden Age, 330–331; Schanz-Hosius 1.555, 568–570.

[11]De Re Rustica 2, Praefatio 4: manus movere maluerunt in theatro ac circo quam in segetibus ac vinetis, (ac) frumentum locamus, qui nobis advehat qui saturi fiamus, ex Africa et Sardinia. But see Rostovtzeff, 497, note 27: "Sicily may have suffered heavily during the later stages of the civil wars when it was the main source of income of Sex. Pompey. But this temporary calamity cannot account for the supposed disappearance of Sicily from the corn producing and exporting countries. The mountainous parts remained, as before, grazing lands. But what happened to the valleys? . . . . At the same time they still produced large quantities of corn." See also Rostovtzeff s. v. Frumentum in Pauly-Wissowa, 7.131. But even if Sicily continued productive, Rome would get none of the grain if Sextus withheld the *decumae*, and it is to the *decumae* that Appian quite clearly refers (5.77).   [12]5.77.

Certain expressions in this chapter make us suspicious of Octavian's attitude. Compare 5.77.1: Καίσαρι δὲ καὶ Πομπηίῳ διελύθησαν αἱ γενόμεναι σπονδαί, κατὰ μὲν αἰτίας, ὡς ὑπενοεῖτο, ἑτέρας, αἱ δὲ ἐς τὸ φανερὸν ὑπὸ τοῦ Καίσαρος ἐκφερόμεναι, and 5.77.3, χαλεπαίνων ⟨Sextus⟩ ὡς ὁ Καῖσαρ ἔλεγεν. . . . There is also the matter of the tortured slaves. Of all the ancients Octavian was the most consummate artist in the astute use of publicity,[13] and we can imagine what capital he made of this bit of 'news.' After the war had begun anew, he still found it necessary to issue propaganda explaining the reason for war:[14]

As the belief still prevailed that this war was a violation of the treaty, Octavian sought to dispel the suspicion. He wrote to the city and he told his soldiers that Pompeius had violated the treaty by encouraging piracy, that the pirates had confessed this, that Menodorus had revealed the whole design, and that Antony knew it, and for that reason had refused to give up the Peloponnesus.

The *periocha* of Livy (128) which deals with this period is careful to make Sextus the villain and Octavian the hero of the piece. Verily it doth protest too much:

Cum Sex. Pompeius rursus latrociniis mare infestum redderet nec pacem, quam acceperat, praestaret, Caesar necessario adversus eum bello suscepto duobus navalibus proeliis cum dubio eventu pugnavit.

This passage is an example of the vicious colors with which official history paints its enemies. The apologetic tone of the word *necessario* is in itself sufficient to render suspect Caesar's attitude in the *bellum susceptum*.

In Velleius,[15] on the other hand, we get an extraordinarily frank avowal regarding the cause of the war: crescente in dies et classe et fama Pompei Caesar ⟨Octavianus⟩ molem belli eius suscipere statuit.

"They were bound, of course," says Dio,[16] "to go to war in any case, even if they had found no excuse." The excuse, Dio goes on to say, was the defection of Menas. Murmurs reached

---

[13]According to Rostovtzeff (29) Octavian probably forged the will of Antony, which he published. Even if the document was genuine, its publication demonstrates Octavian's astuteness in the use of propaganda. For another instance of Octavian's propaganda see Kenneth Scott, Octavian's Propaganda and Antony's *De Sua Ebrietate*, Classical Philology 24 (1929), 133–141.　　　[14]5.80.　　　[15]2.79.1.　　　[16]48.45.5.

the ears of Sextus against the good faith of Menas. Evidence was at hand in the fact that Menas had sent back to Octavian the latter's favorite freedman Helenus. When Menas had taken Sardinia from M. Lurius, Helenus recovered it, but was later himself defeated by Menas and captured.[17] When a man of the character of Menas returned a favorite freedman and trusted lieutenant of Octavian along with other captives, without extorting a handsome ransom, it was evident that he expected his profit in another shape. He desired, in fact, an opening for an accommodation with Octavian.[18]

Sextus therefore summoned Menas in 38 to render an account of his stewardship. But, when Sextus's messengers arrived in Sardinia to deliver the summons, Menas murdered them.[19] Philadelphus, a freedman of Octavian, was already on the island, ostensibly to purchase grain. With this man Menas apparently made his preliminary arrangements. He sent to Italy a certain Micylio, a trusted lieutenant of his own, to complete the bargain. As a result of these negotiations[20] Menas delivered to Octavian Sardinia, Corsica,[21] three legions, a large number of light-armed troops,[22] and probably sixty vessels.[23] There is some disagreement about the time at which Sextus was apprised of the defection of his lieutenant. According to Appian,[24] he heard of it only when Calvisius and Menas were on the point of attacking him. Dio[25] is probably right in placing the defection before the beginning of hostilities. He makes it one of the causes of war:

---

[17]See above, page 88.

[18]Dio 48.30.7–8, 48.45.5. Appian (5.56, 66) is ambiguous on the question of date and is otherwise inexact.   [19]Dio 48.45.6.

[20]Dorn Seiffen finds (19) a difficulty in Dio in the use of ἐκεκοινολόγητο. Where and when might a conference between Sextus and Octavian have been held? But must the word mean 'he conversed with'? May it not mean 'he communicated with'?

[21]The details of the negotiations are all taken from Appian 5.78. He is probably right in including Corsica, which Dio 48.45.6 does not mention.

[22]Appian 5.78. 'Light-armed troops' is a translation of ψιλῶν, which is Schweighäuser's emendation for φίλων.

[23]Appian (5.80), Dio (48.45.6), and Zonaras (10.23) say that Menas surrendered himself and the island, together with the armed forces. Orosius says (6.18.21) that he *deserted* with 60 ships: Mena libertus Pompei cum sexaginta navium classe ad Caesarem defecit eidemque classi ipse iussu Caesaris praefuit. Dio also speaks of the fleet.   [24]5.81.   [25]48.46.1.

Sextus, now, blamed Caesar, not only for harbouring Menas, but for the further reasons that Achaia had been injured and the terms agreed upon were not being carried out either in his case or in that of the restored exiles, and he accordingly sent to Italy Menecrates, another freedman of his, and had him ravage Volturnum and other parts of Campania.

The desertion of Menas gives us an important clue to the character of Sextus. Surely, if Menas could exercise as much power over Pompey as Velleius and his modern followers say he could, he would not have found it necessary to desert to Octavian. Surely, again, Octavian showed himself as cordial to freedmen of dubious morals but practical potentialities as did Sextus himself. Witness Helenᵤs, of whom Dio[26] wrote: ἐξελεύθερόν τε τοῦ Καίσαρος ὄντα καὶ ἀρέσκοντα αὐτῷ τὰ μάλιστα. Witness above all Octavian's reception of Menas himself. Octavian raised the traitor and ex-slave to the equestrian rank[27] and entertained him at his own table.[28]

Gardthausen[29] suggests that a hoard of Roman coins found in Corsica near Aleria was hiddden away by a follower of Pompey. The coins date from this period and are of the mint of Sextus.[30] Coins struck by Antony about this time have been found in large numbers at Olbia, in Sardinia itself.[31] The latter coins may perhaps point to a naval or military detachment which Antony stationed on the island to aid Sextus.[32]

Sextus's request that the runaway, Menas, be returned was of course without result. Charges and counter-charges passed between the supposed colleagues. To this occasion Drumann[33]

---

[26]Dio 48.30.8.

[27]Dio 48.45.7: ἐν τιμῇ μεγάλῃ ἤγαγε δακτυλίοις τε χρυσοῖς ἐκόσμησε καὶ ἐς τὸ τῶν ἱππέων τέλος ἐσέγραψε. See Stein, 37, 111; A. M. Duff, Freedmen in the Early Roman Empire, 87 (Oxford, 1928). For the *Ius Anuli Aurei* see Duff, Appendix II, 214–220, especially 216.

[28]Suetonius, Augustus 74. This show of favor doubtless aroused jealousy and disapproval. Many have thought that Horace, Epode 4, refers to Menas, but there are arguments against this interpretation: see Wickham's introductory note to the poem. In any case the closing lines are apposite; see below, page 166.   [29]1.246, 2.128.

[30]Gardthausen refers (2.127) to an article on the subject, Di Alcuni Repostigli di Monete Romane, in Museo Italiano 1 (1886): 253, Ripostiglio di Fiesole; 283, Ripostiglio di Aleria.

[31]See A. Taramelli, Notizie degli Scavi (1904), 158–175, especially 168.

[32]See Bouchier, 97.

[33]4.574. But the ascription is by no means positive and should not be presented as an assured fact, as Blok presents it (37).

refers an insult reported by Suetonius:[34] Sextus Pompeius ut effeminatum ⟨Octavianum⟩ insectatus est. Considering himself injured especially because the Peloponnese was withheld and because Octavian was harboring Menas, Sextus sent Menecrates with a fleet to ravage Campania.[35] The deep extensions of land at the bay of Cumae with the spacious 'Hen's Forest' behind the bay afforded an excellent retreat for the vessels of Sextus.[36] From this base they harassed all the good harbors in the vicinity of Naples.

Upon news of the descent of Menecrates, Octavian obtained the documents relating to the Treaty of Misenum which had been deposited with the Vestal Virgins,[37] and with solemn reference to the letter of the treaty issued a public manifesto, placing the blame for the renewed warfare upon Sextus.[38] He wrote to Antony asking him to come to Italy to discuss the situation,[39] and also sent to Lepidus for help.[40] The desirable harbors in the neighborhood of Puteoli were menaced by Menecrates. Octavian therefore ordered the building of new vessels at Ravenna and at Rome,[41] neither of which places was convenient to the scene of war.

To the summons of Octavian Lepidus made no response.[42] He had a just grievance, in that he had not been consulted in connection with the Treaty of Misenum. In general he had been relegated to the background after the battle of Philippi, and, as we shall presently see, was already casting about for a scheme whereby he might provide for his own interests. Neither was Antony anxious to make Octavian's way smooth. The war in Sicily was Octavian's own affair, and Antony had had

---

[34]Augustus 68.   [35]Dio 48.46.1.

[36]Strabo 5.4.4: ἐν δὲ τῷ κόλπῳ τούτῳ καὶ ὕλη τίς ἐστι θαμνώδης, ἐπὶ πολλοὺς ἐκτεινομένη σταδίους, ἄνυδρος καὶ ἀμμώδης ἣν Γαλλιναρίαν ὕλην καλοῦσιν. ἐνταῦθα δὴ λῃστήρια συνεστήσαντο οἱ Πομπηίου Σέξτου ναύαρχοι καθ᾿ ὃν καιρὸν Σικελίαν ἀπέστησεν ἐκεῖνος.

[37]Dio 48.46.2.   [38]Appian 5.80.

[39]Dio 48.46.2; Appian 5.78.   [40]Dio 48.46.2.

[41]Appian 5.80. Kromayer (Entwicklung, 448–450), by close and cogent reasoning, calculates that 150–200 vessels were built at this time for Octavian.

[42]Blok is hasty in remarking (41–42): "jam diu dubitabat utrum collegis an Sexto auxilio veniret. Haec erat causa cur classis Lepidi nondum in Siciliam advenisset." His reasoning is as awkward as his Latin. We shall see below (page 143) that Lepidus was as hostile to Sextus as to Octavian.

abundant proof that it was not for him to be overanxious for
Octavian's welfare. He did, however, come as far as Brundisium with a small following,[43] but Octavian happened to be away
in Etruria at the time. Antony would not wait for Octavian,
claiming that the portentous appearance of a wolf in his camp
had warned him to withdraw,[44] and urging, moreover, that the
needs of his projected Parthian campaign made his immediate
departure imperative. Before he left Brundisium, however,
Antony addressed a letter to Octavian in rather peremptory
language, advising him to observe the terms of the recent
alliance. Menas he threatened to demand for punishment,
claiming over him the right of a master, as the slave of Pompey
the Great, whose property he had acquired.[45]

It was now the turn of Sextus to proclaim the righteousness
of his cause. Great capital was made of the attitude of Antony.
Antony, by refusing to take part in the war which Octavian
was preparing, had, it was pointed out, made it sufficiently
clear that he considered Octavian's cause unjust.[46] There must
have been a feeling that the figment of peace had been employed by Octavian to befool Sextus. Such a tradition comes
to light in the expression of Tacitus,[47] sed Pompeium imagine
pacis, sed Lepidum specie amicitiae deceptos.

Octavian swallowed whatever chagrin he felt at the unwilling-
ness of his colleagues to cooperate with him, and energetically
set about prosecuting his plans for the war against Sextus. He
appointed C. Calvisius Sabinus[48] admiral of his fleet, with
Menas to serve as his lieutenant. Their orders were to concentrate all the vessels between Etruria and Puteoli on the coast
of Etruria. They were handicapped there, however, by the
want of a proper harbor. Octavian himself went to Tarentum,

---

[43]Appian 5.79; Dio 48.46.3.

[44]Dorn Seiffen believes (83) that Antony may actually have been frightened by the portent, but it is hard to credit such a story of a man raised in
the school of Julius Caesar.

[45]Appian 5.79. For possible relations between Sextus and Antony at this
time see my remark on the finds of coins at Olbia, page 106, above.

[46]Dio 48.46.4. Appian (5.80), immediately after the account of Antony's
summary departure from Brundisium, tells of steps which Octavian took
"to dispel the suspicion that the war was a violation of the treaty."

[47]Annales 1.10.

[48]For Calvisius see Münzer, in Pauly-Wissowa, 5.1411–1412.

whither the fleet from Ravenna had been despatched under the command of L. Cornificius.[49] A grave omen was seen in the fact that the vessel which was to receive Octavian and to serve as his flagship met with disaster in a storm.[50] The legions from Gaul and Illyria and the interior of Italy were mobilized at Rhegium.[51] Octavian still had little hope of winning a decisive victory on water. His chief aim was to get his legions safely across to Sicily. Once there, their superior numbers and discipline, he felt, would make short work of Sextus's rabble.[52]

To check the two-fold movement of Octavian, Sextus also divided his forces. He himself watched the fleet at Tarentum, and Menecrates he ordered to engage Calvisius and Menas.[53]

Dr. T. Rice Holmes is at his excellent best in reconstructing the movements of ancient battles, but the contest which followed at this time he gives up in despair:[54]

The operations of the ensuing war are described in detail by the Greek compilers, Appian and Dio; but anyone who has studied the verifiable records of modern warfare will perceive that they did not fully comprehend the authorities which they used, and that it is impossible to construct from their statements a satisfactory narrative.

Nevertheless, of the first engagement, at least, Appian[55] gives us a vivid picture, which it may be worth while to reproduce. The hostile fleets of Calvisius and Menecrates sighted each other near the heights of Cumae, toward evening. Calvisius retired into the harbor of Cumae,[56] and Menecrates took his station off the island Aenaria. In the morning he discovered Calvisius's fleet disposed in the figure of a crescent, close to the shore. The passage of Menecrates was blocked, but, on the other hand, the movements of Calvisius's fleet were much restricted. Menecrates directed continual attacks on his enemy, changing his vessels constantly so that the assailants were always fresh. The fleet of Calvisius was unable to effect similar changes in

---

[49]For Cornificius see Pauly-Wissowa, 7.1624–1625.

[50]Appian 5.80.   [51]Appian 5.78–80.   [52]Appian 5.80–81.

[53]Appian 5.81. In this instance, as later in 36, when his forces had to be divided to meet attacks on various fronts, Sextus reserved for himself the post of greatest responsibility. This should serve to remove the charge that he relied wholly upon his freedmen for the conduct of his operations.

[54]Architect, 110.   [55]5.81–82.

[56]For remarks on the ancient and modern topography of the scene of battle see Gardthausen, 1.248, 2.128; Holm, 3.455.

its line and could only suffer itself to be beaten back toward
the shore. From this point I shall let Appian[57] speak:

In this situation Menodorus and Menecrates came in sight
of each other; and, abandoning the rest of the fight, drove at
once against each other with fury and shouting, as though they
had staked the issue of the battle on this encounter, whichever
should be the victor. Their ships came into violent collision
and were badly damaged, Menodorus losing his prow and
Menecrates his oar-blades. Grappling-irons were thrown by
both, and the ships, being fastened together, could no longer
manoeuvre, but the men, as in a battle on land, failed not in
deeds of valour. Showers of javelins, stones, and arrows were
discharged, and bridges for boarding were thrown from one
ship to the other. As the ship of Menodorus was higher than
the other his bridges made a better passage-way for those who
ventured on them, and his missiles were more effective for the
same reason. Many men were already slain, and the remainder
wounded, when Menodorus was pierced in the arm with a dart,
which was, however, drawn out. Menecrates was struck in
the thigh with a Spanish javelin, made wholly of iron with
numerous barbs, which could not be readily extracted. Although Menecrates could no longer take part in the fight, he
remained there all the same, encouraging the others, until his
ship was captured, when he plunged into the depths of the sea.
Menodorus towed the captured ship to the land, but was able
to do nothing more himself.
      Thus had fared the left wing of the naval fight. Calvisius
directed his course from the right to the left and cut off some of
Menecrates' ships from the main body, and when they fled
pursued them to the open sea. Demochares, who was a fellow-
freedman of Menecrates and his lieutenant, fell upon the
remainder of Calvisius' ships, put some of them to flight, broke
others in pieces on the rocks, and set fire to them after the
crews had abandoned them. Finally Calvisius, returning from
the pursuit, led back his own retreating ships and prevented
the burning of any more. As night approached all rested in their
stations of the previous night.[58]

That the engagement took place in the early spring is clear
from Appian,[59] who says, speaking of the later battle at Scyllaeum, οἰόμενοι ταχέως τὸ πνεῦμα ἐνδώσειν ὡς ἐν ἔαρι. Suetonius[60] also indicates that the storm which happened after this
battle took place during the summer season:

---

[57] 5.82–83.
[58] Compare Dio 48.46.4–5; Orosius 6.18.21; Zonaras 10.23.
[59] 5.89.   [60] Augustus 16.1.

Siculum bellum inchoavit in primis, sed diu traxit intermissum saepius, modo reparandarum classium causa, quas tempestatibus duplici naufragio et quidem *per aestatem* amiserat. . . .

I can discover no basis, therefore, for the statement of Ferrero:[61] "The war apparently began about the end of July."

Like his master Sextus, Demochares did not know how best to use a victory. He had but to complete the work of destruction, but, apparently because he did not rely on his own competence, he sailed away to join Sextus at Messana, and left Calvisius unhindered to repair his damaged vessels and to put to sea again.[62]

Octavian had met Cornificius at Tarentum, according to arrangement, and had assumed command of the fleet. Kromayer[63] has demonstrated that the entire fleets of Octavian and Sextus were about equal at this time, each consisting of 200 to 250 vessels. Of Octavian's fleet Calvisius had far the greater portion, for his lieutenant Menas retained command of the sixty vessels he had brought with him.[64] Sextus, it would seem, had only forty ships under his immediate command.[65] The received accounts of what now took place in the Straits of Messina show the behavior of Octavian to have been so irresolute and even puerile that we must agree with Holmes that the compilers did not understand their sources. The staunchest admirers of Octavian have no word of excuse for this behavior,[66] and it remains for Octavian's most mordant critic to suggest that "the ancient historians have neglected to state some vital point which would explain his action."[67]

According to the received account his officers urged Octavian to attack the forty vessels of Sextus with his own greatly superior forces before the remaining ships of Sextus should arrive. But Octavian refused to be hurried into action, and insisted on awaiting the arrival of Calvisius and his division. News of the discomfiture of Calvisius reached Octavian, and he resolved to sail out to meet him. When he had passed Messana and the so-called pillars of Rhegium, the fleet of Sextus, which had had opportunity at its ease to observe his approach, at once fell

[61]3.285.   [62]Appian 5.83–84.   [63]Entwicklung, 450.
[64]See above, page 105.   [65]Appian 5.84.
[66]Compare, for example, Drumann, 4.575; Domaszewski, 1.120; Merivale, 3.194.   [67]Ferrero, 3.286.

upon the rear of his line and blocked his passage, not far from the promontory of Scyllaeum,[68] opposite Pelorum in Sicily. Octavian persisted in his determination not to give battle until he had joined with Calvisius, and his captains waited in vain for the signal to attack. He ordered the vessels to take up a position near the shore, their prows facing out. Here they were helpless against the same sort of unremittent attack to which Calvisius had been subjected at Cumae. The legionaries on the vessels were wearied by the onset of their opponents, who, being constantly changed, came to the attack with ever fresh vigor. Finally Octavian himself leapt on shore.[69]

The commander-in-chief gone, Cornificius and his brother officers determined not to await extermination passively, but raised anchor and sailed out against the foe. This bold stroke stayed the battle for a time, for Cornificius rammed and captured the flag-ship of Demochares, though Demochares himself leapt to another vessel. At this juncture the ships of Sextus, being spread over a larger area, observed the approach of Calvisius and Menas. Octavian's vessels were huddled together, and were therefore unaware of the approach of assistance. Fearing the fresh vigor of the newcomers, the Pompeians retired. The battle could not have continued long in any case, for darkness was falling.[70]

The night was a horrible one for Octavian. He could do no more than signal his fleet with beacon fires. He had no food or shelter himself and could offer his men none. At length the Thirteenth Legion, stationed nearby, was attracted by the beacon fires and brought a few tents and some provisions. At dawn news came that Calvisius had arrived, safe.[71]

One look at the sea revealed his plight to Octavian. The water was strewn with oars and sails and the remains of his burned and battered vessels. The sea-worthy vessels of Calvisius were ranged in front of the hulks that could be repaired, and shipwrights were set to work at once. They continued at their task despite the rise of a storm, which was, they thought, an ordinary fresh wind, natural in spring.[72]

---

[68]For Scyllaeum see Nissen, 2.948.

[69]Gardthausen refers (2.129) to this occasion a passage in Pliny, N. H. 7.148: naufragia Sicula et alia ibi quoque in spelunca occultatio.

[70]Appian 5.84–86; Dio 48.47. Compare Drumann, 4.575–576, and Gardthausen 1.249–250.   [71]Appian 5.87.   [72]See above, note 59.

Menas was an old hand in these treacherous waters, and removed himself to a safe place.[73] I can do no better than cite Appian's own account of the storm and its effects:[74]

As the wind grew more violent everything was thrown into confusion. The ships collided, broke their anchors, and were thrown quivering on the shore or against one another.   Cries of alarm and groans of pain were mingled together, and exhortations that fell upon deaf ears. Orders could not be heard, and there was no distinction between pilot and common sailor, knowledge and authority being alike unavailing. The same destruction awaited those in the ships and those who fell overboard, the latter being crushed by wind, waves, and floating timber. The sea was full of sails, spars, and men, living and dead. Those who sought to escape by swimming to land were dashed against the rocks by the surf. When the convulsion seized the water, as is usual in that strait, they were terrified, being unaccustomed to it, and then their vessels were whirled around and dashed against each other worse than ever. As night came on the wind increased in fury, so that they perished no longer in the light but in the darkness.

Groans were heard throughout the entire night, and the cries of men running along the shore and calling their friends and relatives upon the sea by name, and mourning for them as lost when they could hear no responses; and anon the cries of others lifting their heads above the waves and beseeching aid from those on shore. Nothing could be done on either land or water. Not only was the sea inexorable to those engulfed in it, as well as to those still in the ships, but the danger was almost as great on land as at sea, lest the surf should dash them against the rocks. So distressed were they by this unexampled tempest that those who were nearest the land feared the land, yet could not get sufficient offing to avoid collision with each other, for the narrowness of the place and its naturally difficult outlet, together with the force of the waves, the rotary motion of the wind, caused by the surrounding mountains, and the whirlpool of the deep, holding everything in its grasp, allowed neither tarrying nor escape. The darkness of a very black night added to their distress. And so they perished, no longer even seeing each other, some uttering confused cries, others yielding in silence, accepting their doom, some even hastening it, believing

---

[73]Dio 48.48.2: ὁ γὰρ Μηνᾶς, ἅτε ἐκ πολλοῦ θαλατουργὸς ὤν, τόν τε χειμῶνα προείδετο. . . . Compare Appian 5.89.

[74]Appian 5.89, 90; compare Dio 48.48.1–4. Orosius says (6.18.22): victricem classem paene universam apud Scylaceum naufragio amisit. *Victricem* is absurd, and *Scylaceum* is wrong. Compare also Suetonius, *Augustus* 16.1.

that they were irretrievably doomed. The disaster so far surpassed their experience that it bereft them of the hope of saving
themselves even by chance. Finally, at the approach of daylight, the wind suddenly relaxed its force, and after sunrise
wholly died away; yet even then, although the storm had
ceased, the surges rolled a long time. The fury of the tempest
surpassed the memory of the oldest inhabitants. It was altogether unexampled, and the greater part of Octavian's ships
and men were destroyed by it.[75]

We have become used to the spectacle of Sextus neglecting
opportunities which seemed to be put in his way almost provi-
dentially.[76] If he took the present occasion to reiterate his
claim to descent from Neptune, who shall find fault? Events
certainly had demonstrated an almost personal interest in his
welfare on the part of the deity of the deep.[77] Shall we deny
that Sextus possessed sufficient political acumen to employ
divine machinery for the glorification of his own name among
the common folk? Octavian did not scruple to commission the
first poet of Rome to prove his descent from a weaker deity
than Neptune. It is all a matter of viewpoint, and men's
viewpoint is determined by success. For pride as well as for
cruelty, and certainly for bad generalship, Octavian left as
much room for detractors as did Pompey, and, if the scales
had turned otherwise than they did turn, some obscure student

---

[75]I may observe here, as I shall have occasion to observe later (page 145),
that battle scenes and especially storm scenes are in a sense τόποι in Appian.
The remark applies to Dio also for storms and fights at sea. The raging
waters and shrieking men become familiar. Yet in this, as in other passages
where Appian or Dio is our only source of information, or especially vivid
in description, I feel that it is better to make long excerpts than to attempt
a paraphrase. The paraphrases take us, unnecessarily, one step further
from the source, and seldom effect a saving in space.

[76]See above pages 79, 84.

[77]For his profession of this claim see Dio 48.48.5. He had already made
the claim after his initial success against Salvidienus Rufus. The agitation
of the populace over the statues of Neptune at the *ludi plebei* in November
41 (see above, page 90) proves the point. Merivale, who is consistently
hostile to Sextus, shows his scholarship and his fairness by providing a
footnote to the reference from Dio (3.195): "Such stories against an unpopular and vanquished chieftain must of course be received with suspicion. If they were generally credited at the time, we should expect to
hear them mentioned by Velleius and Horace. Sextus inscribed the figure
of Neptune on his coins, as praefectus classis of the commonwealth by
appointment of the senate."

might be defending Octavian against the slurs of courtly Pompeian writers.

It cannot be denied, however, that here was an opportunity which Sextus did in fact neglect. He paid no attention to the demoralized enemy; they were thus able to mend the remnant of their vessels, less than half their original number,[78] with ropes, as best they could, and to sail off to Vibo with a favorable breeze.[79] A more energetic leader, moreover, might have turned to account the great dissatisfaction of Italy and the popular sentiment in his favor, which was all the stronger precisely because Octavian had entered upon the present war with Sextus without the goodwill and perhaps, indeed, against the wishes of the people of Italy. Sextus's success made his claims seem the more legitimate, and more than ever did it seem that Octavian was waging war not for the welfare of Italy but to ensure his own authority. Peace was the desire of Italy, and bread, and the personality of those who administered the government was a secondary matter. Indeed a change in rulers might be beneficial since the existing one appeared unable to provide peace and bread. Moreover, there must have remained some few liberals, perhaps only of the class that were called 'parlor Bolsheviks' among us some years ago, who still yearned for the 'Republic.' Though the republicanism of Sextus was by this time a doubtful quantity, still the very name of Pompey had a more republican ring that did that of Caesar.

A symptom of the change in sympathy was the fact that the inhabitants of the Aeolic islands off the north coast of Sicily went over to the side of Sextus. The Liparensians Octavian thwarted by removing them from their island and settling them in Campania, where he forced them to live, near Naples, for the duration of the war.[80] A more serious symptom, perhaps, was the fact that the government would not allow Octavian the use of public revenues for renewing his campaign.[81] Appian states specifically[82] that "the people were again harassing him about a new treaty and mocking at the war as being in violation of the old one." The suggestion may be offered that Sextus was at this time in reality a truer patriot than Octavian. He hoped, we may suppose, that popular pressure would enforce

---

[78]Appian 5.92. [79]Appian 5.91.

[80]Dio 48.48.6. [81]Appian 5.92. [82]Appian 5.92.

his claims, and felt that further violence would be needless and therefore criminal, and would only alienate the sympathies of Italy.

Some effort Sextus did put forth. Dio mentions descents on Italy,[83] and the fact that Octavian's first step was to guard the coast of the mainland[84] shows that these descents were effective, perhaps as effective as they were meant to be. Further, Dio reports that Sextus sent Apollophanes to Africa, and that Apollophanes was pursued by Menas.[85] Drumann[86] suggests, with great plausibility, that both men were on missions to Lepidus; the subsequent conduct of Lepidus makes it seem likely.

The power of Sextus was now at its zenith. The most elaborate effort that had been put forth against him had collapsed, whether by reason of the might of his own right hand or by the intervention of the gods, to whom he was entirely willing to ascribe the glory. He had been content with the conditions stipulated at Misenum, and had not sought war. Those who had thrust war upon him were humiliated, and his own position, both moral and physical,[87] seemed

---

[83]48.48.6.　　　[84]Dio 48.48.5.　　　[85]48.48.6.　　　[86]4.577.

[87]Gardthausen (1.251, 2.129) with great ingenuity and some probability refers an epigram in the Greek Anthology (A. P. 11.247) to this period. He supposes it to celebrate Sextus's victory over Octavian, and his absolute lordship over the Mediterranean. I am convinced that Sibylline Oracles 3.475–482 refer to the wars of Sextus. The whole passage deals with the Civil Wars, as 3.464–465 suggests. I quote 3.475–482 in the more readable text of Rzach (Vienna, 1891) rather than in the later text of Geffcken (Leipzig, 1902):

> Καμπανοῖς ἄραβος πέλεται διὰ τὸν πτολίπορθον
> λιμόν· πουλυετῆ δέ τ᾽ ἀποιμώξασα τοκῆα
> Κύρνος καὶ Σαρδὼ μεγάλαις χειμῶνος ἀέλλαις
> καὶ πληγαῖς ἀγίοιο θεοῦ κατὰ βένθεα πόντου
> δύσονται, μέγα θαῦμα θαλασσαίοις τεκέεσσιν.
> αἱ αἱ παρθενικὰς ὁπόσας νυμφεύσεται Ἅιδης,
> κούρους δ᾽ ἀκτερέας ὁπόσους βυθὸς ἀμφιπολεύσει.
> αἱ αἱ νήπια τέκν᾽ ἁλινηχέα καὶ βαρὺς ὄλβος.

H. N. Bate, The Sibylline Oracles III–V, 69 (London, 1918), translates these lines as follows: "The Campanians shall gnash their teeth for the famine that ravages their city, and for many a year (shall they lament their father). Corsica and Sardinia shall be sunk below the depths of the sea by great blasts of storm-winds, by the smiting of the holy god, a great wonder for the children of the sea. Ah, for how many maidens shall death be their bridal, how many youths unburied shall toss in the deep: ah, for little children and great wealth, washed away by the sea!"

faultless. It must be remembered that he was still augur, and still consul designate of the Roman people.

In his preparations against Sextus's power Octavian displayed the greatest resolution and energy. Deprived of the use of public revenues, he collected moneys for the vessels which he had under construction in all parts of Italy, and slaves to row the vessels,

first from his friends, who were supposed to give willingly,[88] and then from the rest—senators and knights and well-to-do plebeians. He also levied heavy-armed troops and gathered money from all the citizens, allies, and subjects, both in Italy and abroad.[89]

The only possible source of naval assistance on a considerable scale was Antony. During the fighting of 38 Antony had preserved a strict neutrality; the war, it must be remembered, had been undertaken in defiance of his advice. Now Octavian sent Maecenas to confer with him and to endeavor to secure the necessary assistance.[90] Before the year 38 was past, cheer-

---

[88]Dio 48.49.1...παρὰ τῶν φίλων ὡς καὶ ἑκόντων διδόντων....Notice the ironic ὡς.   [89]Ibidem. Compare Appian 5.92, ad finem.

[90]Appian 5.92. Horace (Sermones 1.5) probably gives an account of Maecenas's travels to Brundisium on this mission, on which Horace evidently accompanied him, though Gardthausen (see below, page 121), following Kirchner, Franke, Orelli, and Ritter, refers the poem to the actual meeting, which took place near Tarentum (see below, page 121). If that is true, it is difficult to see why Horace stops the journey at Brundisium. The only recorded occasion of an arrangement at Brundisium between Octavian and Antony was the peace of Brundisium, concluded in 40 B.C. (see above, page 89), but Horace was not admitted to intimacy with Maecenas until 38. This leaves the present journey as the only known one that will meet the conditions: see Wickham, 2.60. Kiessling-Heinze, Horatius Satiren[5], 89–90 (Berlin, 1921), refer the journey to the later occasion (when the negotiations were actually carried through near Tarentum). They explain Brundisium as the objective of the journey (in the poem) by the theory that Maecenas was dispatched immediately on the arrival of information that Antony had appeared at Brundisium. But Antony appears not to have lingered at Brundisium for any length of time, and Horace could hardly have been in error regarding the goal of the journey through all the time required for the composition of the poem. It should be added that a further objection to the date that I accept is offered by James Gow (Q. Horati Flacci Saturarum Liber I, 70 [Cambridge, 1901]; compare his note in The Classical Review 15 [1901], 117). He states that Italian frogs (line 14) do not croak in autumn, but only in early spring; the spring of 37 is, therefore, he argues, a more likely date than the

ing news reached Octavian. Antony, for his own interest, to
be sure, promised to give the necessary naval assistance. He
expected in return that Octavian would supply him with the
Roman legionaries which he needed for his projected Parthian
expedition. Agrippa, moreover, had won splendid successes
against the Gauls and the Germans—he was the first general
after Julius Caesar to carry war across the Rhine—, and would
be ready for service against Sextus during 37, the year of his
consulship.[91]

With the consulship for 37 Octavian entrusted to Agrippa
the conduct of the war against Pompey. In the whole conflict
this step was the most intelligent, or at least the most effective,
which Octavian took. Of the ultimate defeat of Sextus and
the share which Agrippa took in this defeat A. Koester and
A. von Nischer[92] have this to say:

Seine ⟨Sextus's⟩ Ueberwindung gelang erst durch das Ein-
greifen des ersten und grössten eigentlichen Seehelden, den
Rom hervorbracht, des M. Vipsanius Agrippa, des einzigen,
dessen Name mit denen der grossen Admirale Griechenlands
und späterer Seenationen genannt zu werden verdient.

Agrippa had as yet had little or no experience of naval warfare, but it wanted only common sense to comprehend the
requirements of the situation. Since Octavian's resources
consisted predominantly of land forces, while Sextus's consisted
of naval forces, the war must be carried into Sicily. To this
end a good harbor must be found as near Sicily as possible.
Furthermore, to ensure the safety of the expedition to Sicily,
ships must be built and crews trained to equal or surpass the
ships and the crews of Sextus. The desired harbor must
therefore be completely sheltered from possible molestation by
Sextus.

Agrippa cast his eye on Lake Avernus and the land-locked
and shallow arm of the sea called the Lucrine Lake, on the
Campanian coast, between Misenum and Puteoli. Lake Avernus was round and spacious, and surrounded by well-wooded
hills of considerable height. The deforestation of the hills,

---

autumn of 38. I am unconvinced. For one thing the frogs may be repro-
duced bodily from Lucilius; for another, Horace may be doing in Sermones
1.5 what he is apparently doing in Sermones 2.6.34–39, combining remi-
niscences of various occasions, regardless of the season.

[91]Appian 5.92.   [92]In Kromayer-Veith, 614.

which took place at this time, provided building materials for the shipwrights. Moreover, having a diameter of about a mile, Lake Avernus was an ideal place for training crews, as it afforded sufficient space for the manoeuvers of the time. Avernus was separated from the Lucrine Lake by a neck of land about a mile in width. The Lucrine Lake, in turn, was separated from the sea by a narrow ridge of sand or shingle which, tradition held, had been formed by Hercules for a short-cut; it was accordingly named Via Herculanea. On the petition of fishermen who used the ridge Julius Caesar had made some repairs on it, which were called Opus Iulium; hence came the name Portus Iulius which was given to the works constructed by Agrippa. The work which he undertook was apparently to unite the two lakes by a canal, to face the exterior ridge with masonry, and to pierce it also with a channel for the admission of vessels. It was probably the difficulty of keeping the channel open which rendered the Portus Iulius useless after the passing of the emergency for which it had been built.[93]

But, during the emergency, 20,000 ex-slaves, who owed their freedom to Octavian, were in training there[94] and practised seamanship daily throughout the winter of 37.[95] Another important contribution of Agrippa was an instrument which he devised, the purpose of which was to neutralize the superior

---

[93]Ancient authorities for the Portus Julius are Dio 48.49-50; Suetonius, Augustus 16; Strabo 5.4; Pliny, N. H. 36.15; Vergil, Georgics 2.161–164 (with the comments of Servius). The account given above is based on Lehmann-Hartleben, 174–175. See this work, and Gardthausen, 2.131–132 for references to modern literature on the subject. The account in the text of Gardthausen (1.257–260) is based on careful autopsy, and gives much more credit to Agrippa than does Lehmann-Hartleben, who says (175): "Was dieser <Agrippa> an künstlichen Anlagen neu geschaffen hat, ist schwer zu sagen." The configuration of the land was greatly altered by the eruption of Monte Nuovo in 1538.

[94]Suetonius, Augustus 16.1. This chapter of Suetonius gives the account of the wars between Sextus and Octavian. Shuckburgh's note to this chapter (pages 31–32) gives an excellent brief summary of the career of Sextus.

[95]Velleius 2.79.2:...cotidianis exercitationibus militem remigemque ad summam...perduxit scientiam. Hac classi Caesar...Pompeio Siciliaeque bellum intulit. Shipley remarks (216) that this war took place in 38 B. C.! Servius says (on Vergil, Aeneid 8.682): Hadrianus scribit Agrippam solitum tempestate orta milites cogere naves in fluctus urgere, ut consuetudine discriminis dempto metu redderet eos adversum pericula fortiores.

naval skill of the Greeks in the service of Sextus, and to convert
any naval battle into a struggle in which the superior fighting
qualities of the legionaries should have free play. This was a
wooden pole about seven feet long, cased with iron, to one end
of which was attached an iron hook, to the other a ring through
which were passed ropes, controlled by a windlass, so that when
the instrument, shot by a catapult, had caught hold of a
hostile ship the ropes could be pulled taut, and the ships could
thus be brought together.[96]

We have seen above[97] that Maecenas had brought a promise
of help from Antony. In fulfilment of this promise, "At the
beginning of spring Antony set sail from Athens to Tarentum
with 30 ships to assist Octavian as he had promised."[98] Plutarch's account of Antony's arrival in Italy[99] is very difficult to
reconcile with the known circumstances. According to this
account the expedition of Antony was hostile, and was directed
against Brundisium. From Brundisium Antony was repelled
by armed resistance, and he coasted along to Tarentum. At
Tarentum he succeeded in averting the hostile intentions of
Octavian by employing Octavia to intercede for him. The
story is accepted at face value by Merivale,[100] though it makes
his account sound unreasonable. Ferrero[101] suggests that the
progress of the preparations under Agrippa, as well as Antony's
own pressing need of troops, emboldened Octavian to his
hostile attitude. Holmes puts his doubts in a foot-note.[102]
Drumann does not allude to the passage in Plutarch. To me
the deciding factor is the circumstance that neither Appian nor
Dio mentions, in the relevant passages, a hostile movement
against Brundisium on the part of Antony or resistance on the

---

[96]Appian 5.118; the instrument was called ἁρπάγον. Compare Holmes,
Architect, 112. Agrippa also invented an improved type of tower for his
vessels: see below, page 131, note 36.

[97]Page 118.

[98]Appian 5.93. The rubric in White (535) reads "B. C. 36." It should of
course be B. C. 37. Kromayer suggests (Begründung, 57–58) May, 37
as the date of Antony's arrival at Tarentum.

[99]Plutarch, Antony 35. [100]3.197.   [101]3.293–294.

[102]Architect, 112, note 3: "According to Plutarch (Ant., 35.1), he had
been [again] excluded from the harbour of Brundisium. By order of
Octavian? If so, why not also from Tarentum? Did Octavian suppose
that Antony would not seek admission there?"

part of Octavian.[103] I feel sure that Plutarch is confusing this arrival of Antony in Italy for the purpose of negotiating again with Octavian with the arrival of Antony in Italy for the same purpose before the Treaty of Brundisium. We have seen above[104] that Antony was treated as an enemy on that occasion.

Upon the failure of Octavian to meet his colleague, Octavia went to plead with Octavian on behalf of her husband, who finally agreed to meet and treat with Antony at the Taras River, between Metapontum and Tarentum.[105] At this meeting an exchange of forces between Octavian and Antony was effected. Octavian received 120 ships against a promise of delivering 20,000 Italian legionaries.[106]

Octavia, begging the favor from Antony made her brother a present of ten three-banked phaseli—a combination of war-ship and merchant vessel—and Octavian gave her in return 1,000 picked men as a body-guard, to be selected by Antony.[107]

In addition, Octavian and Antony agreed to remove Sextus from his priesthood as well as from the consulship which he was to receive,[108] and they also extended the term of their rule for another quinquennium.[109] The hands of Octavian were

---

[103]Appian 5.93; Dio 48.54.1.   [104]Page 88.

[105]Appian 5.93. Gardthausen (1.253) assumes (on the authority of Fischer, Römische Zeittafeln zum J. 717–37) that a preliminary conference of friends of both parties took place at Brundisium. One of Octavian's representatives was Maecenas, and to this present journey to Brundisium Gardthausen refers Horace, Sermones 1.5. It seems simpler to me to refer it to the earlier journey of Maecenas to treat with Antony, as stated in note 90 above. Kromayer, Begründung, includes in an Excursus, Chronologische Bestimmung des Vertrages von Tarent, a thorough discussion (51–57): Kromayer's conclusion is that the meeting took place in September or October of 37. No student of the period can fail to be impressed with the part played by Octavia; she was indeed, as Plutarch (Antony 31) calls her, χρῆμα θαυμαστὸν γυναικός.

[106]Appian 5.95. The figures in Plutarch, Antony 35 are slightly different, but the error which I have pointed out (page 120) in this chapter of Plutarch makes me suspicious of the whole chapter. Gardthausen says (1.253): "Caesar... übergab ihm dafür ein Heer von 20,000 italischen Legionaren." The passage in Appian, as well as subsequent events, shows clearly that Octavian did not actually deliver the legionaries.

[107]Appian 5.95.   [108]Dio 48.54.6.

[109]Appian 5.95; Dio 48.54.6. Holmes, Architect, 231–245, has a learned excursus on the Duration of the Triumvirate, in which he reviews the recent abundant literature on the subject. The agreement here referred to is discussed in pages 232–235, 240.

further strengthened by promises of help from Lepidus in Africa.[110]

Before we proceed to the examination of the naval operations of July, 36, mention must be made of the return of Menas to his former chief.[111] He managed to take with him only seven vessels.[112] The date of this transfer has been in some doubt. Appian says that Octavian dismissed Calvisius, because Menas had gotten away without his knowledge, and appointed Agrippa in his stead. Gardthausen[113] accepts this story, adding that, "⟨Agrippa⟩ grade in diesem Jahre das Consulat bekleidete." This would make the year 37, and the day rather early in the year. But Calvisius had surely demonstrated his incompetence sufficiently before this time, and Octavian would not wait for the desertion of a traitor to replace Calvisius by the best available commander. Dio tells the story of the desertion in the very last line of Book 48, and begins Book 49 with the statement, "All this happened in the winter in which Lucius Gellius and Cocceius Nerva became consuls," that is, at the beginning of 36.[114]

For the student of Sextus, this return of the prodigal is of great significance. The personality of Sextus must have been vigorous enough to attract him. The clemency of Sextus must have been sure enough to make him rely on fair treatment. The resources of Sextus must have been strong enough to lure the shrewdest seaman of his time (Agrippa had not yet shown his mettle) from the master of Rome, who had already shown him how pleasant could be the lot of those whom a ruler delighteth to honor.

---

[110]Dio 49.1.1.   [111]Appian 5.96; Dio 48.54.7.

[112]Appian, 5.96. Orosius says (6.18.25): Mena libertus cum sex navibus ad Pompeium rediit.

[113]1.25.6. Fitzler-Seeck (312) also place the desertion in 37, but do not indicate a more specific date.

[114]Merivale (3.199), for reasons which I do not understand, puts the desertion of Menas in August (or at least after the resumption of hostilities in July). Surely this is too late.

In spite of Menas's return the prospect looked dark for Sextus. For the first time the preparations against him assumed the proportions of a national enterprise. The best general available had at his command every available resource to crush him. Furthermore, for the first time all three Triumvirs were co-operating toward his destruction. It must not be thought, however, that Sextus had remained idle while the elaborate preparations against him were in progress. When Sextus first took Sicily, he had 130 ships.[2] The accession of Murcus[3] and other increments brought the number to nearly 300. This number was reduced by 60 through the desertion of Menas.[4] But, while Agrippa was feverishly building vessels at the Portus Iulius, Sextus was certainly using this time for a similar purpose. At the final battle at Naulochus, we are told,[5] Sextus was master of 350 ships. If these figures are accurate,[6] Sextus must have built a hundred vessels during the winter 37–36.

After performing an elaborate lustration of his fleet at Portus Iulius,[7] Octavian sailed against Sicily, on July 1, 36 B. C.[8] On

[1]For the campaign of 36 see, besides the works cited heretofore, Agatino Aiello, Il Nuovo Piano di Attacco alla Sicilia dopo la Rotta di Tauromenium, in Raccolta, 1.65–126, and La Spedizione di Ottaviano a Tauromenium e la Via di Ritirata di L. Cornificio A. U. C. 718–36, in Raccolta, 2.181–264.

[2]See above, page 66.   [3]See above, page 80.   [4]See above, page 105.

[5]Florus 2.18.9: quippe modo trecentarum quinquaginta navium dominus cum sex septemve fugiebat....; Appian 5.118: τριακόσιαι νῆες ἑκατέρῳ ...., 5.120: νεῶν ἑξακοσίων...ἐκτεταγμένων. There may be here, in reality, no disagreement between Appian (5.118) and Florus; the master of 350 ships probably had 50 of them deployed as lookouts in other waters.

[6]We are assured that they are by Kromayer, Entwicklung, 451–452.

[7]Appian 5.96. The lustratio classis is discussed in G. Wissowa, Religion und Kultus der Römer[2], 390–391 (Munich, 1912).

[8]Appian gives the date specifically (5.97): "The day of Octavian's sailing had been previously communicated to all; it was the tenth day after the summer solstice. This, in the Roman calendar, was the calends of the month which, in honour of the first Caesar, they call July instead of Quintilis. Octavian fixed on this day, perhaps because he considered it propitious on account of his father, who was always victorious." Dio (49.1.1) says the expedition was made "when...spring had set in." Holmes says (Architect, 113, note 5): "I was once inclined to think that there would have been hardly sufficient time for the recorded events of the war

the same day, by prearrangement, Statilius Taurus,[9] who had held the consulship in the previous year, sailed from Tarentum with the fleet which Antony had provided. Of the 130 ships which Antony had supplied Taurus had only 102, having been unable to man the remainder by reason of the number of sailors that had perished during the winter.[10] By prearrangement also Lepidus sailed from Africa on the same day with 70 war vessels, 1,000 ships of burden, twelve legions, and 5,000 Numidian cavalry.[11] The intention was, clearly, that the three fleets should converge upon Sicily from the North, East, and South respectively. To meet this three-fold attack Sextus fortified two islands, Lipara to the North, the island of Cossyra[12] to the South, of Sicily, and stationed L. Plinius[13] at Lilybaeum with one legion and a considerable number of light-armed troops to oppose the landing of the forces of Lepidus.[14] Sextus himself retained the largest and best part of his forces under his immediate command at Messana.[15] Here again we have a means of refuting the charge that Sextus depended wholly on his lieutenants for conducting his campaigns.[16] The charge may be brought against Octavian on much better ground. The fact that Sextus insisted on having personal supervision over the post of greatest danger may suggest a refutation of a criticism which has frequently been made against the strategy of Sextus. It is true that Sextus failed on various occasions to deliver telling blows when opportunity offered. The failure was

---

between July 1 and September 3, the date of the final victory; but Appian's statement is so circumstantial that I feel obliged to accept it." It might be pertinent to cite Suetonius, Augustus 92, which tells of Octavian's superstitious observances; note, for example, observabat et dies quosdam.

[9]For Statilius Taurus see Prosopographia, 3.263 (Number 615), and Klein, 89.   [10]Appian 5.98.

[11]Ibidem. The Loeb translation prints 500 for πεντακισχιλιοις in this passage. Velleius states (2.80.1) that the legions of Lepidus were only half full. Brueggemann (60) does not accept this statement of Velleius.

[12]For Cossyra (Kossura) see Ziegler, in Pauly-Wissowa, 11.1503–1504 (1922).

[13]Appian 5.97. In this section and in 5.98, 122 Appian calls this man Πλένιος. That the spelling I give is the correct Latin spelling is demonstrated by the inscription quoted above, page 100, note 1. See the literature there cited for historical interpretations of the inscription.

[14]For the part of Lepidus in this campaign see especially Brueggemann, 59–73; compare Drumann, 1.9–17.   [15]Appian 5.97.

[16]So too in the campaign of 38; see above, page 109.

most striking in July, 36, when storms had shattered a great part of the elaborate armament that had been prepared against him. Perhaps it was in reality the *want* of trustworthy lieutenants, a want which would be readily intelligible in the circumstances under which Sextus waged war, that made it impossible for Sextus to venture on ambitious military schemes.

The carefully planned campaign of Octavian which had been so auspiciously begun on July 1 seemed shattered by the winds of July 3. Many of the vessels of Lepidus were destroyed by a south wind. Nevertheless he succeeded in reaching his destination, blockaded Lilybaeum, received the surrender of other cities, and took some by storm. The size of Lepidus's armament makes it clear that from the beginning he was planning a conquest for his personal advantage.[17] When Statilius Taurus encountered the storm, he turned about and was carried safely back to Tarentum. The fleet of Octavian and Agrippa, on the other hand, suffered severely off the promontory of Palinurus in Lucania. They succeeded, however, in rounding the promontory with the loss of only one vessel and so reached the shelter of the Bay of Velia. But, when the vessels had reached the bay, the wind veered, so that the vessels could neither ride out to sea nor remain at anchor. Six large vessels, 26 smaller vessels, and a greater number of Liburnian galleys sunk. The others were dashed about on the sea, where many were found and burnt by Menas.[18] The rear squadron of the fleet of Octavian and Agrippa had just crossed the Bay of Naples and was rounding the peninsula of Sorrento when the storm broke. The vessels of this squadron were all scattered and dashed against the rocks.[19]

Octavian buried his dead and cared for his wounded. Thirty days would be required to make his fleet seaworthy again, and, since the sailing season was far advanced, he would naturally have postponed the decisive campaign until the following summer. But scarcity of grain in Rome and the consequent

---

[17]So too Brueggemann, 61; Drumann, 4.579.

[18]Dio 49.1.3. It is remarkable that Appian's account, which is much fuller, does not mention Menas in this connection. Dorn Seiffen therefore thinks (21) the incident identical with the exploit which Appian describes in 5.101, when Menas was preparing for his third desertion.

[19]Appian 5.98; Velleius, 2.79.3; Suetonius, Augustus 16.1; Orosius 6.18.25.

popular dissatisfaction made postponement impossible.[20] Octavian therefore made the round of the military colonies, and encouraged the settlers there, and sent Maecenas to Rome to dispel the dissatisfaction resulting from the continued scarcity, and to assure the people that the war would be vigorously prosecuted in spite of the temporary setback. In his circumstantial account of these proceedings Appian gives the reason for the mission of Maecenas as follows:[21]

In anticipation of more serious misfortune he sent Maecenas to Rome on account of those who were still under the spell of the memory of Pompey the Great, for the fame of that man had not yet lost its influence over them.

It is from such hints as this that we may understand that in Rome Sextus Pompey was looked upon as something more than simply the rebel and pirate our 'official' historians make him. The Romans, apparently, did not condemn him as a wilful outlaw who was disturbing the peace which the righteous Octavian was striving to establish.[22]

Octavian prepared energetically for the resumption of hostilities. The crews saved from the wrecked vessels he turned over to Statilius Taurus to man the vessels of Antony for which no crews could be found before.[23] Then he appeared in Vibo to reassure his land army. He asserted confidently that the men would shortly land in Sicily and conquer the enemy.[24]

Historians of the war, ancient and modern,[25] have found it a cause for blame that Sextus did not make greater use of the unexpected discomfiture of his enemy in this campaign. The truth is that the resumption of hostilities on the part of Octavian so late in the season was unexpected, and before another year should pass much might happen. For Sextus to attempt an

---

[20]Ferrero suggests (4.14) that "Octavianus realised that to postpone the war for another twelve months would expose him to universal ridicule, after his ceremonious opening of the campaign."

[21]Appian 5.99.

[22]Compare Fitzler-Seeck (312): "Und nicht nur durch diesen <den Kornmangel> war das Volk erregt, sondern auch die republikanischen Ideale, als deren Vertreter man den Sohn des grossen Pompeius sehr mit Unrecht betrachtete, gewannen dadurch neue Kraft, dass die Götter selbst sie schon zum zweitenmal mit Sturm und Wetter zu verteidigen schienen."

[23]See above, page 124.   [24]Appian 5.99.

[25]Appian 5.100; Dorn Seiffen, 99; Merivale, 3.199; Drumann, 4.579; Holmes, Architect 115.

incursion into Southern Italy with his inferior land forces against the excellent armies which Octavian controlled would be foolhardy. On the sea it was difficult to find an opening against the prudent Agrippa, who nursed his resources carefully until such time as he should be ready for a telling blow. Furthermore, as has been suggested above (page 125), there was always a question how far Sextus might trust his lieutenants. The damage that an efficient and daring officer could inflict is, indeed, illustrated by the activities of Menas at this time. But Menas is also an example of how little such an officer could be trusted.

To recount the details of the third desertion of Menas seems unnecessary.[26] Travelling at amazing speed and displaying the greatest alertness and dash he raided some lookout ships and grain-carrying merchantmen of Octavian. Once he pretended to be caught fast in a sand bank, and, when his jubilant enemies descended upon him to take him, he rowed away speedily with loud and scornful laughter. Having demonstrated how valuable his services might be, he negotiated through Caninius Rebilus,[27] a senator whom he held captive, and Mindius Marcellus, with whom he had been on friendly terms during his former service under Octavian, and obtained a safe conduct to Octavian from Octavian's lieutenant, Valerius Messala. Octavian welcomed him, but entrusted him with no responsible post. The comment of Ferrero[28] is worth reproducing:

. . . this was the sole punishment inflicted upon this freedman for his treachery, in a state which for centuries had considered merciless severity to ungrateful freedmen as the first social duty of the upper classes.

Menas's excuse for again deserting Sextus was that he had not been entrusted with a responsible command. He had expected the command against Lepidus, which had in fact

---

[26]Appian takes three sections, 5.100-102, to tell the story. Compare Dio 49.1.3–5; Orosius 6.18.25. Gardthausen, 1.265–266, and Drumann, 4. 579–580 give the details.

[27]Rebilus had been a lieutenant of Caesar, and was a relative of Scribonius Libo, with whom he was on friendly terms. He was consul for a few hours on the last day of 45, and thus occasioned Cicero's jest in Fam. 9.30; see the comment in Tyrrell and Purser, 5.229.

[28]4.16.

been given to Demochares[29] on the sea and to Tisienus Gallus on the land. I have ventured the opinion (page 122, above) that the return of Menas to Sextus argues for the personality and the prospects of Sextus. I believe that the argument is strengthened, at least so far as the personality of Sextus is concerned, by the present desertion of Menas. Sextus was prudent in the management of his lieutenants, and refused to be carried away by the needs of the moment. In this final desertion of Menas, Sextus again appears in a more favorable light than Octavian.

Demochares, who had obtained the Pompeian command which Menas had desired, sailed toward Africa and met four legions of Lepidus, which were en route from Africa in merchant ships to strengthen Lepidus's forces in Sicily.

. . . After they had received him as a friend (for they thought that these were ships sent by Lepidus to meet them), ⟨Demochares⟩ destroyed them. Some ships were despatched by Lepidus leisurely, and when these were approaching, the merchant ships that had escaped mistook them for other enemies and fled. So some of them were burned, some captured, some upset, and the rest returned to Africa. Two legions perished in the sea, or, if any of them could swim, Tisienus,[30]

---

[29]Dio calls (49.8.2) the Pompeian commander Demochares, whereas Appian calls him Papias (5.104). The names obviously refer to the same person, as the accounts of the parts in the engagement as signed to the two supposedly different persons correspond exactly. Drumann shows (4.580, note 5) that Demochares is identical with Papias, but is puzzled by the double name. Gardthausen suggests a solution (2.137): "Aber derselbe Freigelassene kann doch nur entweder Demochares oder Papias geheissen haben; ich möchte deshalb statt Papias Papius schreiben; diesen römischen Gentilnamen erhielt er bei der Freilassung und hiess von nun an Papius Demochares. In diesem Sinne ist also der Text des Appian zu corrigiren." F. Münzer, in Pauly-Wissowa 4.2867, Number 7, discusses Demochares; he remains doubtful about the explanation offered by Gardthausen.

[30]The emergence of Tisienus (for whom see Klein, 137) at this point is something of a mystery. Ferrero has the following note (4.13–14): ". . . In v.97, he <Appian> says that a certain Plennius was sent against him <Sextus>; in v. 104, he suddenly brings the admiral Papias on the scene, who destroyed part of the fleet of Lepidus after the disembarkation of the latter; he adds that Lilybaeum was attacked by land, not by Plennius but by Tisienus. This Tisienus was doubtless the general whom Dion calls Gallus as Dion, in xlix. 8, gives his name in full as Tisienus Gallus. Were Tisienus and Plennius one and the same person? As for Papias, it is obvious that his interference in the struggle was the result of sudden

the lieutenant of Pompeius, slew them when they reached the land. The other legions re-embarked and joined Lepidus, some sooner and some later. Papias ⟨=Demochares⟩ sailed back to Pompeius.[31]

Despite the prodigious naval preparations of Octavian he did in fact expect—and the sequel proved him right—that the deciding factor in the war would be his superior land armament. To transport an adequate land army into Sicily had been the endeavor of Octavian since the very commencement of hostilities against Sextus. The key to Sicily and therefore the first objective of Octavian was Messana; here Sextus concentrated the best part of his army and his navy. Octavian planned to attack Messana from the West with his fleet, and from the East with his army. To this end Messala[32] with three legions crossed the instep of Italy to Scylaceum,[33] whither Statilius Taurus had proceeded from Tarentum. From that city they were to cross to the neighborhood of Tauromenium, where, it was planned, Lepidus should join them after traversing the island overland.[34] This force would then be in position to

decision, for Appian clearly says, in chap. xcvii, that Sextus intended to keep his fleet...at Messina and to oppose Lepidus only by land. It seems to me very probable that at the outset of the campaign Papias was at Messina under the orders of Sextus, who sent him against Lepidus when he heard that Sextilius <*sic!*> Taurus and Octavianus were detained by the damage sustained during the storm. Thus we have the reason why Papias could not attack Lepidus, who had already landed, and was only able to destroy that part of his fleet which formed the rear-guard of the expedition."

[31]Appian 5.104.

[32]For Messala's part in this war see J. Hammer, Prolegomena to an Edition of the Panegyricus Messalae, 28–32 (New York, 1925).

[33]For Scylaceum (Scyletium) see Strabo 6.255, 261, and H. Philipp in Pauly-Wissowa, Zweite Reihe, 3.920–927. Vergil (Aeneid 3.552) calls it *navifragum Scylaceum.*

[34]This differs slightly from the account of Appian 5.103 (which is followed by Gardthausen, 1.266). It is clear that Appian is in this chapter reproducing two different sources, without perceiving their contradiction, as Drumann points out (4.580, note 5). Some control, but very little, is offered by Dio 49.1.5. The inaccuracy of the chapter in Appian is illustrated by the sentence: ἐς τὸ Σκυλάκιον ὄρος, ὃ πέραν ἐστὶ Ταυρομενίου. Scylaceum (modern Squillace) is not opposite Tauromenium; furthermore, ὄρος is a peculiar word to use for the destination of a fleet. Casagrandi-Orsini, Il promontorio Taurianum, in Rivista di storia antica die Tropea II, 1.66–70 (Messina, 1896), 'corrects' Ταυρομενίου into Ταυροεντίου. Of this 'correction' Holm offers a criticism (3.456): "Dies Tauroentium, sonst

threaten Sextus from the rear. Three other legions were stationed at the narrowest part of the strait, to await an opportunity for crossing directly to the neighborhood of Messana.

Octavian displayed the greatest energy in supervising the details of the campaign. From Vibo he went to Scylaceum, to see that his orders were properly carried out, and then returned to Vibo to see to the sailing of the fleet to Strongyle (modern Stromboli), one of the Liparaean Islands. The command of the fleet, however, he entrusted to Agrippa. It was observed that a large force of Pompeian vessels was stationed along the Sicilian shore at Pelorum, Mylae, and Tyndaris. From this fact Octavian conjectured that Sextus was present in person with his fleet, and so he desired to seize the opportunity of transporting to Tauromenium the land forces which Messala and Taurus held in readiness at Scylaceum. With the intention, perhaps, of keeping Sextus engaged, that the army might cross undisturbed, Agrippa sailed to Hiera, the most southerly of the Liparaean Islands, and easily dislodged the small Pompeian fleet which held the island. Leaving there a large portion of his fleet he sailed before dawn for Mylae, where he expected to find Demochares with a small fleet of some forty sail. Sextus was aware of the menacing movement of Agrippa, and sent Apollophanes with 45 ships to support Demochares, and then followed himself with 70 others. When Agrippa sighted his enemy, he became aware of the altered circumstances. He therefore summoned the remainder of his own vessels, and sent word to Octavian. For the details of the battle I can do no better, again, than reproduce the account of Appian:[35]

Taurianum bei den Römern genannt, ist das Cap Vaticano. Da nun aber Squillace jetzt erst recht nicht passt, so verbessert er dann p. 70 Σκυλάκιον in Σκύλλαιον, und so haben wir statt Squillace und Taormina: C. Vaticano und Scilla. So ist mit zwei Conjecturen die ganze Begebenheit in ein anderes Meer verlegt, wohin sie jedoch nicht so gut passt. Kap. 109 geht Octavian ἐς Λευκόπετραν ἐκ τοῦ Σκυλακίου; da müsste mit Casagr. wieder corrigirt werden! Die ganze Sache ist eben noch nicht aufgeklärt." See also Viereck's note to Appian 5.103.

[35]5.107, 108. Dio gives (49.2–5) an equally lengthy and ornate account of the battle. In this case, as indeed with respect to all the events of 36 (compare Dorn Seiffen, 18), Dio's information seems more meager than Appian's. Interesting is his report of a belief that Agrippa purposely refrained from pursuing his enemy in order not to rouse the jealousy of

The preparations on both sides were superb. The ships had towers on both stem and stern.[36] When the usual exhortation had been given and the standards raised, they rushed against each other, some coming bow on, others making flank attacks, the shouts of the men and the spray from the ships adding terror to the scene. The Pompeian ships were shorter and lighter, and better adapted to blockading and darting about. Those of Octavian were larger and heavier, and, consequently, slower, yet stronger to give blows and not so easily damaged. The Pompeian crews were better sailors than those of Octavian, but the latter were stronger. Accordingly, the former excelled not so much in close fighting as in the nimbleness of their movements, and they broke oar blades and rudders, cut off oar handles, or separated the enemy's ships entirely, doing them no less harm than by ramming. Those of Octavian sought to cut down with their beaks the hostile ships, which were smaller in size, or shatter them, or break through them. When they came to close quarters, being higher, they could hurl missiles down upon the enemy, and more easily throw the "ravens" and the grappling-irons. The Pompeians whenever they were overpowered in this manner leaped into the sea.

They were picked up by their small boats, which were hovering around for this purpose, but Agrippa bore down directly upon Papias and struck his ship under the bow, shattering it and breaking into the hold. The men in the towers were shaken off, the water rushed into the ship, and all the oarsmen on the lower benches were cut off. The others broke through the deck

Octavian. The Latin authorities for this battle are as follows: Livy, Periocha 129: adversus Pompeium vario eventu navalibus proeliis pugnatum est ita ut ex duabus Caesaris classibus altera cui Agrippa praeerat vinceret....; Velleius 2.79.4:...navali primo proelio apud Mylas ductu Agrippae pugnatum prospere....; Suetonius, Augustus 16.1:...Pompeium inter Mylas et Naulochum superavit.... (In this passage I should like to interpret *inter* as = *apud*. *Inter* governing a single noun is not without sound parallels; see Harpers' Latin Lexicon (New York, 1879), s. v. *inter*, II A, 1, b, *ad finem* for examples. *Inter* may even be a scribal conjecture for *apud*. It is likely that Suetonius is naming the two principal battles in which Pompey was defeated rather than defining the location of the last battle. Our other sources say that the battle was fought *at* Naulochus. If my interpretation of *inter* is not correct, the passage in Suetonius can, of course, not be applied to the battle of Mylae); Orosius 6.18.26: Agrippa inter Mylas et Liparas adversus Democham <*sic!*> et Pompeium navale proelium gessit ac vicit ibique tunc naves triginta aut demersit aut cepit reliquis laceratis.

[36]Servius on Aeneid 8.693 describes a special kind of tower invented by Agrippa: Agrippa primus hoc genus turrium invenit, ut de tabulatis subito erigerentur, simul ac ventum esset in proelium, turres hostibus improvisae in navigando essent occultae.

and escaped by swimming. Papias escaped to a ship alongside of his own, and returned to the battle. Pompeius, who observed from a mountain that his ships were making little headway, and that whenever they came to close quarters with the enemy they were denuded of fighting men, and that reinforcements were coming to Agrippa from Hiera, gave the signal to retire in good order. This they did, advancing and retreating little by little. Agrippa continued to bear down upon them, and they took refuge, not on the beach, but among the shoals formed in the sea by river deposits.

Agrippa's pilots prevented him from running his large ships on the shoals. He cast anchor in the open sea, intending to blockade the enemy and to fight a battle by night if necessary: but his friends advised him not to be carried away by rashness and not to wear out his soldiers with excessive toil and want of sleep and not to trust to that tempestuous sea. So in the evening he reluctantly withdrew. The Pompeians made sail to their harbours, having lost thirty of their ships, and sunk five of the enemy's, and having inflicted considerable other damage and suffered as much in return. Pompeius praised his own men because they had resisted such formidable vessels, saying they had fought against walls rather than against ships; and he rewarded them as though they had been victorious. He encouraged them to believe that, as they were lighter, they would prevail over the enemy in the straits on account of the current. He said also that he would make some addition to the height of his ships.

So ended the naval battle of Mylae, between Agrippa and Papias.[37]

After this engagement Agrippa was received in several towns. He was driven out of Tyndaris after he had entered the town, which seemed ready to surrender. At nightfall he returned to Hiera.[38] This victory of Agrippa was the first success that Octavian's forces had ever won from Sextus. To Sextus, on the other hand, the result of the engagement must have caused

---

[37]A description of the battle which employs modern nautical terminology is to be found in A. Köster, Das Antike Seewesen, 231–232 (Berlin, 1923).

[38]Appian 5.109. Dio says (49.7.4) Sextus sailed back to Lipara; "wahrscheinlich denkt er im Allgemeinen an die liparischen Inseln," says Gardthausen (2.137). Gardthausen might have observed that the reading in Appian to which he makes Dio conform is only an emendation of Dorn Seiffen (22), who reads ἐς Ἱεράν for the meaningless ἐς ἑσπέραν of the MSS. The emendation is embodied in Viereck's text. The purpose of Agrippa in attacking Tyndaris, aside from a natural desire to gain the city, may have been to keep Sextus engaged, that Octavian might effect his crossing undisturbed.

gloomy foreboding. It was on the sea that his strength lay, and yet on the sea the armament of his enemy had proven superior to his own. His encouragement of his men[39] was a tacit admission that the armament of his enemy was superior, and that the enemy would certainly win the victory unless he should be circumvented by some bold stroke.

In point of fact Sextus almost accomplished such a stroke, all but capturing Octavian himself. We have seen above (page 130) that Octavian with the three legions of Messala hurried across from Vibo to Scylaceum; there he joined Statilius Taurus, who was in command of the vessels that had been left by Antony. From Scylaceum the combined land and naval forces proceeded southwards to Leucopetra, a promontory in the southernmost portion of Bruttium. Here Octavian received reports that Sextus was engaged at Mylae by Agrippa, and then that Sextus had been defeated. In the belief, therefore, that Sextus was elsewhere occupied, and seeing, in fact, that the straits were empty of enemies, Octavian abandoned his plan for a surreptitious crossing, and with three legions, 500 cavalry without horses, 1,000 light-armed troops, and 2,000 colonists serving as allies, he sailed for Tauromenium.[40] After the first crossing the vessels were to return for Messala and the remainder of the army. The Pompeians in Tauromenium refused Octavian admission; he therefore

made sail to the river Onobalas[41] and the temple of Venus, and moored his fleet at the shrine of the Archegetes, the god of the

---

[39]Appian 5.108, quoted on page 132. The words of the stern commander to his crestfallen soldiers in the hour of defeat reveal an admirable trait in Sextus's character.

[40]A full treatment of this phase of the war with especial attention to topographical details is given by A. Aiello, La Spedizione di Ottaviano a Tauromenium e la Via di Ritirata di L. Cornificio A. U. C. 718–36 A. C., in Raccolta, 2.181–264. Holm, who gives a good brief account of the war of 36, in 3.206–213, says (209) that there were "Truppen des Antonius" engaged. This is of course absurd. The *vessels* which comprised the fleet of Statilius Taurus were those which Antony had left behind.

[41]Holm says (1.339) Onobalas is an unknown Fiumara near Tauromenium. In 3.456 he suggests that TONONOBAΛAN is an error for TON ABOΛAN. He does this on the basis of Bekker, Anecdota 1.312, which mentions Ἀβόλως ποταμὸς ἐπὶ Ταυρομενίων. V. Casagrandi-Orsini, Il Fiume di Tauromenium Onobalas, Abolas, (Abalas, Abella, Abola, Abolla): Ricerche Storico-Etimologiche, Raccolta, 1.371–392, discusses the matter ex-

Naxians, intending to pitch his camp there and attack Tauromenium.[42]

But the soldiers had only begun the building of their camp
when Sextus was sighted off the coast with a fleet, and hostile
cavalry and infantry appeared on the coast.[43]

The impression given by Appian[44] and the modern scholars[45]
who follow him is that Sextus is to be condemned for letting slip
this opportunity—offered by fate, it is implied—of bringing the
war to a triumphant close by taking Octavian alive. But does
anything prevent us from supposing that such a consummation
was in the mind of Sextus? He must have realized that, in the
normal course of events, his ultimate defeat was inevitable. In
land armament he was hopelessly surpassed by Octavian, and
the victory of Agrippa had demonstrated that his traditional
superiority by sea vanished. Only one thing could save
Sextus, and that was the death or the capture of Octavian.
May not the surprise at Tauromenium, therefore, have been
deliberately planned? Surely many details point to such a
conclusion. He must have known Octavian's objective in
Sicily. Why was Octavian's crossing completely unopposed;
indeed, why was the whole sea free of enemies?[46] Why did
Sextus cut short the engagement with Agrippa? Might it not
have been to free his fleet for his intended stroke?[47] How did
the strong land army happen to arrive at Tauromenium so
promptly? Ferrero[48] is convinced that the trap was deliberately laid by Sextus, and, aside from his usual exuberance of
language and the overstatements which seem inevitable in the
presentation of a novel theory, I can find no fault in his reasoning. That the plan miscarried is due possibly to mismanagement

haustively, without shedding a great deal of light on the subject. Ziegler's
account of the rivers of Sicily (in Pauly-Wissowa, Zweite Reihe, 2.2478–
2479) mentions neither Onobalas nor Obalas. Blok states inaccurately
(47), "Tauromenii exercitum in terram exposuit," and has nothing more
to say. [42]Appian 5.109. [43]Appian 5.109; Dio 49.5.2.
[44]5.110. Dio 49.5.3 may be interpreted to mean that Octavian took to
ship-board as soon as he perceived the danger of a land attack.
[45]Gardthausen, 1.269; Holm, 3.209; Holmes, Architect, 115.
[46]Appian 5.109: κατασκεψάμενος οὖν ἡμέρας τὸ πέλαγος ἐκ τῶν ὁρῶν, ἐπεὶ
καθαρὸν ἔγνω πολεμίων ἔπλει....; compare Dio 49.5.1.
[47]Kromayer argues (Entwicklung, 452–453) that the Pompeian fleet at
Tauromenium was entirely different from the fleet which had faced Agrippa. [48]4.19.

on the part of Sextus's lieutenants, possibly to the Providence which, Caesarian historians assert, watched over Octavian, possibly to the proven capacity of Octavian for extricating himself from embarrassing situations.

Embarrassing indeed to Octavian was the present situation. The northern and the eastern divisions of his fleet were separated by Sextus in such wise that they were unable to cooperate. His army too was so divided that the legions of Messala in Italy could offer no assistance to the isolated troops in Sicily. In the absence of fuller information it is impossible to say why Sextus did not attack at once by land and by sea. It may simply be, as Appian[49] says, because his troops were inexperienced in war, and ignorant of the panic among the troops of Octavian, and unwilling to begin a battle at the approach of nightfall.

Octavian, at any rate, being faced by two dangers, chose that which offered a more likely chance of escape. He turned his army over to Cornificius, ordering him πράσσειν ὅ τι ἐπείγοι,[50] and himself took ship before daylight. Of Octavian's experiences I shall let Appian speak:[51]

He himself took ship before daylight and went seaward lest the enemy should enclose him on this side also, giving the right wing of the fleet to Titinius and the left to Carisius,[52] and embarking himself on a liburnian, with which he sailed around the whole fleet, exhorting them to have courage. Having done this he lowered the general's ensign, as is customary in times of extreme danger. Pompeius put to sea against him, and they encountered each other twice, the battle ending with the night. Some of Octavian's ships were captured and burned;[53] others spread their small sails and made for the Italian coast, contrary to orders. Those of Pompeius followed them a short distance and then turned against the remainder, capturing some and burning others. Some of the crews swam ashore, most of

---

[49]5.110.   [50]Appian 5.111.

[51]Appian 5. 111–112. Dio's account (49.5.3–5) is sketchy. Compare Livy, Periocha 129; Velleius 2.79.4; Orosius 6.18.27.

[52]This name is suggested for the MS Καρκίῳ by Gardthausen, 2.138; he gives cogent reasons for his emendation. Viereck approves Gardthausen's suggestion in a note and embodies it in his text.

[53]This fleet originally consisted of 120–130 vessels; see above, page 124. Appian says (5.139) that 70 were restored to Antony. Octavian's loss at Naulochus was negligible (see Appian 5.121); therefore he must have lost 50–60 ships in the present engagement.

whom were slaughtered or taken prisoners by Pompeius' cavalry. Some of them set out to reach the camp of Cornificius, who sent only his light-armed troops to assist them as they came near, because he did not consider it prudent to move his disheartened legionaries against the enemy's infantry, who were naturally much encouraged by their victory.

Octavian spent the greater part of the night among his small boats, in doubt whether he should go back to Cornificius through the scattered remains of his fleet, or take refuge with Messala. Providence brought him to the harbour of Abala[54] with a single armour-bearer, without friends, attendants, or slaves. Certain persons, who had come down from the mountains to learn the news, found him shattered in body and mind and brought him in rowboats (changing from one to another for the purpose of concealment) to the camp of Messala, which was not far distant. Straightway, and before he had attended to his bodily wants, he dispatched a liburnian to Cornificius, and sent word throughout the mountains that he was safe, and ordered all his forces to help Cornificius, and wrote to him that he would send him aid forthwith. After attending to his own person, and taking a little rest, he set forth by night, accompanied by Messala, to Stylis, where Carinas was stationed with three legions ready to embark, and ordered him to set sail to the other side, whither he would shortly follow. He wrote to Agrippa and urged him to send Laronius with an army to the rescue of Cornificius with all speed. He sent Maecenas again to Rome on account of the revolutionists; and some of these, who were stirring up disorder, were punished. He also sent Messala to Puteoli to bring the first legion to Vibo.[55]

---

[54]Drumann (4.582, note 4) thinks the name corrupt. Hülsen, in Pauly-Wissowa, 1.12, believes that the reference is to Mallias. Nissen suggests (2.968) that the reference is to Balarus, modern Bagnara (see above, page 77). Wijnne, De Fide et Auctoritate Appiani, 96 (Groningae, 1855), cites both Abalus and Balarus as shining examples of Appian's inaccuracy in matters of geography: "<Appianus> tam imperitus geographiae fuit, ut mentionem faciat de Balarum portu, de Abala portu....aliisque locis antiquis et recentioribus plane incognitis." Axt (19–20) offers a suggestion which is very interesting to me and perfectly sound on linguistic grounds. The two names, he says, refer to the same place. Abalus represents the Semitic name of the original Phoenician colony, and Balarus the Grecized form of the name. The names may have survived side by side to designate different parts of the same harbor. For similar changes in transliteration, but in the opposite direction (from Greek to Semitic) see S. Krauss, Griechische und Lateinische Lehnwörter in Talmud und Midrasch, 1.85–87 (Berlin, 1898).

[55]From our point of view the penultimate sentence is very important. There were still those in Rome who favored Pompey, and were willing to give expression to their feeling.

Pliny[56] tells a story that Octavian in despair once besought his friend Proculeius to kill him; the story has been referred to the present flight.[57] From Suetonius[58] we learn that Demochares and Apollophanes[59] pursued Octavian, and that he escaped in a single ship:

Traiecto in Siciliam exercitu, cum partem reliquam copiarum continenti repeteret, oppressus ex inproviso a Demochare et Apollophane praefectis Pompei uno demum navigio aegerrime effugit.

The same section describes a narrow escape:

Again, as he was going on foot to Regium by way of Locri, he saw some of Pompey's biremes coasting along the shore, and taking them for his own ships and going down to the beach, narrowly escaped capture.[59a]

These passages make it clear, it seems to me, that a determined effort was made to hunt Octavian down. Possibly a price had been set on his head, possibly his attempt at suicide was provoked by the knowledge that he was being hunted. If an attempt was really being made to hunt Octavian down, it would tend to prove that the trap at Tauromenium had been deliberately set by Sextus.

Cornificius, whom Octavian had left in charge at Tauromenium, found himself in a situation which was rapidly growing critical. Sextus's forces refrained from attacking, and refused the challenge when Cornificius drew his men up for battle. It would have been poor generalship to attack a superior enemy whom famine and isolation seemed bound to bring into his power in any case. It may be, too, that Sextus was still expecting that his energetic lieutenants would lay hands on the person of Octavian.

A story told by the Elder Pliny[60] may be interpreted as showing that the cause of Sextus showed promise of success at

---

[56]7.45.148.   [57]By Gardthausen, 1.270.

[58]Augustus 16.3. The two are not mentioned in connection with this battle either in Appian or in Dio.

[59]The statement is undoubtedly correct. Sextus himself, as we see from Appian 5.113, remained to watch the movements of Cornificius.

[59a]Suetonius, Augustus 16.3. The translation is that of J. C. Rolfe (The Loeb Classical Library).

[60]N. H. 7.178.

this time.[61] It certainly indicates that even among the enemy
soldiers that cause was not considered unrighteous; among
ordinary citizens there must have been many that favored
Sextus:

Bello Siculo Gabienus Caesaris classium fortissimus captus a
S. Pompeio iussu eius incisa cervice et vix cohaerente iacuit in
litore toto die. Deinde cum advesperavisset, gemitu precibus-
que congregata multitudine petiit uti Pompeius ad se veniret
aut aliquem ex arcanis mitteret, se enim ab inferis remissum
habere quae nuntiaret. Misit complures Pompeius ex amicis,
quibus Gabienus dixit inferis diis placere Pompei causas et
partes pias, proinde eventum futurum quem optaret.

In connection with this passage one should remember
Appian's mention of new disturbances in Rome, quoted and
commented on above.[62]

But one course was left open to Cornificius, and that was to
make his way toward Mylae[63] as best he could. Of his gallant
retreat I shall let Appian tell:[64]

Cornificius, having placed in the centre the unarmed men who
had escaped to him from the ships, took to the road, grievously
exposed to missiles in the open plains from the enemy's horsemen
and in the broken country from the light-armed troops from
Numidia in Africa, who hurled javelins from long distances and
made their escape when charged by their enemies.

On the fourth day, with difficulty, they arrived at the water-
less region which they say was formerly inundated by a stream
of fire that ran down as far as the sea and dried up all the
springs in the district. The inhabitants of the country traverse
it only by night, on account of the stifling heat and the dust
and ashes with which it abounds. Being ignorant of the roads
and fearing ambush, Cornificius and his men did not dare to
march through it by night, especially as there was no moon,[65]

---

[61]The story must be referred to this occasion, because it implies the
presence of Sextus, and the present situation is the only one which the circumstances of the story will fit.   [62]Page 136.

[63]Or to the north coast of Sicily in general, as opposed to the east. I
mention Mylae because Appian (at the end of 5.115) reports that Cornificius escaped to Agrippa at Mylae. But at the beginning of 5.116 Appian
tells us that "the garrison of Pompeius still held Mylae."

[64]5.113–116. Cornificius was rewarded with the consulship (Dio 49.
18.6, 49.33.1) and the extraordinary privilege of riding an elephant whenever he dined out (Dio 49.7.6).

[65]ἀσελήνῳ μάλιστα. Groebe (Drumann, 4.583, note 5) uses this hint to
fix the date of the retreat as August 15, 36: "Gemeint kann nur der
Neumond vom 15. August sein. Der vom 17. Juli wäre zu früh, da

nor could they endure it by day, but even suffocated, and the soles of their feet were burned (especially those who had no shoes), as it was now the hottest part of the summer; and since delay was impossible on account of the tormenting thirst, they no longer resisted their assailants, but received wounds without any means of defence. When they saw the place of exit from this burned district occupied by enemies, the able-bodied ones, heedless of their sick and unprotected companions, dashed at the defile with amazing courage and overpowered the enemy with all their remaining strength. When they found the next defile occupied by hostile forces they gave way to despair and succumbed to thirst and heat. Cornificius aroused them by showing them a spring of water near by; and again they overpowered the enemy, but with heavy loss to themselves. Another body of enemies held possession of the fountain, and now Cornificius' men lost all courage and gave way completely.

While they were in this state Laronius, who had been sent by Agrippa with three legions, made his appearance a long way off. Although it was not yet plain that he was a friend, still, as hope all the time led them to expect a friend, they once more recovered their spirits. When they saw the enemy abandon the water in order not to be exposed to attack on both sides, they shouted for joy with all their strength; and when the troops of Laronius shouted in return, they ran and seized the fountain.[66]

Laronius[67] escorted the army of Cornificius to the north coast. With the escape of this army went Sextus's best oppor-

---

Oktavian nach den ersten Unfällen im Anfang des Juli (App. V 97, 404. 98, 408) dreissig Tage brauchte, um wieder kampfbereit zu sein (App. V 99, 412); der vom 13. September zu spät, da bereits am 3. September, nach der Seeschlacht bei Naulochus, das Heer des Lepidus sich ergab (CIL I² p. 328)." Additional proof that August is the month in question may be derived from Suetonius, Augustus 31.2: Sextilem mensem e suo cognomine nuncupavit magis quam Septembrem quo erat natus, quod hoc sibi et primus consulatus et insignes victoriae optigissent.

[66]Compare Dio 49.6.3–49.7.5; Velleius 2.79.4. Holm gives interesting topographical details (2.210): "Der Marsch...war höchst beschwerlich, besonders deswegen, weil ein Ausbruch des Aetna, der nach Norden gerechtet war, kaum sein Ende gefunden hatte.... Cornificius muss in dem Thale des Alcantara aufwärts gezogen sein, und zwar auf dem linken, nördlichen Ufer desselben. Die Feinde suchten dem Heere den Aufgang auf den Kamm des Gebirges, das es überschreiten musste, zu verwehren. Der Weg, der allein den Kriegern frei blieb, war überdies von Wasser fast entblösst, und so litten sie ausserordentlich von Durst." This account of Holm is based largely on Aiello, especially pages 216–264, where a very careful study of the terrain is given.

[67]For Laronius see Pauly-Wissowa 12.876.

tunity of winning any considerable victory by land. Apparently, however, he considered his success sufficient to justify
placing IMP. ITER. on his coins.[68]

We have seen that Octavian made his way to land. As soon
as he reached his friends, he showed extraordinary energy in
planning and supervising renewed efforts against Sextus. To
the display of renewed energy on the part of Octavian may be
referred the origin of a story which Dio[69] places at the close of
his account of Octavian's escape:

His confidence was not restored until a fish of its own accord
leaped out of the sea and fell at his feet; this incident gave him
courage once more, for he believed the soothsayers who told
him that he should make the sea his slave.

Octavian succeeded in transporting the remainder of his
army to Sicily. His forces on the island now amounted to
twenty-one legions of infantry, 20,000 cavalry, and more than
5,000 light-armed troops. Agrippa had in the meanwhile been
successful at Tyndaris, and with the stronghold, which was
admirably situated for naval warfare, he took large stores of
munitions and provisions.[70] We have seen[71] that Lepidus had
twelve legions and 5,000 Numidian cavalry. Whatever as-

---

[68]Babelon, Numbers 21–27. Gardthausen (2.138) was doubtful about
the ascription of these coins to this period: "Drumann...meint Pompeius
habe für diesen Erfolg zum zweiten Mal sich als Imperator begrüssen
lassen, da er sich auf Münzen...imperator iterum nennt. Allein das
bezieht sich wohl auf frühere Zeit; nach diesem Sieg hat Pompeius schwer-
lich noch viele Münzen prägen lassen." But the inscription quoted above
(page 100), which was found two years after the publication of Gardthausen's book, makes it clear that Pompey did not call himself Imperator
Iterum in July, 36. Compare also V. Casagrandi-Orsini, Il Cursus honorum
di Sesto Pompeo Magno Pio sulla Lapide lilibetana, in Raccolta 2.143–
180, especially 161–162.

[69]Pliny (N. H. 9.55) almost certainly refers to the same incident: Siculo
bello ambulante in litore Augusto piscis e mari ad pedes eius exilivit quo
argumento vates respondere Neptunum patrem adoptante tum sibi Sexto
Pompeio—tanta erat navalis rei gloria—sub pedibus Caesaris futuros qui
maria tempore illo tenerent. So also does a passage in Suetonius, Augustus
96.2: Pridie quam Siciliensem pugnam classe committeret, deambulanti in
litore piscis e mari exsilvit et ad pedes iacuit. Gardthausen cites the
passage in Pliny, but refers it to Octavian's second expedition to Sicily,
saying: "Plinius spricht von einem Vorzeichen, das sich zeitlich nicht
näher bestimmen lässt." Gardthausen does not mention the version of
what is certainly the same story in Dio. The *zeitliche Bestimmung* of Dio
seems logical enough.   [70]Appian 5.116.   [71]See above, page 124.

persions may be made upon the generalship of Sextus must be offset by reflection on the huge armament which was now gathered against him. What a glorious climax for the career of a pirate chief, if indeed it is a mere pirate chief with whom we are dealing!

Even so the situation of Sextus was not entirely desperate. From Pelorum at the northeastern tip of Sicily Sextus controlled the northern coast as far east as Mylae, and the eastern coast as far south as Tauromenium. Between these two points there is only a small stretch of comparatively hilly country. The most important point, Messana, which lies south of Pelorum, is completely protected on the land side by a mountain range which was in the possession of Sextus. But, when Agrippa threatened Pelorum, Sextus withdrew his garrisons from the territory about Mylae, so that Octavian[72] was enabled to take Mylae and the neighboring Artemisium. It became clear to Sextus that his sole hope of defense lay in northeastern Sicily. He therefore summoned Tisienus Gallus, who had been watching Lepidus in the western part of the island.[73] Octavian naturally sought to intercept Tisienus before he should join Sextus, but lost his way around Mount Myconium.

There was heavy rainfall as often occurs in the Autumn,[74] and some of his armour-bearers held a Gallic shield over his head the whole night. Harsh mutterings and prolonged roars from Mount Etna were heard, accompanied by flames which lighted up the camp. . . .[75]
On the next day or so Octavian met Lepidus, who had marched toward Messana from the western part of the island.[76]

---

[72]Holm says (3.211) that Agrippa took these places. The statement in Appian 5.116 as well as succeeding events shows that Octavian was the general.

[73]Appian 5.104; see above, page 128. Tisienus had fought against Octavian in the Perusine War: Appian 5.32. See Klein, 137.

[74]ὄμβρου τε πολλοῦ καταρραγέντος, οἷος ἐν φθινοπώρῳ γίγνεται. The autumn (φθινόπωρον) began with the early rising of Arcturus: see F. K. Ginzel, Handbuch der Mathematischen und Technischen Chronologie, 1.250–251 (Leipzig, 1911). [75]Appian 5.117.

[76]Appian 5.117; Dio 49.8.2. Appian says the meeting took place in Παλαιστηνῶν γῆ. It has become the fashion to disbelieve entirely any geographical information which Appian gives. I have quoted the opinion of Wijnne, above, page 136. Schwartz (Pauly-Wissowa, 2.235) calls Appian "...ein durch geographische Unwissenheit sich auszeichnender Autor..." And Dorn Seiffen (21) says: "Utut est, rem geographicam non magnopere

The concluding scene of the war was fast approaching. Octavian and Lepidus[77] stood ready to besiege Messana by land, and Agrippa blocked the approach by sea. The small extent of land under the control of Sextus would not suffice for the maintenance of his forces, and Statilius Taurus was picking off one by one the cities which were his bases of supply. Just how the concluding naval battle took its start it is difficult to say. In the accounts of both Dio and Appian rhetorical flourishes fail to conceal an ignorance of what actually happened. Dio tells the story as follows:[78]

... but Lepidus quarreled with Caesar, since he claimed the privilege, as a colleague, of managing everything on equal terms with Caesar, whereas Caesar treated him in all respects as a lieutenant; therefore he inclined to Sextus and secretly held communication with him. Caesar suspected this, but dared not make it known. ... Hence he determined to risk a decisive encounter as soon as possible, before there should be any defection, although on other accounts he was by no means in haste; for Sextus had neither food nor money, and therefore he hoped to overthrow him without a battle before a great while. When, therefore, he had once reached this decision, he himself led out the army on land and marshalled it in front of the camp, while at the same time Agrippa sailed in and lay at anchor, for Sextus, whose forces were far inferior to theirs, would not come out to meet them on either element. This lasted for several days. But finally, becoming afraid that he might be despised for his behaviour and so be deserted by his allies, Sextus gave orders at last for the ships to put out to battle; for in these he reposed his chief trust.

---

calluit Appianus; Abalas enim portus, et Scylacius mons in Italia, Onobalas flumen...Palaestinorum ager in Sicilia, antiquis et hodiernis ignota sunt." The false location of well-known places is a fault that can be understood, but names which happen not to be mentioned by other authors are not necessarily made by Appian out of whole cloth. Viereck lists (622) a number of guesses regarding the present location, and then says, correctly, *quorum nihil probabile*. The most reasonable explanation, which is also the simplest, he does not mention. Axt suggests (35) that the name is correct exactly as the MSS have it, and was applied to an original Phoenician settlement. In the second century A. D. Apuleius (11.5) calls the Sicilians *trilingues*.

[77]In his desire for compression Marsh (193) is led into a misstatement of fact: "...in a naval battle he \<Agrippa\> broke the maritime power of Sextus for ever. It only remained to stamp out the last remnants of the young Pompey's forces in Sicily, and to assist in this Octavian called on Lepidus to bring his legions from Africa." We have seen (page 122) that Octavian called on Lepidus in the spring of 36.   [78]Dio 49.8.3–6.

The clandestine correspondence between Sextus and Lepidus here mentioned by Dio offers an interesting theme for speculation. But it is probable that Dio is only embroidering his tale, for we get no hint of the matter in Appian or elsewhere. Felix Brueggemann[79] insists that Lepidus was as hostile to Sextus as to Octavian:

> Apud Dionem autem scriptum legimus, Lepidum clandestina —per litteras sive per legatos—colloquia eo tempore fecisse cum Sexto Pompeio et de societate cum eo facienda egisse. At haec Dionis relatio minimam per se meretur fidem, cum ea, quae sibi voluerit Lepidus, non minus adversa fuerint Pompeio quam Octaviano. Etiamsi huic quidem societas Sexti cum Lepido periculosissima fortasse facta esset, tamen id Lepido dubium videri nullo pacto potuit, quin Sextus superior discedens sibi ipsi fructum perciperet Siciliamque retineret.

Appian's account of the beginning of the battle is quite different:[80]

> Since he ⟨Sextus⟩ feared the enemy's infantry, but had confidence in his own ships, he sent and asked Octavian if he would allow the war to be decided by a naval engagement. Octavian, although he dreaded all naval encounters, which until now had turned out badly for him, considered it base to refuse, and accordingly accepted the challenge. A day was fixed by them, for which 300 ships were put in readiness on either side, provided with missiles of all kinds, with towers and whatever machines they could think of.

Even by sea, as it developed, and indeed, as might easily have been foretold, Agrippa was the stronger. By land Sextus's prospects were hopeless. If a battle was to be fought, therefore, Sextus would by all means prefer to have it a sea-battle. Perhaps Sextus forced the battle at sea. Perhaps Appian's formal challenge and chivalrous acceptance are his embroidered version of a more prosaic account in the source he used. Gardthausen,[81] indeed, and Fitzler-Seeck[82] accept Appian at face value. But, though Octavian may have had complete confidence in his sea forces, the stakes were certainly too great and his former ex-

---

[79]Page 62.   [80]5.118.

[81]1.273. Gardthausen makes the incident an instance of Octavian's chivalry.

[82]Fitzler-Seeck, 315. A more reasonable basis for crediting Appian is given here, namely that Octavian accepted the challenge because he feared Sextus would unite with Lepidus.

periences of the sea too harrowing for him to yield to such an
impulse of generosity, when he knew that he must in any case
win by land.   One would naturally inquire for established
instances of similar chivalry on the part of Octavian.

Of the battle itself it is needless to say much in this place.
One is tempted to reproduce the vivid account in Dio,[83] but
this account is a patent borrowing from Thucydides's classic
description of the sea-battle between the Athenians and the
Sicilians of an earlier day,[84] with whole sentences 'lifted' almost
unaltered.   The account of Appian[85] is equally ornate, though
his pattern is not so clearly distinguishable.   Three hundred
vessels[86] were engaged on each side.   Prodigies of valor were
displayed, the carnage was immense, the fact that Romans
were engaged on both sides made it difficult for the combatants
to distinguish friend from foe— the details are familiar from
accounts of other contests in the Civil Wars.[87]   The device of

---

[83]49.9–10.

[84]7.71.   So obvious is the dependence of Dio on Thucydides in this
passage that commentators on Thucydides (Classen, for example) cite
the peculiar use of συστάσει in Dio to explain ξύστασιν in Thucydides.

[85]5.119–121.

[86]Ferrero (4.21) says, without authority, that Pompey had only 180.
The only possible basis for this figure, and its fallacy, are shown in note 92,
below.

[87]An item that arouses my suspicion is the following detail from Appian
5.120: "It was no longer easy to distinguish an enemy from a friend, as they
used the same weapons for the most part...", and 5.121: "Judging from
the colours of the towers, which constituted the only difference between
them, Agrippa with difficulty made out that Pompeius' ships had sustained
the greater loss..."   The similarity of armaments and ships is made much
of in all the modern accounts of the battle.   Compare Drumann, 4.586:
"...bei der im ganzen gleichen Rüstung und Sprache Freunde und Feinde
nur noch an der Bauart der Flotte und an der Farbe der Türme unterschied
..."; Gardthausen, 1.275: "...Niemand mehr Freund und Feind unterscheiden konnte, höchstens an der verschiedene Farbe der Schiffsthürme;"
Holm, 3.211: "Die Verwirrung der Schlacht wurde dadurch vermehrt, dass
beide Parteien sich der lateinischen Sprache zum Feldgeschrei bedienten
und die Schiffe beider Flotten gleichmässig gebaut waren und theilweise nur
an der Farbe der Thürme als Octavianisch oder Pompeianisch erkannt
werden konnten;" Domaszewski, 1.128: "Nichts unterschied die kamp-
fenden Schiffe mehr als die Farbe der Türme...;" Dorn Seiffen, 118–119.
But in the accounts of the Battle of Mylae, which was fought approximately only two weeks before Naulochus, both Appian (5.106) and Dio
(49.3) emphasize the great disparity between the ships of the contending

Agrippa for harpooning the enemy vessels[88] was especially effective. But, after reading the verbose accounts of the struggle in Dio and Appian, one is brought up with a start to find that only "Three of Octavian's ships were sunk in the fight. Pompeius lost twenty-eight in this way . . ."[89] Nevertheless, the victory of Octavian was quite complete, for, when Sextus's fleet attempted to retire in the direction of Messana, Agrippa cut off their retreat, so that only Sextus himself with seventeen ships got clear of Agrippa; the crews of these ships threw their towers overboard, and succeeded in escaping.[90] Orosius[91] tells us that Agrippa captured or sunk 163 ships, but it appears that he captured that number.[92]

For determining the date of the Battle of Naulochus we have inscriptional evidence. The Fasti Amiterni[93] inform us:

navies. The present passage I should, therefore, be inclined to characterize as a τόπος for the description of a naval battle in a civil war. I have the feeling that the same sort of criticism may be applied to much else in Appian (and Dio), for example to the vivid descriptions of storms at sea. In his description of the battle of Pharsalus (2.80) Appian also comments on the similarity of arms and speech: ὡς Ἰταλῶν ὁμοιτρόπως ἐσκευασμένων τε καὶ φωνὴν ὁμοίαν ἀφιέντων.

[88]See above, page 120. The device is described by Appian as if it were invented and installed immediately before this battle, but I believe it probable that Agrippa's ships had been equipped with the instrument at Portus Julius. The fact that Appian enlarges on its use in the present battle and fails to mention it in the battle at Mylae may simply reflect an emphasis in Appian's sources. The device was after all only an adaptation of the instrument used by Brutus at Massilia (Caesar, B. C. 1.37).

[89]Appian 5.121.

[90]Other references for the battle are Livy, Periocha 129; Velleius 2.79.5; Suetonius, Augustus 16.4; Pseudo-Victor 84.4; Florus 2.18.7; Zonaras 10.25. Modern accounts are to be found e.g. in Drumann, 4.585–586; Gardthausen, 1.274–275; Holm, 3.211–212; Domaszewski, 1.128–129.

[91]6.18.29: Agrippa...centum sexaginta et tres naves aut demersit aut cepit. Pompeius cum decem et septem navibus vix elapsus evasit.

[92]This is the basis for the figure given by Ferrero (163 + 17), mentioned above in note 86. Gardthausen is puzzled (2.141), and suggests that the number, if it is accurate, must refer to large vessels only. But Kromayer (Entwicklung, 456, note 17) maintains that the number is correct for the ships *captured* by Octavian, and supports his contentions logically. The mistake in Orosius lies in the careless use of the words *aut demersit aut cepit*. "Aber das ist eine bei Orosius häufig wiederkehrende Floskel (z. B. kurz vorher VI 18, 26 und 2, 21) auf die daher kein Wert zu legen ist. Orosius Zahlenangaben sind dagegen in diesem ganzen Abschnitte gut und mit Appian übereinstimmend..."

[93]C. I. L. 1².328. Compare Fasti Arvales, C. I. L. 1².214: q(uod) e(o) d(ie) Caesar August(us) in Sicilia vicit.

III·NON·SEPT· Fer(iae) et supplicationes aput omnia pulvinaria quod eo die Caes(ar) divi f. vicit in Sicilia Censorin(o) et Calvis(io) cos.

For the period between August 19 and September 23 the Feriale Cumanum[94] gives this note: exerCITVS · LEPIDI · TRADIDIT · SE · CAESARI · SVPPLIcAtio. Mommsen[95] assumes that both inscriptions refer to the same event, namely the surrender of the troops of Lepidus. Since he fixes the date of this surrender at September 3, and the surrender took place some time after the Battle of Naulochus,[96] Mommsen asserts that the battle must have taken place during the last days of August.

But the reasoning of Mommsen is not sound. "The word *vicit* plainly means 'won the battle,' not 'accepted the surrender of Lepidus,' "[97] and Mommsen had no justification for inserting *iii Non. Septembr.* in the Feriale Cumanum. There are two other considerations which make a later date for the Battle of Naulochus desirable. First, there is hardly time enough between the Battle of Mylae and the date conjecturally fixed by Mommsen for the events which took place between the two battles.[98] Secondly, Appian[99] informs us that the autumnal rains had begun before the Battle of Naulochus.

In connection with the great defeat of Sextus a few words regarding the capacities of the opposing leaders may be in place. Sextus saw himself inexorably hemmed in by overwhelmingly superior forces, fought his battle, lost it, and made his escape. His father had done the same, and Antony, unless we heed his advocates,[100] was to do much worse. The fact that Sextus was able to maintain authority over his ill-assorted forces, and plan and execute even an unsuccessful defense, speaks well for his generalship. Indeed, that he could achieve at all the power which he did in fact achieve, and maintain it during the period

---

[94]C. I. L. 1².229.

[95]Hermes 17 (1882), 633. His reasoning is accepted by Groebe in Drumann, 4.585, note 9.

[96]Appian 5.122.   [97]Holmes, Architect, 221.

[98]Fitzler-Seeck, 316.   [99]5.117; see above, note 74.

[100]See, for example, the Appendix on the Battle of Actium in Ferrero, 4.259–277. Ferrero shows that Antony's desertion of his army and withdrawal to the fleet of Cleopatra was really a well-planned but badly executed strategic move.

of years during which he did in fact maintain it bespeaks an organizing and executive ability of a high order. "Er verdankte es aber nur den Umständen," Drumann[101] warns us, "seinem Namen . . . den erneuerten bürgerlichen Unruhen . . . der Schwäche Oktavians." Gardthausen[102] follows him: "⟨Sextus⟩ verdankte es seinem Namen . . . und der allgemeinen Kopflosigkeit und Verwirrung nach der Ermordung Caesars." I should say, in reply, that, if the government at Rome had been functioning normally and efficiently, Sextus might not have attained the power he did (very probably he would have attained high distinction as a legitimate servant of the government), but, however great the *Kopflosigkeit* and *Verwirrung* of others might have been, Sextus could never have kept his power unless he were himself a person of real ability.

What of Octavian? We have seen that his timidity almost cost him his fleet on one occasion, and that he jumped ashore and left Cornificius to save himself and his fleet as best he could.[103] At Tauromenium, again, he left Cornificius in a perilous position while he himself took the safer course; even then, in despair, he was tempted to take his own life.[104] In the Battle of Naulochus his conduct was not much better. He appears to have been in a daze all through the battle, and to have refused to look out at the contending navies:[105]

. . . sub horam pugnae tam arto repente somno devinctus, ut ad dandum signum ab amicis excitaretur. Unde praebitam Antonio materiam putem exprobrandi, ne rectis quidem oculis eum aspicere potuisse instructam aciem, verum supinum, caelum intuentem, stupidum cubuisse, nec prius surrexisse ac militibus in conspectum venisse quam a M. Agrippa fugatae sint hostium naves.

Octavian prevailed over Sextus because by the year 36 the significant part of the Roman world had come to realize that its interests were bound up with the success of Octavian, and Octavian had at his disposal the best the Roman world could offer in men and in money. Without doubt it was to the interest of civilization that Octavian prevail. But in personal capacity it is hard to deny that Sextus compares very favorably with his conqueror.

---

[101]4.591. [102]1.312. [103]See page 135. [104]See page 137.
[105]Suetonius, Augustus 16.4; see Shuckburgh's note.

IX. THE END OF THE HOUSE OF POMPEY

In his haste to reach Messana Sextus neglected to leave instructions for his land army. There was, therefore, nothing left for Tisienus Gallus and the other Pompeian leaders to do but to capitulate and deliver their forces to Octavian.[1] Plinius with the legion that had defended Lilybaeum against Lepidus[2] had been summoned to the northeastern part of the island. Plinius picked up seven additional Pompeian legions outside Messana, and succeeded in making his way into the city with his eight legions.[3] But, by the time Plinius entered the city, Sextus had already put on board his seventeen vessels the most valuable of his treasures and his young daughter Pompeia,[4] changed his general's attire for that of a private person, and sailed off as speedily as possible, before the town should be beleaguered both by land and by sea. At sea he extinguished the light on his vessel to escape detection, and also, according to Florus,[5] removed his seal ring from his finger in order not to be recognized. His goal was the headquarters of Antony, of whom he expected asylum in return for the protection he had previously given to Antony's mother.[6]

With his eight legions Plinius might have defended Messana for some time, but there was no motive for further resistance, and so he sued for peace to Agrippa and Lepidus, who had blockaded the town. Agrippa wished to await the arrival of Octavian for consummating the negotiations, but Lepidus

---

[1]Dio 49.11.   [2]See page 124.

[3]Appian wrongly says (5.122) that Plinius brought eight legions from Lilybaeum; Appian himself states (5.97) that Plinius's forces consisted of a single legion. That Plinius's forces were increased to eight legions by the accession of the Pompeian land forces stationed at Naulochus may be inferred from Appian 5.123: "Including this new accession <i. e. of Plinius's legions> Lepidus now had twenty-two legions of infantry..." He had brought over twelve legions originally, had been joined by two additional legions, and now by the eight of Plinius; see Brueggemann, 68.

[4]Is the fact that Sextus's wife is not mentioned in the accounts of the escape proof that she had died before 36? Drumann thinks so (4.591).

[5]Dio 49.17.2; Florus 2.18.9.

[6]Appian 5.122; compare above, page 85. Other references for Sextus's flight are Dio 49.11.1; Strabo 3.2.2, 6.1.6; Velleius 2.79.5; Seneca, Quaestiones Naturales 4, Praefatio 22.

hastened to make a private arrangement with the Pompeian
soldiers, whereby they joined his forces and with them plundered
the city of the luckless Messanians.[7] The designs which he
had certainly long been cherishing were revealed to the light
of day. He wished to win for himself the power over Sicily
which Sextus had enjoyed.

But his bitterest enemies must admit that Sextus was forced
to retain his hold on Sicily because there was no other place
in the Roman world for him. He had been a hunted man and
an outlaw, except for short intervals, from before the time he
had attained manhood. It was only by the sword that he
could live. In his early years in Sicily he might well have
considered that he had the right, nay, perhaps even the patriotic
duty, to oppose Octavian.[8] Though the revolving years had
made it clear to Italy generally that true patriotism required
the support of Octavian, a man in the position of Sextus may
well have remained unconvinced; in any event he had so far
committed himself that retraction was impossible. But Lepidus
was a Triumvir, and held a share in the government. If his
share was less than that of his colleagues, it was as large as his
capacity and energies deserved. Lepidus, we must remember,
was within the law, and had every reason to follow the course
which patriotism demanded. If, then, Lepidus could show
himself both rebellious and selfish to the highest degree, and
still—what is most significant—return to his position as
Pontifex Maximus, with its social if not political implications,
how can we condemn Sextus except from the point of view of
his failure, and of the ultimate interest of civilization? Considered absolutely, therefore, the conduct of Sextus may have
been morally wrong, but considered against the background of
his contemporaries he cannot be condemned as easily as
Niebuhr,[9] for example, condemns him: "Sextus Pompeius war
ein blosser Condottierre, er dachte an nichts weiter als sich in
Sicilien und diesen Gegenden zu behaupten."

I have chosen this point for a word of defense for Sextus,
partly because of the opportunity for comparison with Lepidus,
and partly because I do not believe that Sextus's conduct

---

[7]See Holmes, Architect, 117; Gardthausen, 1.276–277; Drumann, 1.17;
Fitzler-Seeck, 316–317; Brueggemann, 68–71.
[8]See above, page 115.   [9]Vorträge, 105.

subsequent to his flight from Messana is as justifiable as his earlier career, though that conduct can certainly be explained. The attempt he made was in fact no worse morally than the attempt of Lepidus just referred to, and much easier to understand in a man in Pompey's position.

From Messana, Sextus directed his course toward the East. The West had no haven for him, and his former relations with Antony constituted some claim on Antony's generosity.[10] It was easy to see, furthermore, that Antony and Octavian must eventually come to blows, and Antony might therefore welcome Sextus in order to conciliate whatever following he might still have.   Sextus's first stop was at the Lacinian promontory, where he appropriated the treasures stored in the Temple of Juno.[11]   Thence he directed his course to the Ionian Islands. Here, according to Dio,[12] at Cephallenia, he met scattered remnants of his fleet, which had collected at that place.   In a formal speech he advised those of his men who were present to scatter in diverse directions in order to minimize the chances of detection.[13]   With the few that remained he continued on his journey eastward, with the intention of going directly to Antony.

When he reached Lesbos, however, and learned that Antony had gone on a campaign against the Medes and that Caesar and Lepidus had gone to war with each other, he decided to winter where he was; and in fact the Lesbians welcomed him with great enthusiasm on account of their recollection of his father, and tried to keep him there.[14]

At first Sextus lived quietly as a private citizen, awaiting the return of Antony from his expedition to make his plea before

---

[10]I refer not only to the fact that Sextus sheltered Antony's mother, but also to the temporary alliance in 38; see page 85. Compare my remark on the find of coins at Olbia, page 106.

[11]Appian 5.133. The ruins of the celebrated temple have given the modern name to the promontory, Capo delle Colonne.

[12]49.17.

[13]Dio (49.17.3) says that he removed his σκευὴν τὴν στρατηγικήν on this occasion. Appian (5.122) says that even before Pompey reached Messana τήν τε ἐσθῆτα ἤλλαξεν ἐς ἰδιώτην ἀπ' αὐτοκράτορος.   Appian's story seems more logical; Dio's Appomatox has an artificial ring.

[14]Dio 49.17.4; compare Appian 5.133. For Sextus's earlier sojourn in Lesbos as a place of refuge, and for the friendship of the Lesbians for the house of Pompey, see pages 15, 22.

him. But, when more and more unfavorable reports of the situation of Antony in Media reached him, Sextus again thought of acquiring an independent power in the Mediterranean. If Antony and his army should be destroyed, as reports may well have indicated as a likely probability, Sextus would naturally come forward as the most celebrated Roman commander in the East. The most sweeping successes of Rome in the East had been won under the Elder Pompey, and the feebler Romans that had subsequently fought in the East only served to enhance Pompey's fame. How much magic the name of Pompey still possessed Sextus's reception by the Lesbians will serve to indicate.

The psychologic influence which the world's memory of his father's greatness exercised on Sextus, and his *pietas* in avenging his father's shameful end and maintaining the family tradition of military prowess are matters which may not be ignored. There can be no doubt that Marcus Brutus was impelled to assassinate his benefactor Julius Caesar by the circumstance that an ancestor of his, several centuries removed, was reported to have assassinated the 'tyrant' of his day. If the exploits of Pompey the Great were not sufficiently remote to have become legendary, yet were they near enough and magnificent enough to form a great tradition. The explanation of the entire career of Sextus may well be comprised in the single word *pietas*. Such is the solution which Niese[15] hints at in a sentence:

Sextus hat eine eigenartige Stellung, er betrachtet sich als Rechtsnachfolger und Rächer seines Vaters, in dessen Spuren er wandeln will; deshalb legte er sich den Beinamen *Pius* zu.

This view seems to be illustrated with considerable clarity by certain expressions in the last few chapters of Appian's Civil Wars:

(1) 5.133: ἔπεμπε δὲ καὶ ἐς Παρθναίους, ἐλπίσας . . . αὐτοὺς δέξεσθαι προθύμως στρατηγὸν Ῥωμαῖόν τε καὶ παῖδα Μάγνου μάλιστα.

(2) 5.135: μέγα κλέος εἰ τὸν Μάγνου παῖδα περισῴζοις.

(3) 5.140: ⟨When Sextus was pursued by Furnius and Titius, he sought an interview with Furnius alone, though Furnius was the subordinate officer, and though Titius was

---

[15]Page 267.

under some obligation to him[16]): ἠξίωσεν ἐς λόγους ἐλθεῖν
Φουρνίῳ φίλῳ τε Μάγνου γεγενομένῳ.

(4) 5.142: ἐπὶ δὲ τῇ ὀργῇ καὶ ἠδόξει, Πομήιος ὤν, ἐπὶ
Τιτίῳ γενέσθαι, οὐκ ἐπιφανεῖ πάνυ ἀνδρί.

From these (and many similar) passages one gets the impression that something more than mere pride of race is involved. Sextus seems to have felt that his descent imposed a certain obligation upon him, and at the same time upon others, to render to the last of the Pompeys the recognition which was the family's proper due.

Another and better indication that *pietas* was Sextus's motive impulse is offered by the fact that he assumed the cognomen Pius.[17] Practically all his coins[18] show the word Pius, and the title can have been meant for no other purpose than to proclaim his motives to the world. That Sextus consciously made capital of his father's name and fame there can be no doubt. But it is my feeling that the underlying motive was sincere, as I have tried to indicate by the analogy of Marcus Brutus. There is, it seems to me, a splendid impracticality in the personality of Sextus with which such a feeling as I attribute to him fits admirably. Consider, for example, his challenge to Octavian at Naulochus,[19] his generous reception of the proscripts,[20] his exuberant celebration of the discomfiture of Salvidienus,[21] even his restraint in the matter of raiding the shores of Italy. In this latter connection Gardthausen,[22] somewhat reluctantly, it seems, makes this admission: "Aber Pompeius war nicht nur auf der einen Seite Seeräuberkönig, sondern auf der anderen auch römischer Bürger."

The tendency of the political and military power of the great Roman families to become hereditary must be taken into full

[16]See above, page 89. For a discussion of the events referred to in this passage see below, page 158.

[17]Compare Mras, 289: "Das Attribut *Pius* nahm Sextus an, um damit seine Pietät dem Andenken seines Vaters gegenüber ins helle Licht zu setzen." At the Battle of Munda the watchword of the Pompeians was εὐσέβεια (= *pietas*): see Appian 2.104.

[18]Babelon, 350–354, Numbers 16–27.

[19]See above, page 143. There I question Octavian's response to the challenge, and not the challenge itself.

[20]See pages 74–75. It is certainly a mistake to attribute Sextus's attitude toward the proscripts to strictly selfish motives.

[21]See above, page 78.   [22]1.221.

account in any appraisal of the career of Sextus. I cannot expatiate on this phase of Roman life in this place. E. von Nischer[23] has written a concise and lucid account of the military aspect of the "Hausmachtpolitik," and because of the clear light it throws on the circumstances governing the career of Sextus I reproduce portions of a paragraph:

Diese freie Stellung der Feldherren, die sich dessen bewusst waren, ohne und unter Umständen gegen die Staatsgewalt ihre eigene Politik mit militärischen Mitteln durchkämpfen zu müssen, zeitigte eine die Strategie natürlich vielfach beeinflussende Erscheinung, die, virtuell auf dem prokonsularischen Imperium beruhend, in freilich sehr übertragenem Sinne, aber durchaus zutreffend, als eine Art Hausmachtpolitik bezeichnet werden kann. Das Vorbild war die spanische Politik der Barkiden: der Feldherr schuf sich ausserhalb des Staatszentrums eine persönliche, territorial fundierte Machtsphäre und -stellung, die es ihm ermöglichte, selbständig grosse Politik zu treiben, unter Umstände dieselbe dem Staate aufzuzwingen, und die ihm zugleich auch die strategische Basis zur Durchführung seiner Pläne bot. Es ist freilich nur ein Zufall, dass der erste Römer dieses Stiles, Sertorius, räumlich an Hamilkar Barkas anknüpfte. Der nächste war Caesar, und wie alles, was dieser gewaltige Geist unternahm, in geschlossener Einheitlichkeit ersteht, so ist auch in seiner gallischen "Hausmacht" das politische Element von strategischen nicht zu trennen. . . . Noch vor seiner Vollendung wurde das caesarianische Gallien zum Vorbild für die Machtsphären, die nun seine Verbündeten und Rivalen Pompeius und Crassus in Spanien bezw. Syrien zu gründen sich anschickten. Ersterer hat seinen Plan durchgeführt—die Tatsache dass er gar nicht persönlich seine Provinzen verwaltet, sondern in der Hauptstadt sitzend sie durch seine Legaten verwalten liess, zeigt am krassesten den hausmachtartigen Character dieser Statthalterschaften—und Spanien hat ihm denn auch tatsächlich im Bürgerkriege als strategische Basis und militärische Kraftquelle die erwarteten Dienste geleistet; des Crassus Plan hat bei Carrhae seinen Schöpfer ins Grab gerissen.—Mit Caesar's Sieg und Alleinherrschaft waren natürlich alle andern "Hausmachten" ausgeschaltet; erst nach seinem Tode hat sich Sextus Pompeius, nicht unähnlich dem Sertorius, eine Neue in Sizilien gegründet, und sie leitet äusserlich über zu der nur graduell, nicht prinzipiell verschiedenen krassesten Form, der triumviralen Reichsteilung, in deren Rahmen ja der Seeräuberstaat des Pompeius eine Zeitlang noch Platz gefunden hat.

This transmission of power within the great families explains

---

[23] In Kromayer-Veith, 464–465.

and condones a great deal in the career of Sextus.[24]   It shows
us also why Sextus always managed to obtain a nucleus for a
military force, in Spain, in Sicily, and in Asia Minor.   In all
these places followers of the house of Pompey—adherents of
its "Hausmacht"—were to be found.

Considerations such as these must temper our estimate of
Sextus not only for the earlier part of his career, but also, and
especially, for the period between his escape to Lesbos and his
death.   In point of fact, his conduct after the Battle of Naulochus is the most illegitimate (I am tempted to say, the only
illegitimate) part of his career.   The defeat of 36 B. C. should
have convinced him that Octavian was now the legitimate ruler
of Rome, however shady the means he employed to attain his
power.   Sextus should have acknowledged himself persuaded,
by the argument of force if not by the force of argument; he
should have bided his time, and then have sued for restoration
to Rome.   Octavian's lenity to Lepidus, his desire to conciliate
republican feeling, his impending contest with Antony make it
reasonable to suppose that even Sextus might have received
amnesty; whatever else he was, he had not been one of the
conspirators of 44.   The fact that a Sextus Pompey was consul
in 35 would indicate, it seems to me, that Octavian was disposed
to show favor to one who bore the name.[25]   From the point of
view of his personality, however, we should be disappointed to
see Sextus cringe before Octavian, and the course he followed,
impractical or revolutionary as it may have been, is exactly
the course we should have expected him to take.

The plans which Sextus had formed, possibly only for the
eventuality of Antony's death, appeared so promising, or
perhaps had progressed so far, that he persisted in them even
after Antony returned safe from his disastrous expedition.   I
have indicated[26] that Sertorius may have been Sextus's model
for his conduct in Spain.   It is more than likely that, in the

---

[24]An extremely suggestive work for this phase of Roman history is the
book of Münzer; his closing chapter (409–428) gives a brief resumé of
the contents of his book.

[25]Dio (50.1.3) reports that, when Octavian reproached Antony for
having put Sextus to death, he declared that he himself would have willingly spared him.

[26]Page 54.

present instance, he took the exploit of Q. Labienus[27] as a model. After the Battle of Philippi Labienus had found himself unable to remain in territory controlled by Octavian, and had established a realm in Parthia, striking his own coins and displaying other external manifestations of independent rule. Sextus contemplated carving out a similar realm for himself in Asia Minor, with the assistance of a Parthian army.[28] He resumed the dress of a general and summoned his old comrades in arms.[29] He strengthened his fleet, and sent emissaries to the princes of Pontus and Thrace to bespeak their friendship in case he should need to march to Armenia. At the same time he sent ambassadors to the Parthians, offering his services for the war against Antony, and also to Antony, reminding him of past favors and requesting an honorable connection with his army.[30]

But Antony's agents intercepted the ambassadors to the Parthians. After Antony had heard the ambassadors that were sent to him, and had indicated a disposition to be friendly, he received the proof of Sextus's double dealing, and confronted the ambassadors with the letters which Sextus had sent to the Parthians. The ambassadors made what excuses they could, and promised on behalf of Sextus that he would remain loyal to Antony if Antony would indeed receive him. Antony allowed himself to be persuaded, and said he would be content with the steps he had already taken.[31] He had ordered Titius[32] to take a position near Mitylene with his fleet, and from that point to keep Sextus under surveillance. Titius was to contest vigorously any hostile move that Sextus might undertake, but was to treat him honorably if he should be disposed to be friendly.[33]

For a while nothing more is head of Titius. From Lesbos Sextus crossed to Asia Minor, in the early part of 35.[34] Fur-

---

[27]A good account of Labienus's career is given in Gardthausen, 1.225–228. Compare Münzer, in Pauly-Wissowa, 12.258–260 (1924). Dorn Seiffen wrongly gives his name as T. Atius Labienus.

[28]Appian 5.133.   [29]Dio 49.17.6.

[30]Appian 5.133.

[31]Appian 5.136.

[32]For Titius see Prosopographia, 3.328 (Number 196).

[33]Appian 5.134.

[34]Blok (57) is surely wrong in putting this event in 36.

nius,[35] the governor of the province, was at first disposed to be
friendly to him, but he could not help observing that Sextus
was recruiting an army and strengthening his navy. Being
himself but poorly supplied with forces to check Sextus, Furnius
called to his assistance Cn. Domitius Ahenobarbus, who had
an army in Bithynia, and Amyntas, King of Galatia. Sextus
reproached Furnius for regarding him as an enemy, saying that
he was in communication with Antony, and only awaiting his
reply:

While he was saying this he was meditating the project of
seizing Ahenobarbus, with the connivance of Curius, one of
Ahenobarbus' officers, intending to hold that general as a
valuable hostage to exchange for himself in case of need. The
treachery was discovered and Curius was convicted before the
Romans present and put to death. Pompeius put to death his
freedman Theodorus, the only person who was privy to the
plan, believing that he had divulged it.[36]

Sextus had committed himself openly, and his part now was
to act swiftly. He possessed himself of Lampsacus by treachery,
and by the offer of high rewards induced the numerous Italians
who had been settled there by Julius Caesar to join his forces.
Next he attacked Cyzicus by land and by sea, but was repulsed
by the garrison which Antony kept there for the purpose of
guarding his gladiators. He then retired to the Harbor of the
Achaeans in the Troas,[37] and collected provisions.[38]

Furnius followed Sextus, and encamped nearby, but Sextus
succeeded in driving him from his camp. Sextus's great need
was cavalry, and so, when he heard of a troop which Octavia
was sending to her husband Antony, he sent messengers with
large bribes to waylay and corrupt the troop in Macedonia.
Again his emissaries and the money they bore were apprehended.[39] But, in spite of all, his forces grew rapidly. The provincials whom Rome had impoverished and oppressed gladly
flocked to the great Roman who was fighting against Rome.
The capture and plunder of Nicaea and Nicomedia provided
Sextus with abundant supplies and money, and by enhancing
his reputation promoted his recruiting.

[35]I cannot discover why Risse (50) introduces Furnius by saying that he
was *Sexti inimicus*. Appian (5.140) says that he was a friend of Pompey
the Great. [36]Appian 5.137. [37]See Hirschfeld, in Pauly-Wissowa, 1.205.
[38]Appian 5.137.   [39]Appian 5.138.

Since Appian is our only authority for the final scene,[40] it will serve the interest of economy as well as clarity to reproduce his account:[41]

But Furnius, who was camping not far away from him, was reinforced, at the beginning of spring, first with seventy ships that had come from Sicily, which had been saved from those that Antony had lent to Octavian against Pompeius; for after the close of the war in Sicily Octavian had dismissed them. Then Titius arrived from Syria with 120 additional ships and a large army; and all these had landed at Proconnesus. So Pompeius became alarmed and burned his own ships and armed his oarsmen, believing that he could fight to better advantage with all of his forces combined on land. Cassius of Parma, Nasidius, Saturninus, Thermus, Antistius, and the other distinguished men of his party who were still with him as friends, and Fannius, who held the highest rank of all, and Pompeius' father-in-law, Libo, when they saw that he did not desist from war against superior forces even after Titius, to whom Antony had given entire charge, had arrived, despaired of him, and having made terms for themselves, went over to Antony.[42]

Pompeius, now deserted by his friends, withdrew to the interior of Bithynia, being reported as making his way to Armenia. One night as he marched out of his camp quietly, Furnius and Titius followed him, and Amyntas joined in the pursuit. After a hot chase they came up with him toward evening, and each encamped by himself around a certain hill without ditch or palisade, as it was late and they were tired. While they were in this state, Pompeius made a night attack with 300 light troops and killed many who were still asleep or springing out of bed. The rest took to disgraceful flight half dressed as they were. It is evident that if Pompeius had made this night attack with his entire army, or if he had followed up energetically the victory he did win, he would have overcome them completely. But, misled by some evil genius, he let slip these opportunities also, and he gained no other advantage from the affair than to penetrate farther into the interior of the country. His enemies, having formed a junction, followed him and cut him off from supplies, until he was in danger from want. Then he sought an interview with Furnius, who had been a friend of Pompey the Great, and who was of higher rank and of a more trustworthy character than the others.

[40] The brief paragraphs in Dio 49.18.1–5 do not disagree with Appian's account, but suffer badly from foreshortening.

[41] 5.139–140.

[42] That they remained with him up to this point is as fine a testimonium as one could wish for Sextus. For references for the various names see Gardthausen, 2.157–158.

The interview was fruitless. Furnius disclaimed authority to act, and to Titius Pompey refused to surrender.[43]

The opinion prevailed in the camp of Furnius that, for want of other resources, Pompeius would deliver himself up to Titius on the following day. When night came Pompeius left the customary fires burning, and the trumpets giving the usual signal at intervals through the night, while he quietly withdrew from the camp with a well-prepared band, who had not previously been advised whither they were to go. He intended to go to the sea-shore and burn Titius' fleet, and perhaps would have done so had not Scaurus deserted from him and communicated the fact of his departure and the road he had taken, although ignorant of his design. Amyntas, with 1,500 horse, pursued Pompeius, who had no cavalry. When Amyntas drew near, Pompeius' men passed over to him, some privately, others openly. Pompeius, being almost entirely deserted and afraid of his own men, surrendered himself to Amyntas without conditions, although he had scorned to surrender to Titius with conditions.[44]

Appian then gives a summary of Sextus's career[45] and proceeds to retail the various reports of his death:[46]

After such a career Pompeius was taken prisoner. Titius brought Pompeius' soldiers into Antony's service and put Pompeius himself to death at Miletus in the fortieth year of his age. This he did either on his own account, angry at some former insult, and ungrateful for the subsequent kindness, or in pursuance of Antony's order. Some say that Plancus, not Antony, gave this order. They think that Plancus, while governing Syria, was authorized by letters to sign Antony's name in cases of urgency and to use his seal. Some think that it was written by Plancus with Antony's knowledge, but that the latter was ashamed to write it on account of the name Pompeius, and because Cleopatra was favourable to him on account of Pompey the Great. Others think that Plancus, being cognizant of these facts, took it upon himself to give the order as a matter of precaution, lest Pompeius, with the co-operation of Cleopatra, should disturb the auspicious respect between Antony and Octavian.

Dio[47] has a different version:

Titus and Furnius pursued him, and overtaking him at Midaeum in Phrygia, surrounded him and captured him alive. When

---

[43]Appian 5.141–142. [44]Appian 5.142.
[45]5.143. [46]5.144.
[47]49.18.4–6.

Antony learned of this, he at once in anger sent word to them that Sextus should be put to death, but repenting again not long afterward, wrote that his life should be spared. . . . Now the bearer of the second letter arrived before the other; and Titius later received the letter ordering Sextus' death, and either believing that it was really the second or else knowing the truth but not caring to heed it, he followed the order of the arrival of the two, but not their intention. So Sextus was executed in the consulship of Lucius Cornificius and one Sextus Pompeius. Caesar held games in the Circus in honour of the event, and set up for Antony a chariot in front of the rostra and statues in the temple of Concord. . . .

Strabo says, wrongly, that Sextus was killed as well as captured at Midaion.[48] The other sources add nothing to our information.[49] The date of the death of Sextus is not mentioned, but it must have fallen toward the end of 35.[50]

Although, as we have seen in the passage just quoted from Dio, Octavian celebrated the death of Sextus with games, when the rupture with Antony came he reproached Antony with having killed Sextus.[51] Since Octavian was making it his business at the time to alienate Italian feeling from Antony and to render the people favorably disposed to actual warfare against his colleague, we may well believe that this sudden concern over the fate of Sextus was dictated by a desire to propitiate that section of the people which still cherished the memory of Sextus. That such people existed in Rome is clear from the plain statement of the historian most hostile to Sextus:[52]

Cui in tantum duravit hoc facinore ⟨the death of Sextus⟩ contractum odium, ut mox ludos in theatro Pompei faciens ⟨Titius⟩ execratione populi spectaculo quod praebebat pelleretur.[53]

[48]3.2.2.

[49]Zonaras 10.25; Livy, Periocha 131; Seneca, Consolatio ad Polybium 15.1; Eutropius 7.6.1; Orosius 6.19.3. Velleius (2.79.5) says he was killed *iussu M. Antonii*, but Antony was a more serious menace to the house of Caesar than Sextus had been. It was natural, therefore, for Velleius to lay the unpopular (see below) deed at his door.

[50]So Drumann (4.590) takes it.   [51]Dio 50.1.3.   [52]Velleius 2.79.6.

[53]Such an incident, it seems to me, is in itself sufficient to disprove the opinion of Merivale (3.205): "The last of the Pompeii died unhonored and unlamented. He had cut himself adrift from the parties of the senate and the forum, and the remnant of the father's faction disdained to flatter the memory of a degenerate son."

Sympathy for the fate of Sextus remained a tradition in Rome, for we cannot imagine Martial celebrating in his verse a person whose name would be anathema to any considerable section of the population of Rome:[54]

> Pompeios iuvenes Asia atque Europa, sed ipsum
>   terra tegit Libyae, si tamen ulla tegit.
> Quid mirum toto si spargitur orbe? Iacere
>   uno non poterat tanta ruina loco.

---

[54]5.74. L. Friedlaender, M. Valerii Martialis Epigrammaton Libri 1.425 (Leipzig, 1886), gives the following note: "Vgl. Seneca Epigr. 10–14. 64–66 (Baehrens Plm IV p. 59; p. 82). 10, 2 (Fortuna) Tam late sparsit funera, Magne, tua. 12, 5 divisa ruina est: Uno non potuit jacere loco. 13 Aut Asia aut Europa tegit aut Africa Magnos: Quanta domus toto quae jacet orbe, fuit! 14, 1 Quantus quam parvo vix tegeris tumulo. 66, 1 Diversis juvenes Asia atque Europa sepulcris Distinet; infida, Magne, jaces Libya."

X. APPRAISAL OF SEXTUS POMPEY: THE SOURCES

The normal closing for the study of a career is formed by a characterization and an appreciation of the subject of the study. In the present case such a summary is superfluous, inasmuch as I have taken the occasion, at each significant turn in the career of Sextus, to make whatever comments I thought necessary or desirable.[1] However, because conclusions in regard to the life of Sextus differing from my conclusions have been pronounced with great emphasis, I feel that it is advisable to say a word in reply to those who set forth such views.

Drumann,[2] Gardthausen,[3] and the others agree that Sextus possessed personal bravery in the highest degree, but insist that he was a poor commander. Dorn Seiffen[4] puts it eloquently:

Nulla tamen fuit Sexto bellica virtus et prudentia, nulla bellandi peritia et calliditas, nullum in hostibus adoriendis consilium, nulla victoriis utendi cura et sollertia. . . . Tumidus in rebus secundis, timidus in dubiis. . . .

To recall here the entire military career of Sextus is futile, but one remark may be in place. In view of the scale of the preparations which were made against him, and the resources in men and in money which his enemies possessed, it is no proof of bad generalship on the part of Pompey that he was defeated. Indeed, what we know of his generalship is quite favorable. His sins, according to his critics, were sins of omission—the several instances of his neglect of opportunities for damaging his enemies. But do we know enough of the inner resources and the organization of Sextus's forces to make such a charge just? May it not be suggested that Sextus *preferred* to gain his ends by blockade rather than by bringing a bloody war into Italy? Ascription of generous motives to any of the leaders of the Civil Wars is a dangerous proceeding; but let us not forget that the Elder Pompey—inexplicably, as the historians say—laid down his arms when he returned from the East with an irresistible army loyal to himself, and let us remember that, as we have seen, Sextus made a conscious

---

[1]See for example pages 51, 68, 149. [4]4.590–591.
[3]1.313.

161

attempt to follow in his father's footsteps. Sextus is derided
for letting wind and wave fight his battles. Was it only luck
that protected him from the elements and exposed his enemies
to them? For the culture and moral qualities of Sextus we
must not accept the testimony of Velleius. But Velleius was
himself a soldier, and his praise of Sextus's fighting qualities is
fair praise indeed, coming, as it does, from the enemy camp.
After calling Sextus *studiis rudis sermone barbarus*, Velleius[5]
goes on to say that he was *impetu strenuus, manu promptus,
cogitatu celer*.

I have suggested comparisons with other figures of Roman
history, whose careers may help us to view the career of Sextus
in a fairer light. Sertorius[6] had held Spain against Rome, and
Labienus[7] (who does not deserve to be mentioned with Sertorius) maintained a realm in Parthia. Octavian's motives in
claiming his heritage were no loftier than were the motives of
Sextus in claiming his.[8] By his attempt to possess himself of
Sicily when he was under no personal necessity to do so and
when his attempt constituted a grave offense against patriotism,
Lepidus[9] illustrates the moral level of the politics of the period
and makes it easy for us to condone Sextus. I should like to
add one other figure to show how little blameworthy Sextus
was for defying the legitimized power of Rome. Marcus Brutus
was the idealist among the conspirators. Of him, if of none of
the others, might it be said that he was moved by a genuine
love for republican institutions. Yet Brutus presumed to
strike his own coinage without constitutional authority, and
ornamented his coins with his own likeness.[10]

Sextus being no worse, if no better, than his contemporaries,
how did it come about that historians have conspired, as it
were, to blacken his name? The answer is that our histories of
the period in which Sextus figured are derived from a source or
sources hostile to Sextus. The science of 'Quellenforschung'
has produced some results that are reasonably certain. This
science has made it clear that for the period of the Civil Wars

---

[5]2.73.1.   [6]Page 54.
[7]Page 155.   [8]Page 48.
[9]See page 148.
[10]Dio 47.25.3; Appian 4.75. The coins are figured in Babelon, 2.117–119
(Numbers 43, 45, 52). Compare also Drumann, 4.37.

Dio drew largely on Livy.[11] Eduard Meyer[12] grants that Dio's
use of Livy is beyond doubt. Livy, it is well known, was a
great admirer of Augustus, and doubtless used Augustus's
memoirs as a source.[13] What Livy thought of Sextus becomes
clear from a careful reading of Periocha 128:

Cum Sex. Pompeius rursus latrociniis mare infestum redderet
nec pacem, quam acceperat, praestaret, Caesar necessario
adversus eum bello suscepto duobus navalibus proeliis cum
dubio eventu pugnavit.[14]

Lucan[15] has some disparaging lines about Sextus:

> Turbae sed mixtus inerti
> Sextus erat, Magno proles indigna parente,
> cui mox Scyllaeis exul grassatus in undis
> polluit aequoreos Siculus pirata triumphos.

It is the thesis of René Pichon[16] that Lucan's source was
Livy,[17] and Pichon cites these lines as an example of Livian
influence.[18] It may occasion some surprise that Livy, whose
Pompeian sympathies are well known, should so scorn the son
of Pompey. Pichon offers a very satisfactory answer:[19]

Quant à prétendre que Tite-Live était trop pompéien pour
parler en termes si durs de Sextus Pompée, c'est, en vérité,
jouer sur les mots. Le "pompéianisme" de Tite-Live,—qui ne
l'empêchait pas d'être l'ami d'Auguste,—ne l'obligeait pas à
être le panégyriste de Sextus. On pouvait admirer la gloire du
père sans fermer les yeux sur les défaut du fils. Il semble bien

---

[11]Cary, 1.xv; E. Schwartz, in Pauly-Wissowa, 3.1709–1710. For a
bibliography of studies on the historicity and sources of Dio see the Praefatio in the splendid edition of U. P. Boissevain, 1.CI (Berlin, 1895). It
might be remarked here that the fourth and final volume of this edition
(1926) is an Index Historicus, which is of great help to the student.

[12]Page 611: "Dass Dio den Livius hier wie sonst im weitem Umfang,
aber keineswegs als einzige Quelle, benutzt hat, ist zweifellos."

[13]Schwartz, Vertheilung, 208: "Dass Livius Augustus Memoiren benutzt
hat steht fest." For the character of these Memoirs see the work of
Blumenthal. Miss Henrica Malcovati's striking comment on their bias
is quoted in Note 172, page 99 above.

[14]This Periocha is discussed above, page 104.

[15]6.419–422.

[16]Les Sources de Lucain (Paris, 1912).

[17]Pichon's theory is accepted by Postgate VIII, Introduction, xi–xii:
"Of these sources the chief or perhaps the sole one was the lost *Civil War* of
Livy." See the remarks of Professor Gertrude M. Hirst in The Classical
Weekly 13 (1919), 69.

[18]Page 96.   [19]Ibidem.

que ç'ait été la façon de penser la plus habituelle. J'en trouve
un vestige dans la phrase où Florus oppose l'un à l'autre les
deux Pompées, l'un destructeur des pirates de Cilicie, et l'autre
chef de nouveaux pirates ⟨6.8.2⟩. Cette antithèse est à retentir:
elle ressemble au vers de Lucain sur "ce pirate de Sicile qui
souille les triomphes paternels;" et, comme Florus . . . il est fort
probable que nous avons là un souvenir de Tite-Live. Ce n'est
donc pas l'opinion de Lucain sur Sextus.

Eduard Meyer also speaks of Livy's independent attitude in
his praise of Pompey, despite his great admiration for Augustus.[20]
But we can easily understand that Livy's feeling for the Elder
Pompey would not embrace Sextus, because Sextus had seriously threatened Augustus's regeneration of Rome, and it was
his regeneration of Rome that endeared Augustus to Livy.[21]

Of Appian too it is clear that his sympathies are thoroughly
Caesarian.[22] For Appian's treatment of the period from the
so-called First Triumvirate to the death of Sextus (2.8–5.144)
Schwartz declares (on what have been universally applauded
as sufficient grounds) that the principal source is Livy or Asinius
Pollio,[23] who would naturally be more Catholic than the Pope
and more Royalist than the King.

For Appian and Plutarch and Dio and Livy Eduard Meyer,
the dean of modern writers on ancient history, posits a single
great historical work as a source:[24]

Somit müssen wir als Grundlage für die gesamte Ueberlieferung
über diese Zeit ein grosses, alle Vorgänge bis ins einzelnste
verfolgendes Geschichtswerk betrachten, auf dem direkt oder
indirekt alle späteren Bearbeitungen fussen. Im Grunde ist
die Aufgabe der modernen Geschichtsforschung nichts anderes,
als dies Werk zu rekonstruieren und durch Einfügung des
ciceronischen Materials zu kontrollieren und gelegentlich zu
ergänzen; in der Auffassung und Beurteilung der so ermittelten
Tatsachen und der Persönlichkeiten mag man dann seine eignen
Wege gehn. Wer der Verfasser gewesen ist, wird sich freilich

---

[20]Pages 612–613. These remarks are contained in an excursus, Beilage
IV —Die Quellen.

[21]The thesis of Meyer's entire book is that Augustus was the natural
successor not of Julius Caesar but of Pompey.

[22]E. Schwartz, in Pauly-Wissowa, 2.226: "Ferner ist der Standpunkt
entschieden Caesarianisch."

[23]The monograph of P. Bailleu, Quo Modo Appianus in Bellorum Civi-
lium Libris II–IV Usus Sit Asinii Pollionis Historiis (Göttingen, 1874), is a
plausible attempt to prove Appian's dependence on Pollio.

[24]Meyer, 613.

kaum ermitteln lassen; dafür ist eben unsere Kunde von der historischen Literatur viel zu dürftig, Fragmente fehlen für all die zahllosen Historiker nach Posidonius fast vollständig. Natürlich wird sich einem jeden zunächst der grosse Name des Asinius Pollio aufdrängen.

Meyer goes on to say that Asinius Pollio is probably not the great source he posits. Kornemann[25] suggests that Cremutius Cordus was the immediate source for Appian's Civil Wars, but Cichorius[26] is sure that he could not have been: "Auf keinen Fall aber hat das Buch ⟨des Cremutius Cordus⟩ auf die spätere Tradition irgendwelchen tiefen Einfluss geübt." But the personality of the author of the great history does not matter. If such a single person or even a group of persons existed, minded as were Pollio and Livy and Velleius, the fact would explain the *vox omnis antiquitatis* united to condemn Sextus. And yet not quite *omnis antiquitas*, for it must always be remembered that Cicero offers a first class control for the later, professed historians, and, though it may be argued that Cicero did not live to know the worst about Sextus, yet his attitude, as Dorn Seiffen[27] well expressed it, is that of a man who "disseruit de eo tanquam de spectato et sibi caro iuvene."

Further, it must not be forgotten that both Dio and Appian were imperial office-holders. By the second century the Empire was so well established and so prosperous that any other order of things must have seemed preposterous to these two Easterners. Anyone who had defied the existing order as personified in the divine Augustus must have been a monster. Consider, for example, Dio's "systematisch durchgeführte Glorificierung Caesars und Herabsetzung des Antonius,"[28] which is to be ascribed to similar reasons. Appian, it is true, treats Antony more gently, but the Alexandrian may have considered Antony sufficiently important or praiseworthy on other grounds to accept a divergent tradition concerning him. But Sextus's resistance was neither important nor persistent enough to persuade the third-hand and fourth-hand authors to exert themselves in his behalf.

---

[25]Die Unmittelbare Vorlage von Appians Emphyllia, in Klio 17 (1921), 33–43.

[26]Pauly-Wissowa, 4.1703–1704.   [27]Page 3.

[28]Schwartz, Vertheilung, 207.

I have mentioned the disparaging lines of Lucan. It is a commonplace that singers have more influence on the thought of a people than do those who make their laws, and a slighting half-line in the canonical writings of the court poets Vergil and Horace would be enormously effective in prejudicing the opinion of all posterity against Sextus. G. Romeo[29] has with much ingenuity contrived to gather quite a list of passages in Horace, Vergil, and Ovid which refer in some way to Sextus and the Sicilian War. I shall reproduce here three passages from Horace,[30] which have a bearing on my thesis:

(1) Carm. 3.16.15–16:

> munera navium
> saevos illaqueant duces.[31]

(2) Epod. 4.17–20:

> Quid attinet tot ora navium gravi
> rostrata duci pondere
> contra latrones atque servilem manum
> hoc, hoc tribuno militum?[32]

(3) Epod. 9.7–10:

> ut nuper, actus cum freto Neptunius
> dux fugit ustis navibus,
> minatus Urbi vincla, quae detraxerat
> servis amicus perfidis.

Note the expressions *saevos duces, latrones, servilem manum, minatus Urbi vincla, servis amicus perfidis*—hard words all; yet who would dare gainsay them, uttered by Rome's most beloved poet, and endorsed by Rome's greatest Emperor?

---

[29]Ricerche e Commento delle Fonti della Guerra Sicula in Orazio, Vergilio, Ovidio, in Raccolta, 1.17–64.

[30]The best passage in Vergil (for the present purpose) is the one in the so-called Messianic Eclogue (4.31–36), which I have discussed, page 101. None of the passages cited from Ovid suits my requirements. But Ovid wrote after the passions of the Sicilian War were allayed, and in any case was no great favorite with Augustus.

[31]"Horace is generally supposed to be taking an instance from contemporary history, and to aim at Menas or Menodorus, the freedman of Sextus Pompeius and chief captain of his fleet...": so Wickham, in his Introduction to the poem.

[32]This passage I have discussed on page 106.

LIST OF ABBREVIATIONS

Amend—Andreas Amend, Über die Bedeutung von **MEIPA-KION** und **ANTIΠAIΣ** (Dissertation, Dillingen, 1893).

Axt—Otto Axt, Zur Topographie von Rhegion und Messana (Grimma, 1887).

Babelon—E. Babelon, Description Historique et Chronologique des Monnaies de la Republique Romaine. 2 volumes (Paris, 1885-1886).

Blok—P. J. Blok, Sextus Pompeius Magnus Gnaei Filius (Dissertation, Lugduni Batavorum, 1879).

Blumenthal—Fritz Blumenthal, Die Autobiographie des Augustus, Wiener Studien 35 (1913), 113-130, 267-288; 36 (1914), 84-103.

Blümner—H. Blümner, Römische Privataltertümer (Munich, 1911).

Bouchier—E. S. Bouchier, Sardinia in Ancient Times (Oxford, 1917).

Brueggemann—F. Brueggemann, De Marci Aemilii Lepidi Vita et Rebus Gestis (Dissertation, Monasterii Guestfalorum, 1887).

Cary—Earnest Cary, Dio's Roman History (on the basis of the version of Herbert Baldwin Foster). The Loeb Classical Library. 9 volumes (London and New York, 1914-1927).

Cichorius—Conrad Cichorius, Römische Studien (Leipzig, 1922).

Dittenberger—W. Dittenberger, Sylloge Inscriptionum Graecarum³. 4 volumes (Leipzig, 1915-1923).

Domaszewski—Alfred von Domaszewski, Geschichte der Römischen Kaiser³. Volume one (Leipzig, 1922).

Dorn Seiffen—I. Dorn Seiffen, De Sex. Pompeio Magno Cn. Magni F. (Dissertation, Traiecti ad Rhenum, 1846).

Drumann—W. Drumann, Geschichte Roms in seinem Übergange von der Republikanischen zur Monarchischen Verfassung, Zweite Auflage, Herausgegeben von P. Groebe. 5 volumes to date (Leipzig, 1899-1919).

Duff—J. Wight Duff, A Literary History of Rome in the Silver Age, from Tiberius to Hadrian (London, 1927).

Duff, Golden Age—J. Wight Duff, A Literary History of Rome from the Origins to the Close of the Golden Age (London, 1910).

Ferrero—G. Ferrero, The Greatness and Decline of Rome. Translated by A. H. Zimmern and H. J. Chaytor. 5 volumes (New York, 1909).

Fitzler-Seeck—K. Fitzler and O. Seeck, Article *Iulius Augustus* in Pauly-Wissowa, 10.275–381 (1917).

Fowler—W. Warde Fowler, Social Life at Rome in the Age of Cicero (New York, 1909).

Frank—Tenney Frank, Roman Imperialism (New York, 1914).

Gardthausen—V. Gardthausen, Augustus und Seine Zeit. 2 volumes, in six parts (Leipzig, 1891–1904).

Groebe, Quaestiones—P. Groebe, De Legibus et Senatus Consultis Anni 710 Quaestiones Chronologicae (Dissertation, Leipzig, 1893).

Gwynn—A. Gwynn, Roman Education from Cicero to Quintilian (Oxford, 1926).

Heitland—W. E. Heitland, The Roman Republic. 3 volumes (Cambridge, 1923).

Hill—G. F. Hill, Historical Roman Coins (London, 1909).

Hitze—Aemilius Hitze, De Sexto Pompeio (Dissertation, Vratislaviae, 1883).

Holm—Ad. Holm, Geschichte Siciliens in Alterthum. 3 volumes (Leipzig, 1870–1898).

Holmes—T. Rice Holmes, The Roman Republic and the Founder of the Empire. 3 volumes (Oxford, 1923).

Holmes, Architect—T. Rice Holmes, The Architect of the Roman Empire (Oxford, 1928).

Klein—J. Klein, Die Verwaltungsbeamten von Sicilien und Sardinien (Bonn, 1878).

Kloevekorn—H. Kloevekorn, De Proscriptionibus A. A. Chr. 43 a M. Antonio, M. Aemilio Lepido, C. Iulio Octaviano Triumviris Factis (Dissertation, Regimonti, 1891).

Klotz—Alfred Klotz, Kommentar zum Bellum Hispaniense (Leipzig, 1927).

Kromayer, Begründung—J. Kromayer, Die Rechtliche Begründung des Principats (Dissertation, Marburg, 1888).

Kromayer, Entwicklung—J. Kromayer, Die Entwicklung der Römischen Flotte von Seeräuberkriege bis zur Schlacht von Actium, Philologus 56 (1897), 426–491.

Kromayer, Kleine Forschungen—J. Kromayer, Kleine Forschungen zur Geschichte des Zweiten Triumvirats, I, Hermes 29 (1894), 556–563.

Kromayer-Veith—J. Kromayer and G. Veith, Heerwesen und Kriegsführung der Römer (Munich, 1928).

Lehmann-Hartleben—Karl Lehmann-Hartleben, Die Antiken Hafenanlagen des Mittelmeeres (Leipzig, 1923).

Lübker—F. Lübker, Reallexikon des Klassischen Altertums[8] (Leipzig, 1914).

Marsh—Frank Burr Marsh, The Founding of the Roman Empire[2] (Oxford, 1927).

Merivale—C. Merivale, A History of the Romans under the Empire. 7 volumes (New York, 1873).

Meyer—Eduard Meyer, Caesars Monarchie und das Principat des Pompeius[2] (Stuttgart and Berlin, 1919). (A third edition of this work appeared in 1922).

Mommsen, History—Theodor Mommsen, The History of Rome. Translated by W. P. Dickson, and Reprinted in Everyman's Library. 4 volumes (London, 1911).

Mommsen, Staatsrecht—Theodor Mommsen, Römisches Staatsrecht[3] (Leipzig, 1887).

Mras—K. Mras, Der Magnus-Titel des Sex. Pompeius und der Imperator-Titel des Augustus, Wiener Studien 25 (1903), 288–292.

Münzer—Friedrich Münzer, Römische Adelsparteien und Adelsfamilien (Stuttgart, 1920).

Niebuhr, Lectures—B. G. Niebuhr, Lectures on the History of Rome. Translated by L. Schmitz. 3 volumes (London, 1849).

Niebuhr, Römische Geschichte—B. G. Niebuhr, Römische Geschichte. 3 volumes (Berlin, 1873).

Niese—B. Niese, Grundriss der Römischen Geschichte, Fünfte Auflage...von E. Hohl (Munich, 1923).

Nissen—H. Nissen, Italische Landeskunde. 2 volumes (Berlin, 1883–1902).

Ormerod—H. A. Ormerod, Piracy in the Ancient World (Liverpool and London, 1924).

Parker—H. M. D. Parker, The Roman Legions (Oxford, 1928).

Pichon—René Pichon, Les Sources de Lucain (Paris, 1912).

Prosopographia—Prosopographia Imperii Romani, Saec. I. II. III. 3 volumes (Berlin, 1898).

Raccolta—V. Casagrandi (ed.), Raccolta di Studi di Storia Antica. 2 volumes (Catania, 1893–1896).

Risse—Casparus Risse, De Gestis Sexti Pompei (Dissertation, Monasterii Guestfalorum, 1882).

Rosenberg—A. Rosenberg, Einleitung und Quellenkunde zur Römischen Geschichte (Berlin, 1921).

Rostovtzeff—M. Rostovtzeff, Social and Economic History of the Roman Empire (Oxford, 1926).

Sandys—J. E. Sandys, A History of Classical Scholarship. 3 volumes: 1³, (Cambridge, 1921).

Schanz-Hosius—M. Schanz and C. Hosius, Geschichte der Römischen Literatur 1⁴ (Munich, 1927).

Schulten—Adolf Schulten, Sertorius (Leipzig, 1926).

Schwartz, Vertheilung—Ed. Schwartz, Die Vertheilung der Roemischen Provinzen nach Caesars Tod, Hermes 33 (1898), 185–244.

Shipley—F. W. Shipley, Velleius Paterculus and Res Gestae Divi Augusti. The Loeb Classical Library (London and New York, 1924).

Shuckburgh—E. S. Shuckburgh, C. Suetoni Tranquilli Divus Augustus (Cambridge, 1896).

Stein—A. Stein, Der Römische Ritterstand (Munich, 1927).

Tyrrell and Purser—R. Y. Tyrrell and L. C. Purser, The Correspondence of M. Tullius Cicero. 6 volumes and Index: volumes 1–5 in second edition (Dublin and London, 1885–1915).

Veith, Caesar—G. Veith, Caesar (Leipzig, 1912).

Veith, Geschichte—G. Veith, Geschichte der Feldzüge C. Julius Caesars (Vienna, 1906).

Viereck—P. Viereck, Appiani Historia Romana ex Recensione Ludovici Mendelssohnii (Leipzig, 1905).

Wickham—E. C. Wickham, The Works of Horace. 2 volumes: 1³ (Oxford, 1896).

White—Horace White, Appian's Roman History. The Loeb Classical Library. 4 volumes (London and New York, 1912–1913).

INDEX

NOTE: Page references are to the text or to the notes on the pages cited, indifferently; "Caesar" always denotes Julius Caesar, and "Pompey" denotes Pompey the Great

Abalas, harbor, refuge of Salvidienus, 77, of Octavian, 136
Abalas, Semitic form of *Balarus*, 136
Acron, Interpretation by, of Horace, Carm. 1.14, 78
Actium, Battle of, 146
Admirals of Sextus, character of, 70; eastern origin of, 83
Adriatic, in 48, 31; shipbuilding in, because Sextus occupies the West, 76
Adulescens, meaning of, 6, 8
Advice, handicap to Sextus, 95; explains Sextus's 'cruelty,' 79
Aenaria, island off Campanian coast, 94
Aeolic Islands, inhabitants of, favor Sextus and are transplanted by Octavian to Naples, 115; as scene of engagements, 123–148, *passim*
Africa, refuge of Republicans after Pharsalus, 38; penetrated by Sextus, 89
Agrippa, as praetor, 86; competence of, 118, 127; at Battle of Mylae, 130–132, at Battle of Naulochus, 142–145; as inventor of devices for naval warfare, 120, 131, 145; in storm, July 36, 125
Ahenobarbus, Domitius, in command, of Corfinium, 28, of republican fleet, 66, 80, of army, in Bithynia in 35, 156; helps to cause scarcity of grain in Rome, 84; shares in Peace of Misenum, 99
Aiello, A., cited, 72, 123, 133, 139
Alcaeus, memories of, in Lesbos, 34
Alcantara, scene of Cornificius's retreat, 139
Alexandria, death of Pompey near, 37
Amend, Andreas, quoted, 7
Amphipolis, station in Pompey's flight, 37
Amyntas, King of Galatia, assists in final campaign against Sextus, 156–157
Anthology, Greek, cited, 116
Antioch, refuses shelter to Pompey in flight, 37
Antistius, loyal to Sextus until the end, 157
Antithesis, in Appian, 7
Antony, conduct of, after Ides, 56–58; relations of, with Sextus, in 44, 62–66; forms Triumvirate with Octavian and Lepidus, 67; reaches understanding with Sextus, 85; cooperates with Sextus, 88; betrays Sextus in Peace of Brundisium, 89; loyalty of veterans to, 89; refuses to surrender the Peloponnese to Sextus, 102; coins of, at Olbia, may point to relations with Sextus, 106; refuses to cooperate with Octavian, 107–108; again asked for help by Octavian, 117; has misunderstanding with Octavian, but lends him 120 ships, 120–121; goal of Sextus's flight after Naulochus, 150; deceived by Sextus, 155; agents of, kill Sextus, 157; reproached by Octavian for death of Sextus, 159; at Battle of Actium, 146. See also Fulvia, Julia, Parthians
Apollophanes, lieutenant of Sextus, 83; on mission to Lepidus, 116; in Battle of Mylae, 130; pursues Octavian, 137
Aponius, Quintus, insurgent leader in Spain, 45
Appian, cited, *passim;* in error, 42, 97; criticism of, 7, 114, 142, 164
Apsus, scene of Caesar's camp in 48, 33
Apuleius, cited, for Roman education, 13, for light on Sicilian languages, 142
Arabio, son of Masinissa, supports Sextus in Spain, 54
Arae Perusinae, illustrate Octavian's cruelty, 79
Archegetes, to define locality near Tauromenium, 133
Aristodemus, teacher of Sextus, 13, 16
Armament, character of Pompey's, at Pharsalus, 33, of Gnaeus's, in Spain, 43, 45; of Lepidus in March 44, 56; size of, in 40, 86; at Rhegium in 38, 109; Octavian's, at Tauromenium, 133; total of Octavian's, in Sicily, 140; Lepidus's, in Sicily, 124, 140; Plinius's, at Messana, 148. See also Fleets
Armenia, goal of Pompey in 35, 155, 157
Armies, motives of, in the later Republic, 1
Arruntius, L., leaves Sextus for Rome after the Peace of Misenum, 99
Artemisium, taken by Octavian in 36, 141

171

Ascurum, in Mauretania, assaulted by Gnaeus, 45

Ashby, T., cited, 20

Asia Minor, Labienus in, 155; Sextus in, 155–159

Assassination of Caesar, events following, 56–58; Sextus not a participant in, 67, a fact which might have procured him pardon, 154

Assassins of Caesar, subject to Lex Pedia, 66; excluded from amnesty at Misenum, 97

Aternum, occupied by Caesar, 27

Athens, Pompey a student in, 15; Sextus sends Julia to meet Antony at, 85

Atticus, daughter of, taught by Caecilius Epirota, 16

Augurship, Sextus suggested for, by Cicero, 65; alluded to, by *lituus* on coins 79; of Sextus, as a condition in the Peace of Misenum, 97; involved in error of Appian, 97; insisted upon, in Sextus's inscription at Lilybaeum, 100

Augustus: see Octavian

Aürelian: see Pseudo-Victor

Axt, Otto, equates Abalas and Balarus, 77, 136; explains Palaestini, 142

Babelon, E., cited, for coins of Sextus, 58, 69, 78, 140, 152; for coins of Brutus, 162

Baedeker, cited for Bagnara, 77

Baetica, rises against Caesar, 45; garrisoned by Caesar, 53

Bagnara: see Balarus

Bailleu, P., cited for Appian's use of Pollio, 164

Balarus, Salvidienus runs into, 77

Balarus, equated with *Abalas*, 136

Balearic Islands, occupied by Gnaeus, 45

Barea, in Spain, captured by Sextus, 55, 58

Bate, H. N., translation of Oracula Sibyllina by, cited, 116

Battles, descriptions of: Cumae, 110, Scyllaeum, 112, Mylae, 131–132, Naulochus, 144; stereotyped character of descriptions of, 144

Bekker, cited for Onobalas River, 133

Bellum Africanum, cited, 6, 40–44

Bellum Hispaniense, cited, 6, 42–52, *passim;* criticism of, 49

Bernoulli, cited, 42

Berrhoea, Pompey's headquarters in 48, 31, 32

Bias, of ancient authorities, against Sextus, 71, 104, 163–166

Bithynia, scene of Sextus's last stand, 156, 157

Bithynicus, A. Pompeius, governor of Sicily, 72; shares rule of Sicily with Sextus, 73; murder of, by Sextus, 79

Blok, P. J., cited, 10, 38, 86; quoted, 71; criticized, 78, 81, 106, 107, 134, 155

Blumenthal, Fritz, cited, 79, 88, 99, 163

Blümner, H., cited, 13, 14, 19

Boissevain, U. P., cited, 163

Bossier, G., cited 41

Bouchier, E. S., cited, 87, 106

Brueggemann, Felix, cited, 62, 124, 125, 143, 148, 149

Brundisium, point of departure for campaign that ended at Pharsalus, 26, 28, 29; Antony excluded from, 88; Antony fails to await Octavian at, 108, but returns to, later, 120; in Horace, Sermones 1.5, 117

Brundisium, Peace of, 89; Sextus excluded from, 89

Bruttium, attacked by Sextus, 76, 88

Brutus, Marcus, motives of, in assassination of Caesar, illustrate psychology of Sextus, 151; unconstitutional conduct of, in the East, justifies the career of Sextus, 162

Brutus, Marcus, father of the murderer of Caesar, 4

Brutus and Cassius in the East, 75

Butler and Cary, criticized, 42

Caecilius Epirota, *grammaticus*, 16

Caesar, Julius, position of, in history of period covered by this book, 1; at Luca, 14, 21; crosses Rubicon, 21; in Epirus, 31; at Dyrrachium, 33; at Pharsalus, 37; revolution against, in Spain, 42; at Thapsus, 43; at Munda, 50–51; ignores Sextus in Spain, 53; assassination of, 56; effect of assassination of, on Sextus, 55, 58; works of, at Portus Julius, 119; settles Italians at Lampsacus, 156; De Bello Civili of, cited, 22–37 *passim*, 145

Calabria, Greek element in, 77

Calpurnia, delivers Caesar's papers to Antony, 56

Calvisius Sabinus, lieutenant of Octavian, 108; commander in campaign of 38, 105, 108–112; dismissed, 122

Campania, ravaged by Menecrates, 107

Canusium, on route of Pompey, 28

Capo delle Colonne, station in flight of Sextus, 150

Capua, Pompey at, in 49, 27

Caralis, capital of Sardinia, 88
Caria: see Nysa
Carinae, at Rome, residence of Pompey on, 20
Carinae, pun of Sextus on, 98
Carisius, lieutenant of Octavian in 36, 135
Carrinas, C., lieutenant of Caesar in Spain, 54; of Octavian in 36, 136
Carteia, in possession of Gnaeus, 51, of Caesar, 53, of Sextus, 55
Cary, E., cited on authority of Dio, 163
Casagrandi, cited, 72, 100, 129, 133, 140
Cassius, Q., Caesarian governor of Spain, 42, 45
Cassius of Parma, loyal to Sextus until the end, 157
Castrum Truentinum, Pompey at, 27
Cato, leader of the Republican forces, 38–43; suicide of, 43; allusion to integrity of, 48
Cavalry, use of, to repel raids of Sextus, 83; Octavia sends, to Antony, 156
Cephallenia, scene of Sextus's farewell to his associates, 150
Chios, station on flight of Pompey, 37
Christ, W. v., cited, 16
Chronology, of birth of Sextus, 3–9; of Sextus's movements in 48, 25–36; of offer of restitution tendered to Sextus, 62–64; of Sextus's coins, 78; of the year 40, 84; of the understanding between Antony and Sextus, 85; of Sextus's raids on Southern Italy, 86; of the meeting between Octavian and Lepidus, 141; of the Battle of Naulochus, 145–146
Cicero, pupil of Gnipho, 16; position of, after Ides, 59–60; 'restores' Republic, 64–65; proposes decree to honor Sextus, 65, and to create him augur, 65; attitude of, toward Sextus, 82, 165; works of, cited, 6–67 *passim*, 72, 73, 82, 97; criticism of, 18; value of correspondence of, for the history of 44, 59
Cicero, son of the great orator, joins Sextus, 80
Cichorius, C., cited, 34, 74, 165
Circus, games in, for death of Sextus, 159. See Ludi
Classen, on Thucydides, cited, 144
Claudius, Emperor, devotion of, to freedmen, 16
Cleopatra, in company of Antony, 85; at Battle of Actium, 146; possible ally of Sextus, 158
Cobet, cited, 96
Cohen, H., cited 58

Coins of Brutus, 152
Coins, hoards of, from Italy in the year 41, 84, from Aleria in Corsica, 106, from Olbia in Sardinia, 106
Coins of Sextus, classes of, 58; legends on, 66; figuring oak crown, 69, figuring Neptune, 78; chronology of, 140
Colson, F. H., cited, 13
Commentaries of Octavian, influence of, on authorities, 99, 163
Comparison of Sextus and Octavian, as successors to Pompey and Caesar, 2; as to motives for waging war, 61; as to use of freedmen, 81; as to relations to Menas, 106; as to claim of divine descent, 114; as to personal supervision of operations, 124; as to personal courage, 147
Comparison, of Sextus and Lepidus, 82, 149; of Sextus and Brutus; see Brutus
Comparison of Sextus and the Triumvirs, 82
Comparison of Pompey and Antony, 37
Comparison of Scipio and Cato to Brutus and Cassius, 40
Conjectures: see Emendations
Compensation, for property of Sextus, 63, 97
Confiscations, as cause for unrest, 86
Consentia, attacked by Sextus, 88
Conway, R. S., cited, 101
Corcyra, Republican rallying place after Pharsalus, 38
Corduba, Sextus in charge of (under Gnaeus) 43, 50; taken by Caesar, 52
Cordus, Cremutius, possible source for ancient authorities, 165
Corfinium, held by Ahenobarbus, but taken by Caesar, 28
Cornelia, step-mother of Sextus, 8; education of, 15; seeks safety with Sextus in Lesbos, 22–24, because of literary and other associations of Mitylene, 34; witnesses death of Pompey, 37; pardoned by Caesar, 44
Cornificius, L., lieutenant of Octavian in campaign of 38, 109–112; in campaign of 36, 135–137; retreat of, from Tauromenium, 138–139
Cornificius, Q., senatorial governor of Africa, supports Sextus, 74
Corpus Inscriptionum Latinarum, cited, 139, 145–146
Corsica, in possession of Sextus, 89, 96, 105
Cossyra (Kossura), fortified by Sextus, 124
Crassus, Triumvir, 14, 21

Cumae, Battle of, 109–110, 112. See 'Hen's Forest'

Curius, connives with Sextus to seize Ahenobarbus, 156

Cyprus, station of Pompey in flight from Pharsalus, 37; of Sextus in flight from Egypt, 38

Cyrene, station of Republicans (including Sextus) between Corcyra and Africa, 38

Cyzicus, attacked by Sextus, 156

Decumae, of Sicily, withheld, 103

Deiotarus, refuses to receive Pompey, 44

Demochares, lieutenant of Sextus 83; commander in campaign of 38, 110–112; part of, in campaign of 36, 130; pursues Octavian, 137

Demochares, as equivalence of name to Papias, and explanation of that fact, 128

Demostrations against Octavian, 91, 126, 138. See Disorders, Popular feeling

Descriptions of battles: see Battles

Dictatorship, 'abolition' of, 62

Didius, naval lieutenant of Caesar in Spain, 45; destroys Gnaeus's fleet, 51

Dio, cited, *passim;* at fault, 52, 92, 94, 95, 98, 132, 135, 143, 157; criticism of, 114, 144, 150, 163, 165

Disorders at Rome, contribute to Sextus's success, 83; arise because Sextus was excluded from Treaty of Brundisium, 90; force Octavian to the Peace of Misenum, 92. See Popular feeling

Dittenberger, W., cited, 15, 26

Doijer, D., cited, 25

Dolabella, buys Pompey's property, 46

Domaszewski, A. v., cited, 58, 98, 111, 144, 145

Domitius: see Ahenobarbus

Dorn Seiffen, I., cited, 9, 10, 19, 25, 33, 63, 75, 79, 86, 95, 105, 108, 125, 126, 130, 132, 165; criticized, 26, 144, 155, 161

Drakenborch, edition of Livy by, contains Freinshemius, 58

Drumann, cited, *passim;* criticized, 18, 58, 136, 144, 148

Duff, A. M., cited, 106

Duff, J. W., cited, 17, 23, 103

Dyrrachium, 22–32, *passim;* Battle of, 32

Education, of Sextus, 10–20; of Pompey, 15; of Cornelia, 15

Egypt, scene of Pompey's death, 37

Emendations and corrections: Epirus, 71; Laeetani, 52; *ex continenti*, 71; Hirrus, 73; Nasidienus, 75; augur, 97; Demochares = Papias, 128; *inter = apud*, 131; Carisius, 135: Paliurus, 39; Scribonia, 96; Plinius, 100; light-armed, 105; Hiera, 132

Epicadus, freedman of Sulla, *grammaticus*, 16

Epirus, scene of first phase of campaign of Pharsalus, 21, 28, 31; Epirus, name, emendation involving, 71

Erichtho, Thessalian witch, 22

Etna, Mount, volcanic disturbances of, 141

Eutropius, cited, 3, 6, 14, 40, 43, 48, 51, 52, 159

Expertness, of Sextus's seamen, 76

Expropriated cities, help Sextus, 74

Famine: see Scarcity

Fannius, as envoy to Sextus, 65; mediates between Sextus and Bithynicus, 73; loyal to Sextus until the end, 157

Fasces, Sextus denies Claudius Nero the use of, 85; involved in Pliny's compliment to Pompey, 15

Fasti Amiterni, cited, 145

Faustus Sulla, brother-in-law of Sextus, 39, 40

Feriale Cumanum, cited, 146

Ferrero, G., cited, 93, 101, 102, 120, 126–130, 134, 146; criticized, 111, 144–145

Firmum, Pompey at, 28

Fischer, cited, 121

Fitzler-Seeck, cited, 58, 79, 88, 102, 122, 126, 143, 146, 149

Fleets, size of Sextus's when he became Praefectus, 66; Republican, under Murcus and Ahenobarbus, 80; size of combined anti-Octavian, 86; of Sextus's, in 38, 111, in 36, 123; of Octavian (Agrippa, Taurus, Lepidus) in 36, 124; division in Octavian's (Tauromenium and the Aeolic Islands), 135; losses of, at Naulochus, 144–145. See Armament

Florus, cited, 4, 6, 18, 19, 37, 43, 44, 48, 51–53, 56. 69, 70, 74, 123, 145, 148

Fougeres, G., cited, 102

Fowler, W. W., cited, 11, 12, 19, 86

Francken, C. N., cited, 39

Frank, T., cited, 1

Freedmen, attitude of Sextus toward, 81, 93, 128; attitude of Octavian toward, 81, 106; comparison of attitudes of Sextus and Octavian

toward, 81; position of, in camp of Sextus, 79, 93
Freinshemius, quality of chronicle of, 58
Fretum Siculum, 76
Friedlaender, L., quoted, 160
Frogs, as evidence for determining date of Horace, Sermones 1.5, 117
Fulvia, wife of Antony, foments Perusine War, 84; dies, 89
Furnius, Antony's lieutenant against Sextus, 151, 156–157

Gallus, Cornelius, poet, 16
Gabienus, subject of Pliny's necromantic story, 138
Gabinian Law and Pompey's command against the pirates, 11
Gardthausen, V., cited, 66–161, *passim;* criticized, 121, 132, 134, 140, 144
Gaul, penetrated by Sextus, 89
Gellius, cited, 16
General's cloak, discarded by Pollio in retreat in Spain, 58; discarded by Sextus in flight, 150
Ginzel, F. K., cited, 141
Gnaeus, elder brother of Sextus, birth of, 3; age of, 8; in command of naval squadron in 48, 19–20; at Corcyra, where he almost kills Cicero, 38; in Africa, 40; goes to Spain, 42, in command there, 45; death of, 51; character of, 41
Gnipho, teacher of Caesar and Cicero, 16
Gow, James, cited, 117
Graefe, F., cited, 78
Grammatici, 16–17
Groebe, Paul, cited, 5, 62, 64, 67, 138, 146
Gsell, S., cited, 39
Gwynn, A., cited, 12–14

Hadrumentum, Caesar lands at, in 47, 43
Hahn, L., cited, 1
Hall, C. M., cited, 53
Hammer, Jacob, cited, 17, 129
Harbor of the Achaeans, occupied by Sextus, 156
Harpagon, naval device, invented by Agrippa, 120, 145
Harpers' Lexicon, cited, 131
Haskins, cited, 23, 24
Hausmacht, 1, 153; of Pompey, 151, 154; employed by Sextus in Spain, 45, 52; 72, 73; in Asia Minor, 154
Heitland, W. E., cited, 1–87, *passim*

Helenus, favorite of Octavian, 105; takes Sardinia, 81; defeated by Menas, 88
'Hen's Forest', behind Bay of Cumae, retreat of Sextus, 107
Hereditary character of political position: see *Hausmacht*
Hiera, taken by Agrippa, 130; Agrippa's base, 132
Hiera, name emendation of, 132
Hill, G. F., cited, 78
Hirrus, Lucilius, Partizan of Sextus, 73; emendation in the name, 73
Hirschfeld, cited, 156
Hirst, Gertrude M., cited, 163
Hirtius, error for Hirrus, 73
Hirtius, consul of 44, 58
Hispania Ulterior, Pollio governor of, 55
Hitze, Aemilius, cited, 5, 6, 19; criticized, 8–9
Holm, Ad., cited, 109, 121, 129, 139, 145; criticized, 133, 134, 141, 144
Holmes, T. R., cited, 4–149, *passim;* criticized, 76, 87, 134
Horace, cited, 44, 75, 78, 106, 117, 121, 166
Hospitality, of Sextus (and Pompeia), 85
Hülsen, Ch., cited, 136

Imperator Iterum, date of Sextus's assumption of the title, 78, 140
Inscription(s), attesting Cornelia's *sophrosyne,* 15; relating to Sextus's augurship, 100; on bullet, 58. See also Coins and Corpus
Institutio puerilis, 13
Interference of nobles, in military camps, at Pharsalus, 36, with Sextus, 83, 93; explains Sextus's trust of freedmen, 93
Ionian Islands, station of Sextus, in flight, 150

Jenison, Elsie S., cited, 72
Jerome, cited, 11
Juba, relations of, with Republican leaders, 40; treatment of, by Caesar, 54
Julia, wife of Pompey, 14, 15
Julia, mother of Antony, protected by Sextus, 85, a fact which constitutes claim of Sextus on Antony, 148
Juno, temple of, plundered by Sextus, 150

Kiessling-Heinze, on Horace, cited, 117
Klein, J., on Sicilian magistrates, cited, 72, 88, 100, 124, 128, 141

Kloevekorn, H., cited, 67, 80
Klotz, A., cited, 42, 49, 52
Knapp, Charles, cited, 78
Kornemann, E., cited, 165
Köster, A., cited 132
Köster-von Nischer, quoted, 118
Krauss, S., cited, 136
Kromayer, J., cited, 76, 80, 84, 86, 107, 111, 120, 121, 134, 145; criticized, 19
Kromayer-Veith, cited, 66, 85, 118, 153

Labienus, former lieutenant of Caesar, in Corcyra, 38, in Spain, 43
Labienus, insurgent leader, in Asia Minor, 155, 162
Laeetani, 52
Lake Avernus, 119
Lake Lucrine, 119
Lambinus, conjecture of, in Horace, 75
Lampsacus, taken by Sextus, 156
Larinum, Pompey in, 27
Larissa, station in Pompey's flight, 37
Laronius, lieutenant of Octavian, relieves Cornificius, 136, 139
Lauron, scene of death of Gnaeus, 51
Leather boats, employed by Salvidienus, 76; mocked by Sextus, 78
Legati, Gnaeus and Sextus as, 19, 26
Lehmann-Hartleben, Karl, cited, 31, 119
Lenaeus, freedman of Pompey, 16
Lepidus, Marcus Aemilius, attempts to undo the reforms of Sulla, 3–4
Lepidus, Marcus Aemilius, Triumvir, 67; Pontifex Maximus, 57; attempted revolution by, 149; relations of, with Sextus, in 44, 62; for reconciling Sextus is honored with *supplicatio*, 64, and statue, 65; Octavian applies to, for help in 38, in vain, 107; apparently engaged in negotiations both with Octavian and with Sextus, 116; promises Octavian help in 36, 122; armament of, in attack on Lilybaeum, 124; losses of, in storm, 125; detachment of, defeated by Demochares, 128; marches across Sicily, 129, and meets Octavian, 141, with whom he quarrels, 142; makes private arrangement with Sextus's soldiers, 149, thus revealing his treacherous intentions, 149, 125; reported negotiations of, with Sextus, 142; comparison of, with Sextus, 82
Lesbos, friendly to Sextus, 15, 150, 155; Cornelia and Sextus take refuge in, 22–24
Leucopetra, station of Octavian in 36, 133

Lex Pedia, condemns assassins of Caesar, 66
Lex Titia, legalizes Triumvirate, 67
Libo: see Scribonius
Libya, station of Republicans between Corcyra and Africa, 38
Lilybaeum, attacked by unknown forces, 72, 74; inscription found at, 100; Lepidus attacks, 124; scene of Plinius's activity, 148
Lipara (Liparensians), go over to Sextus and are expatriated by Octavian, 115; fortified by Sextus, 124; objective of Octavian's fleet, 130
Lissus, scene of activity of Gnaeus, 26
Livia, takes refuge with Sextus, 85; beloved of Octavian, 102
Livy (or Periochae), cited, 3, 4, 37–79, *passim*, 97, 99, 131, 135, 145, 159; criticism of, 104, 163
Longinus, C. Cassius, lieutenant of Pompey, 78
Lübker, *Reallexikon*, cited, 3, 20, 31, 80
Luca, scene of meeting of 'First' Triumvirate, 14, 21
Lucan, cited, 22, 35–38, 70, 163; criticism of, 23–24, 163
Luceria, station of Pompey in 49, 27, 29
Ludi Apollinares, explain absence of Agrippa, 86
Ludi Plebei, occasion for demonstration in favor of Sextus, 90
Lurius, M., holds Sardinia for Octavian, 88, 105
Lustration, of fleets, 123

Macedonia, scene of campaign that ended at Pharsalus, 21–34, *passim*; Sextus attempts to waylay Antony's cavalry in, 156
Maecenas, agent of Octavian, to seek help from Antony, 117, 120, to pacify malcontents in Rome, 126, 136
Magnus, in name of Sextus, 100
Malcovati, Henrica, quoted, 99, 163
Manilian Law, gives command in East to Pompey, 11
Manilius, quoted, 69
Marcellus, Marcus, betrothed to daughter of Sextus, 98
Marius, military reforms of, 1, 48
Marquardt, cited, 86
Marriages, political character of, among Romans, 87
Marsh, F. B., quoted, 48; criticized, 142
Martial, quoted, 37, 75, 160

Massilia, station of Sextus in 44, 65; use of naval device at, 145

Mather, M. W., cited, 20

Mattingly, Harold, cited, 59

Maximus, Q. Fabius, Caesarian governor of Spain, 45

Mauretania, attacked by Gnaeus, 44; Bocchus, King of, 54

Meirakion, meaning of, 7

Memoirs of Octavian: see Commentaries

Menas, lieutenant of Sextus, freedman of Pompey, 70; takes Sardinia, 88; attempts to dissuade Sextus from Peace of Misenum, 94; deserts to Octavian, 105; reception of, by Octavian, 106; character of Sextus illustrated by his relations with, 106, 122, 128; serves under Calvisius, 108; furious encounter of, with Menecrates, 110; returns to Sextus, 122; active against Octavian, 125; deserts again to Octavian, 127. See also Comparison of Sextus and Octavian, as to use of freedmen

Menecrates, lieutenant of Sextus, freedman, 70; ravages Campania, 107; commands at Battle of Cumae, 109; death of, by drowning, 110

Menodorus, longer form of *Menas*, 70

Merivale, C., cited, 79, 83, 96, 98, 101, 111, 114, 120, 126; criticized, 87, 122, 159

Messala Corvinus, lieutenant of Octavian, favored by Velleius, 17; part of, in campaign of 36, 129–133

Messana, Sextus repulsed from, in 44, 73; Sextus's headquarters at, 111, 124; objective of Octavian, 129–130; Sextus's last stronghold in Sicily, 141, which his lieutenants surrender after he escapes, 148–149

Messina: see Messana

Meyer, Eduard, cited, 4, 32, 52, 163–164

Micylio, intermediary between Menas and Octavian, 105

Midaeum, scene of capture of Sextus, 158–159

Milazzo: see Mylae

Miletus, scene of Sextus's death, 158

Mindius Marcellus, intermediary between Menas and Octavian, 127

Misenum, Peace of, 95–99

Mitylene, refuge for Cornelia and Sextus, 8; attractions of, for Cornelia, 15; relations of, with the house of Pompey, 34; Sextus kept under surveillance near, 155. See also Lesbos

Moberly, C. E., cited, 19

Mommsen, M., cited, 41, 52, 85, 96–99; criticized, 146

Monarchy, tendency toward, under the Republic, 1

Monte Nuovo, 119

Monumentum Ancyranum, cited, 47, 70

Moore, F. G., cited, 8

Motives, of Gnaeus and Sextus, in Spain, 46; of Sextus and Octavian, compared, 61; of Lepidus, in Sicily, 125, 149. For motives of Sextus see also *Pietas* and *Hausmacht*

Mras, Karl, cited, 100, 152

Mucia, mother of Sextus, 3; faithful wife in 77, 5; divorced in 62, 11; urged to further Peace of Misenum, 93

Mucius Scaevola, father of Mucia, 3

Munda, Battle of, 49–51; Caesar hard pressed at, 50; Pompeian watchword at, 152

Münzer, F., cited, 54, 73, 74, 87, 108, 128, 154, 155

Murcus, L. Staius, in command of Republican fleet, 66, 80; joins Sextus, 80; death of, at instigation of Sextus, 94

Mutina, Pompey at, 4; Battles of, 58; Sextus refuses to relieve Republicans in, 65

Myconium, Mount, scene of meeting between Octavian and Lepidus, 141

Mylae, taken by Sextus, 72; vessels of Sextus stationed there, 130; Battle of, 131–132; objective of Cornificius, 138; Sextus withdraws from, 141; description of vessels engaged at, 144; bearing of, on chronology of Naulochus, 146

Nasidius, loyal to Sextus to the end, 157

Naulochus, Battle of, 144–145

Navalia, at Thessalonica, 31

Naval tactics, at Cumae, 109; at Scyllaeum, 112; devices, invented or developed by Agrippa, 120, at Mylae, 131, at Naulochus, 144–145. See also Battles, descriptions of

Necromancy, of Erichtho, 22; of Gabienus (Pliny), 138

Neos, meaning of a, 8

Neptune, Sextus claims descent from, 78; disturbances concerning missing image of, at Ludi Plebei, 90; justification for Sextus's claim, 114; coins figuring, 78

Nero, Claudius, finds refuge with Sextus, 85, 99

New Carthage, besieged by Gnaeus, 45

Nicaea, captured by Sextus, 156

Nicias, teacher in Pompey's household, 16

Nicolaus of Damascus, cited, 53

Nicomedia, captured by Sextus, 156

Niebuhr, cited, 70; criticized, 17, 149

Niese, B., cited, 89, 151

von Nischer, E., quoted, 153

Nissen, H., cited, 77, 112, 136

Nobles, particular objects of proscriptions, 67, from which they are saved by Sextus, 74–75, who gives them due rank, 74; free in giving advice to Sextus, 79; urge Sextus to accede to Peace of Misenum, 94, after which many of them return to Rome, 99. See also Advice

Nysa (Caria), birth-place of Aristodemus, teacher of Sextus, 13

Obsequens, Julius, quoted, 6

Octavia, sister of Octavian, intercedes between Antony and Octavian, 120–121; sends cavalry to Antony, 156

Octavian, meets Julius Caesar in Spain, 53; claims heritage of Julius, 57; cooperates with Senate, 58, 64; becomes consul, 66; Triumvir, 67; ignores Sextus, 71, 75; sends Salvidienus against Sextus, 76; expects to win by land, 76, 129, 143; is forced to circumnavigate Sicily to meet Antony in 42, 77; uses cavalry in attempt to repel raids of Sextus, 83; in Perusian War, 84; measures of, against Antony, 86; marries Scribonia, 87; makes Peace of Brundisium, 89; at Peace of Misenum, 95–99; plans renewal of hostilities, 101; divorces Scribonia, 102; much exercised to excuse conduct, in renewing war with Sextus, 104; prepares campaign of 38, 108; disgraceful conduct of, at Scyllaeum, 111; Italian sympathy against, 115; preparations of, for campaign of 36, 117–122; disaster suffered by, in storm, 125; preparations of, for final campaign, 130; crosses to Tauromenium, 133; almost captured, 135–136; meditates suicide, 137; in Sicily again, 140–142; accepts challenge of Sextus, 143; in a daze at Naulochus, 147; celebrates death of Sextus, but later reproaches Antony with the deed, 159; motives of, 61, 162; see also Motives; cruelty of: see Arae Perusinae; relations of,

with freedmen, 81: see also Menas; stubbornness of, 92; cowardice of, 112, 135, 147; poor generalship of, 111–112, 147; popular demonstrations against, 91, 126, 138: see also Maecenas; selfjustification of, influences our authorities, 99, 107, 163: see also Commentaries; mastery of propaganda by, 104; imitation of name-device of Sextus by, 100; energy of, 117, 126. See also Comparison of Sextus and Octavian, Comparison of Sextus and Lepidus, Sextus

Octavius: see Octavian

Odyssey, favorite Roman reading, 68

Olbia, hoard of coins found at, 106

Onobalas, unidentified river in Sicily, 133

Opportunities neglected by Sextus, at Mutina, 61, at Philippi, 81; of combining with Ahenobarbus, 81; during Perusian War, 84; after Octavian's disaster of 38, 114; after the storms of July 1, 36, 126; perhaps to be explained by want of dependable lieutenants, 124

Ordo equester, Theophanes's descendants in, 16; Menas inscribed in, 106

Oricum, scene of Gnaeus's activity in 49, 26

Ormerod, H. A., cited, 54, 68

Orosius, cited, *passim;* criticized, 145

Ovid, 166

Palaestini, correct name for a group in Sicily, 142

Palinurus, confused with Paliurus, 39; Octavian's fleet shipwrecked off, 125

Paliurus (Cyrene), station of Republicans in flight to Africa, 39. See also Palinurus

Papias, equivalent to *Demochares*, 128. See Demochares

Pansa, consul of 44, 58

Parker, H. M. D., cited, 1, 28

Parthians, expedition of Antony against, 108, 118, 150, 154; Sextus in communication with, 155

Patrae, seized by Cato, 39

Patriotism of Sextus, possible explanation for his restraint in raiding coasts of Italy, 115, 161

Paullus, L. Aemilius, envoy of Senate to Sextus in 44, 65

Pedius, Q., Caesarian governor of Spain, 45

Pedius, Q., colleague of Octavian in consulship, 66

Peloponnese, to be surrendered to Sextus according to the Treaty of Misenum, 96; Antony refuses to surrender, 101–103
Pelorum, in possession of Sextus, 112, 130,171,
Pelusium, scene of Pompey's death, 37, 44
Pergamum, inscription found in, 15
Periochae, 58. See also Livy
Perperna, slayer of Sertorius, 4
Perusian War, 84
Peskett, A. G., cited, 20
Peter, H., cited, 7
Petreius, suicide of, in Africa, 43
Pharsalus, Battle of, 22, 36–37, 145
Philadelphus, freedman of Octavian, 105
Philipp, H., cited, 87, 129
Philippi, Battle of, 80, 107, 155
Philosophers, heard by Pompey, 15
Photius, cited, 15
Picenum, Pompeian recruiting ground, 73
Pichon, R., cited, 163–164
Pierce, Elizabeth D., cited, 55
Pietas of Sextus, motive for his conduct, 46, 151
Pietas, watchword at Munda, 152
Piracy, Sextus's warfare regarded as, 70, 149 (but for the other side see 52, 68)
Pirates, Pompey's attitude toward, 69; tortured by Octavian, 103
Pius, as part of Sextus's name, 151–152
Plancus, Munatius, joins Sextus, 84
Plinius, lieutenant of Sextus, 124, 148; correct spelling of name of, 100
Pliny the Elder, cited, 15, 16, 112, 119, 137, 138, 140
Plutarch, cited, 3–52, *passim*, 69, 70, 85, 97, 98; at fault, 120–121
Pollio, Asinius, favored by Velleius, 17; Caesarian governor in Spain, 55; mediates between Antony and Ahenobarbus, 81; as historian, 164
Pompeia, sister of Sextus, birth of, 3; in Africa, 40; hospitality of, 85
Pompeia, daughter of Sextus, betrothed to Marcellus, 98; escapes with father, 148
Pompey (the Great), importance of position of, 1, 20, 40, 41; movements of, in 77, 4–5; influence of, on Sextus's education, 11, 15; movements of, in 49–48, 21–22, 27–30; death of, 37; devotion of, to sea and sailing, 69, 66; sympathy of, with pirates, 69; laments failure to use his fleet, 39, 69; traditions of, 41;

see also *Hausmacht;* property of, 46; refusal of, to usurp power, 161
Pontus, Sextus's relations with, 155
Popular feeling, for Sextus or against Octavian, 67, 84, 89, 91, 96, 101, 108, 115, 136, 159–160
Portents, 22, 108, 109, 138, 140
Portus Julius, 118–119
Posidonius, teacher of Cicero and Pompey, 15
Postgate, J. P., cited, 23, 25, 27, 37, 44, 163
Pott, A. F., cited 77
Proconessus, scene of activity of Sextus, 157
Proculeius, Octavian requests to assist him in suicide, 137
Propertius, cited, 87, 98
Property, Sextus's compensation for, 63, 97
Proscriptions, horrors of, 69; Sextus's services in, 69, 75, 152
Prosopographia, cited, 16, 155
Pseudo-Victor, cited, 3, 6, 37, 43, 51, 78, 98, 145
Purser: see Tyrrell and Purser
Puteoli, 94, 107, 108, 136

Quellenforschung, 162
Quintilian, cited, 13

Raids of Sextus, on Bruttium, 83; chronology of, 86; on Thurii and Consentia, 88; restraint of, possibly due to patriotism, 115, 161
Ravenna, Octavian builds ships at, because Sextus holds West, 107, 109
Rebilus, Caninius, lieutenant of Octavian, 127
Regium: see Rhegium
Recruiting, for Sextus, 84; by Hirrus, 73. See also *Hausmacht*
Republican feeling persistent at Rome, 47. See also popular feeling
Republican leaders, incompetence of, 36, 39, 40, 56, 60; low morality of, 61; preliminary successes of, 43. See also Cato, Scipio Metellus, Gnaeus
Restitution to Sextus, date of, 62–64; amount of, 63, 97
Rhegium, Salvidienus at, 75; Octavian makes promises to, 77; legions mobilized at, 109; Octavian at, 137
Rhodes, Pompey at, 15; refuses admission to Pompey, 37
Risse, C., cited, 10–44, *passim*, 79, 86, 96; criticized, 98, 156
Rolfe, J. C., cited, 137
Romeo, G., cited, 166
Rose, H. J., cited, 22

Rosenberg, A., cited, 7, 17, 19
Rossbach, O, at fault, 71
Rostovtzeff, M., cited, 59, 103, 104
Route of Sextus and Cornelia, to Lesbos, 34, from Egypt, 39; of Pompey's flight to Egypt, 37; of Republicans' flight to Africa, 38; of Sextus's flight to the East, 150
Rubicon, Caesar crosses, 21, 29
Rzach, cited, 116

Saburra, general of Juba, 54
St. Maria di Tindaro: see Tyndaris
Salinas, cited, 100
Sallust, cited, 4
Salvidienus Rufus, operations against Sextus, 75–78
Sandys, J. E., cited, 12, 58
Sappho, association of, with Lesbos, 34
Sardinia, assigned to Octavian, 67; importance of, 87; taken by Menas, 87, who deserts there, 105
Saturninus, C. Sentius, escorts Julia to Athens, 85; leaves Sextus for Rome, 99, but is with him again at the end, 157
Scaccia-Scarafoni, cited, 102
Scampa, Pompey at, 32
Scapula, T. Quinctius, insurgent leader, 45
Scarcity of food at Rome, in 43, 75; in 40, 84, 86; in 39, 89, 91; after Peace of Misenum, 102; in 36, 125–126
Scaurus, deserts Sextus, 158
Schanz, M. cited, 17
Schanz-Hosius, cited, 16, 103
Schulten, A., cited, 4, 54
Schur, W., cited, 1
Schwartz, E., cited, 56, 63, 64, 141, 163, 164
Schweighäuser, cited, 96, 105
Scipio Africanus, 1
Scipio, Metellus, father of Cornelia, 14; leader in Africa, 38; suicide, 43
Scott, K., cited, 104
Scribonia, marriage of, to Octavian, 87; divorced, by Octavian, 102
Scribonius Libo, father-in-law of Sextus, intermediary between Sextus and Cicero, 18, 60; escorts Julia to Athens, 85; promotes marriage of Scribonia, 87; intermediary between Sextus and Octavian, 92; with Sextus until the end, 157
Scylaceum (Squillace), Octavian at, 129–130, 133
Scyllaeum, Salvidienus engaged at, 76; Octavian engaged at, 110–112
Seeck: see Fitzler-Seeck

Semitic name, of Abalas, 136; of Palaestini, 142
'Senate', at Thessalonica, 31–32
Seneca, cited, 79, 148, 159
Sertorius, career of, in Spain similar to Sextus's, 54, 154, 162
Servius, quoted, 119, 131
Sextus (other references will be found under other lemmata), birth of, 3; education of, 10–20; in Lesbos, 22–24; in Cyrene and Africa, 38; resumé of career of, until his service in Spain, 44; career of, in Spain, 44–55; *Imperator (Iterum)*, 58, 140; courted by Senate, 59; ultimatum of, after Ides, 60; *Praefectus*, 63; position of, after Lex Titia, 68; in proscriptions, 69; at war with Antony, 68, 147; in the East, 148–158; death of, 158; conduct of, legitimate, 2, 68, 71, 79, 100, 116, 154, or justifiable, 47, 49, 154, 161–163; competent general, 52, 141, 146, 161–162; avoided battles with superior forces in Spain, 54, 55; himself retained posts of responsibility, 109; encouraged his soldiers, 132–133, 150; almost traps Octavian, 134; trust of, in naval rather than in land forces, 143; organization of forces of, unknown, 161; movements of, restricted, perhaps, by want of trustworthy lieutenants, 124, 127; failure of, to exploit Republican sympathy, 82; success of, due in part to disorders at Rome, 83; treatment of associates by, 94; wit of, 98; challenge of, to Octavian, 143; exuberance of, 152; personality of, 78, 154, 157; double dealing of, 155; pride of, 158; inheritor of Pompey's traits, 2, 61, 78, 93, 146, 151, 161–162
Sextus Pompey, consul in 35, as boy, 20, an appointment which shows Octavian's recognition of Sextus's following, 154; dates Sextus's death, 159
Shakespeare, characterizes Domitius Ahenobarbus, 81
Sham battle, illustrates Sextus's personality, 78
Shipley, F. W., in error, 3, 119
Shuckburgh, E. S., cited, 79, 87, 102, 119
Sibylline Oracles, cited, 116
Sicilians, trilingual, 142
Sicily, granary of Rome, 103; assigned to Octavian by Lex Titia, 67; suitability of, for Sextus's purposes, 72; Pompeian influence in, 72; won by Sextus, 74, and used by him as fortress, 83

Silanus, M. Junius, leaves Sextus for Rome, 99
Similarity of armament, of Sextus and Octavian, 144
Sittius, lieutenant of Caesar, 54
Slaves, emancipated as combatants in Spain, 45; in camp of Sextus, 69; trained for Octavian at Portus Julius, 118
Sophrosyne, of Cornelia lauded, 15
Sorrento, Octavian caught in storm at, 125
Sosius, consul designate, 99
Spain, character of, 53; Pompey in, 4, 11; Caesar in, 31; Sextus in, 44–55
Statilius Taurus, lieutenant of Octavian in campaigns of 36, 124–142 *passim*
Stein, A., cited, 16, 106
Step-mothers, 15
Storms, descriptions of, 113–114, 125
Strabo, cited, 14, 15, 27, 39, 51, 52, 70, 77, 107, 119, 148, 159
Strongyle, objective of Octavian, 130
Stylis, Octavian at, 136
Suetonius, cited, 4–20, *passim*, 56, 66, 79, 85, 102–147 *passim*
Sulla, 1, 4, 16, 71; refuses to recognize government which outlawed him, 68
Sulpicius, Servius, 62
Supplicatio, for Lepidus, 64
Syracuse, in control of Sextus, 74
Syria, Pompey in, 15; officers from, take Sextus, 157, 158

Taormina: see Tauromenium
Tacitus, cited, 11, 12, 17, 87, 97, 108
Taramelli, cited, 106
Taras River, 121
Tarentum, Octavian at, 108, 111; meets Antony at, 120; Statilius Taurus proceeds from, 124, 129
Tarraconensis, Hispania, Gnaeus killed in, 51
Tauromenium, scene of Octavian's unfortunate venture in 36, 129–141, *passim*
Teanum Sidicinum, Pompey at, 27
Thapsus, Battle of, 43
Theodorus, freedman executed by Sextus, 156
Theophanes, favorite freedman of Pompey, 16, 34
Thermus, envoy of Senate to Sextus, 65; loyal to Sextus at the end, 157
Thessalonica, seat of Republican government in 49–48, 27–32
Thessaly, Sextus in, to consult witch, 22, 24
Thomas, P., cited, 94
Thrace, Sextus in relations with, 155

Thucydides, on piracy, 68; model for Dio, 144
Thurii, besieged by Sextus, 88
Tiberius, Emperor, favored by Velleius, 17; entertained by Sextus, 85
Tirocinium militiae, 19
Tisienus Gallus, lieutenant of Sextus, 128, 141, 148
Titinius, lieutenant of Octavian, 135
Titius, M., taken by Sextus, 99; return of, to Rome, 99; Sextus refuses to surrender to, because of his ingratitude, 151, 157
Topos, descriptions of battles have character of, 145
Trebonius, Caesarian governor in Spain, 45
Tribunus militum, 20
Triumvirate, of Caesar, Pompey, Crassus, 21; of Antony, Octavian, Lepidus, 67
Tyndaris, taken by Sextus, 72; action at, in 36, 130, 132, 140
Tyre, Sextus and Cornelia in, 38
Tyrrell and Purser, cited, 18–80, *passim*, 127

Ulia, besieged by Gnaeus, 50
Utica, Republican headquarters, 40

Valerius Maximus, cited, 3, 6, 74
Varro, cited, 103
Varus, Attius, joins Gnaeus in Spain, 43
Veith, G., cited, 27, 28, 41, 43
Velia, Bay of, Octavian takes shelter in, 125
Velleius, cited, *passim;* criticism of, 17
Vergil, cited, 101, 119, 129, 166
Vestal Virgins, documents deposited with, 97, 107; pray to stop exodus of slaves, 75
Veterans, ill-disposed to Octavian, 89
Via Egnatia, used by Pompey, 31, 32
Vibo, Octavian makes promises to inhabitants of, 77; station of Octavian, 115, 126, 130, 133, 136
Viereck, P., cited, 96, 130, 132, 135, 142
Vigintivirate, 20

White, H., cited, 7, 97; at fault, 120, 124
Wickham, E. C., cited, 75, 78, 106, 117, 166
Wife of Sextus, 148
Wijnne, cited, 136
Wissowa, G., cited, 123

Ziegler, cited, 76, 134
Zonaras, cited, 67–159, *passim*